Why America Stopped Voting

The American Social Experience
SERIES

James Kirby Martin
GENERAL EDITOR

Paula S. Fass, Steven H. Mintz, Carl Prince, James W. Reed & Peter N. Stearns
EDITORS

Why America Stopped Voting

The Decline of Participatory Democracy and the Emergence of Modern American Politics

MARK LAWRENCE KORNBLUH

NEW YORK UNIVERSITY PRESS

New York and London

149205

NEW YORK UNIVERSITY PRESS
New York and London

© 2000 by New York University
All rights reserved

Library of Congress Cataloging-in-Publication Data
Kornbluh, Mark Lawrence, 1955–
Why America stopped voting : the decline of participatory democracy
and the emergence of modern American politics / Mark Lawrence Kornbluh.
p.   cm.
Includes bibliographical references and index.
ISBN 0-8147-4708-6 (cloth : alk. paper)
1. Voting—United States—History. 2. Political participation—
United States—History. 3. Political parties—United States—History.
4. United States—Politics and government.   I. Title.
JK1965 .K67 1999
324.973—dc21   99-006956

New York University Press books are printed on acid-free paper,
and their binding materials are chosen for strength and durability.

Manufactured in the United States of America

10 9 8 7 6 5 4 3 2 1

Contents

Preface

Americans today rarely vote. When Bill Clinton was elected president in 1996, only 49 percent of the eligible electorate cast ballots. Turnout levels were not much higher in 1992 or in 1988 when George Bush was elected president. Indeed, Ronald Reagan's "mandate" election in 1980 was based upon the active support of only 27 percent of the electorate. It is not only presidential races that turn off voters. Off-year congressional elections draw scarcely four out of ten eligible voters, and voter turnout diminishes to 10–20 percent for state and local elections concerning schools, safety, quality of services, and taxes. Voter participation in all elections has fallen to its lowest levels since the mass electorate was first incorporated into the political system in the nineteenth century.

The decline has drawn considerable attention from government officials, party leaders, media analysts, and scholars. In 1988 Jesse Jackson's campaign for the presidency placed this issue squarely on the political agenda, and it has been discussed during every subsequent national election. What the discussion of nonvoting lacks, however, is a historical perspective on its structural roots. Although part of the explanation for the exceptionally poor turnouts in recent elections lies in the particularly political events of the last four decades, the core of the problem is buried much deeper. Voter turnout has not exceeded two-thirds of the eligible electorate since 1900, and the drop-off from high profile national elections to congressional, state, and local elections has been consistently severe. Not once since World War I has even half the electorate cast ballots in an off-year election. Nonvoting is, quite simply, endemic in modern American politics.

Yet, before the turn of the century, American electoral politics was intensely participatory. Integrated into the electoral system in the 1830s and 1840s, this country's mass electorate remained highly mobilized throughout the nineteenth century. In presidential elections, voter turnout averaged nearly 80 percent nationwide and 85 percent in the North, figures that are astounding considering all the factors such as illness, bad weather, work, travel, and relocation that weighed heavily on that highly mobile, largely rural population. In late-nineteenth-century America, virtually everyone who was eligible to vote and able to do so went to the polls. And they did so in nearly every election, off-year contests as well as presidential elections, local and state races as well as national ones.

The turning point in American politics came during the first two decades of the twentieth century. From unmatched heights in the 1890s, turnout fell repeatedly election after election. By the eve of America's entry into World War I, national voter participation had dropped to barely 60 percent; even in the North only slightly more than two-thirds of the eligible electorate continued to participate. Fewer people voted, and those who did voted less frequently. This demobilization of the mass electorate was unprecedented and enduring. Voter participation rates have fluctuated during the succeeding eight decades but have never risen much above World War I levels. Over the space of a political generation, the modern American electorate emerged, characterized not only by low turnout and minimal popular involvement, but also by severe socioeconomic, ethnic, and age biases.

An essential transformation of American electoral politics thus occurred during the Progressive Era. A half-century of industrial development and urban growth had fundamentally altered social relations and created new social problems that transfixed the nation. By the turn of the century, the scale of the corporate economy and the scope of modern urban society had outgrown individual and community control. In response, early-twentieth-century Americans fashioned new institutions in an attempt to restore order, secure prosperity, and ensure continued development.[1]

Every corner of society was touched. Reform reshaped the political system; new forms of social organizations and economic combinations restructured the way Americans lived; and the proliferation of new outlets of mass culture and intellectual developments in universities provided new ways to think about the world. In the process American society began to reorganize along largely functional lines, and social relations became increasingly bureaucratic. This transformation severely undermined the nineteenth-century American system of electoral politics, which was firmly rooted in community-based social relations.

At the same time, economic and social development required the expansion of political authority and insulation from popular politics. The result was the eclipse of mass voter participation, which set the stage for the development of the modern administrative state. To understand this fundamental shift from participatory to administrative politics, we must look at both the process of social change and the results of political action. Only then can we develop a complete picture of modern American electoral politics and explain the historical roots of nonvoting in the United States.

Over the many years in which I have been involved with this project, I have benefited greatly from the insights, assistance, and support of colleagues, friends, and family. This book has its origins in the first years of my graduate work at the Johns Hopkins University. I owe debts that I will never fully repay to Lou Galambos, who guided my development as a historian, and Rick Rubinson, who introduced me to the study of political behavior. They each contributed greatly to my intellectual development, and this work reflects much that I learned from them. John Higham challenged me to tackle this topic and inspired me to always look at the big picture. Graduate school colleagues and friends assisted enormously. Naomi and David Lamoreaux, Brian Balogh, Chris Tomlins, Deborah Rubin, and Ida Altman each read my work with a critical and supportive eye.

As my notes testify, I have accumulated numerous intellectual debts to a wide range of scholars. Walter Dean Burnham's work was the starting point for this project and has been an inspiration throughout. My basic approach to the topic was influenced greatly by the work of Samuel P. Hays, Grant McConnell, E. E. Schattschneider, Robert Wiebe, and Charles Tilly. Ed Ayers, Jean Baker, Paula Baker, Ballard Campbell, Richard Jensen, Paul Kleppner, J. Morgan Kousser, Richard L. McCormick, Michael McGerr,

Jack Reynolds, Jerrold Rusk, and Stephen Skowronek will find that I relied on much of their scholarship, although I sometimes disagreed with each of them.

In completing this book, New York University Press and Niko Pfund and Despina Papazoglou Gimbel have provided encouragement, patience, and excellent editing advice. I have benefited greatly from the support of friends, colleagues, and students. Encouragement and assistance was always forthcoming from Roger Biles, Jim Huston, and Glenna Mathews. John Allswang, Peter Argersinger, David Burner, Ballard Campbell, Paula Fass, Ron Formissano, Richard Jensen, Morton Keller, Sam McSeveney, Jack Reynolds, Rick Vallely, and Bob Wiebe provided valuable advice along the way. Long into too many nights, Engin Akarli and Jeannie Attie helped greatly as I began the process to rewrite and expand. Peter Knupfer, Steve Mintz, and Jim Sleight provided on-going encouragement.

At Michigan State University, Dean John Eadie and my two chairs, Gordon Stewart and Henry Silverman, helped me by providing the time, resources, and encouragement to complete the task. David Bailey, Lisa Fine, and Leslie Moch have been pillars of support. My secretary, Jacque Shoppell, has provided encouragement, tolerance, and support. Investing much of his time and his keen editorial eye, Harold Marcus taught me much about turning a dissertation into a book. Melanie Shell Weiss has read every word of this book many times over and assisted me in innumerable tasks both large and small. This work is all the better for the assistance of both Harold and Melanie. I am forever grateful to them.

The encouragement and support of friends and family members has meant a great deal to me. My dear friends Mathew Hermann, Susan Lydon, Rick Lockwood, and Cynthia Hahn; my brother and his wife, David Kornbluh and Diane Siegel; and my sister and her husband, Julie and Kelly Smith, have been pillars of support. My grandparents, Rose and Murray Kornbluh, Eve and Jack Epstein, Mina and Joe Rennert, and Sarah Behar, and my mother-in-law and father-in-law, Isaac and Trudi Behar, offered me nothing but love and encouragement. I owe my parents, Walter and Joan Kornbluh, a special debt. They both experienced this project as I did, offering substantive suggestions and valued support. I appreciated greatly that my family was willing to read my work, quantitative analysis included, all along the way.

The project began long before my children, Evan and Allie, were born, and it is a special pleasure to know they are now old enough to appreciate what it means that "Daddy is finishing his book." I thank them for their patience with the long hours that I have sat at my computer. I have drawn inspiration as I watch their ravenous appetite for knowledge. Finally, to my wife, Miriam Behar, no words will suffice to express my gratitude. She read and reread every idea and sentence contained here innumerable times and aided me in every way possible large and small. I truly could not have completed this without her love, encouragement, and continuous help.

Introduction

Voting is both an individual and a collective act.[1] Since voting is not compulsory in the United States, individuals must choose to cast a ballot. A voter must physically go to the polls on Election Day or else make special arrangements to vote by absentee ballot. But electoral participation is more than just the sum of individual decision making. Political parties and other political, social, economic, religious, and cultural organizations and groups mobilize voters. Government institutions and the legal system determine who can vote and how elections are to be conducted. Analysis of voting as collective action requires us to pay attention not only to individual costs and rewards but also to organization, mobilization, collective resources, political opportunity, and power.[2]

The extent of mass participation in electoral politics is an aggregate-level question. To understand the low levels of voting in modern American politics, we must examine the structural factors that facilitate or hinder mass participation. The question is not so much why individuals choose to vote in given elections, but rather why the extensive political participation that characterized the nineteenth-century American electoral system is absent from modern American politics.

Most scholarly explanations have focused on discrete political factors—shifts in the party system and/or institutional and electoral

1

reforms.[3] There are two schools of thought in the historiography. The first, represented most notably by Walter Dean Burnham and Paul Kleppner, blames the decline on the 1896 realignment of the party system, since it undercut electoral competition throughout the nation and altered the composition of party alliances. The second position, which includes such pluralist scholars as Philip Converse and Jerrold Rusk, explains the falloff as the result of specific changes in the legal and institutional structure of electoral politics. Most scholars who hold this position regard falling turnout as an artifact of Progressive reforms (especially ballot reform) that purified electoral politics, although some radical scholars, among them Frances Piven and Richard Cloward, argue that reform (particularly voter registration) was designed to exclude the lower class from political participation.[4] Not surprisingly, the most detailed studies of state and local politics have found both electoral change and political reform to be important.[5]

Without a doubt, both realignment and reform played significant roles in restructuring the American electorate. To a large extent, they provided the immediate mechanisms by which electoral participation was altered. These factors, however—either alone or in combination—fail to provide a sufficient causal explanation for the demise of mass voter participation in this country. My analysis shows that voting does not drop suddenly after 1896 with the emergence of the fourth party system. Nor, except in the South, does it fall sharply in response to the passage of specific legislation. On the contrary, regression analysis of voter turnout figures indicates that a long-term, gradual, cumulative process was at work.[6] The shape of this decline and its secular nature is incompatible with the literature that focuses on discrete political events to explain the demobilization of the electorate.

We need a broader perspective to understand this long-term and enduring change. Michael McGerr's *Decline of Popular Politics: The American North, 1865–1928* (1986) provides a partial step in that direction. McGerr vividly illustrates that a particular "style" of popular politics in the nineteenth century characterized mass participation. Individual involvement declined as that style was replaced by educational and advertising campaigns. Nonetheless, McGerr's work, which sees the change in political style largely as the result of Gilded Age reformers, still casts the issue far too narrowly.

Missing from the scholarly discussion has been an understanding of the social roots of mass participation in the nineteenth century and the role that social change played in eroding that system over time. Electoral participation needs to be understood within the larger context of American culture and society.[7] The social analysis of politics has been subjected to considerable criticism for neglecting the political side of politics.[8] There is nothing inherent in a social analysis, however, that precludes political acumen. Understanding politics within a broader social context is essential if we are to analyze the stakes involved in political participation. The problem with the scholarly literature on the decline in voting has not been a neglect of politics, but a failure to locate the decline of political participation within the larger history of American social and political development.

As I demonstrate in this book, the fundamental social changes that restructured every aspect of American life during the late nineteenth and early twentieth centuries also eroded the social basis of the nation's participatory politics. The same social changes provide the context for the political forces that realigned and reformed the modern American electoral system. By combining social and political analysis, I have developed a causal explanation for the decline of voting in the United States. And within that explanation, it becomes clear that the transformation of electoral politics was a central ingredient in the emergence of modern America.

To explore participation in American electoral politics, it is necessary to go beyond the level of the articulate elite and examine mass political behavior. Aggregate election returns can provide a unique window on public involvement because they enable us to recover information about the actions of ordinary Americans. Through quantitative analysis we can learn how many and what types of Americans voted, how often they went to the polls, and whom they favored. The political actions of the American electorate can be examined directly rather than through the filtering lens of literate sources.

Voting, of course, is not the only type of political involvement. Americans participate in politics by campaigning for candidates, running for office, lobbying officeholders, publicizing political positions, bringing court cases, protesting, forming voluntary associations, donating to causes, writing letters, rioting, and acting politically in innumerable other ways.[9] A focus on electoral politics, therefore, does not capture the full spectrum of American political activism. A huge variety of political actions ranging from routine day-to-day contacts between citizens and government to extrainstitutional expressions of political protest are left out.

Unfortunately, large parts of the population are also excluded. Throughout American history, the political realm has been sharply divided along gender and racial lines. In the late nineteenth and early twentieth centuries, blacks were forced out of electoral politics throughout the South. Though women were politically active in a wide range of voluntary associations and reform movements, electoral politics belonged largely to men; women generally were denied the franchise.[10] The division of political participation along gender and racial lines means that the view of American mass politics offered by analysis of electoral politics is incomplete. We must also consider those nonvoters and their relationship to the electoral system.

Nonetheless, electoral politics was the primary arena through which late-nineteenth-century Americans were incorporated into the political system and chose their government. Elections marked the route to state power, and even the nonvoting women were not fully excluded from this arena. Not only did they participate directly in many of the activities leading up to casting a ballot, but also, as inhabitants of a culture that divided functions along gender lines, their concerns were to some extent mediated through the male electorate.[11] Sensitivity to gender divisions and political differences between men and women in the nineteenth century does not negate the value of electoral analysis; on the contrary, it can broaden and enrich our understanding of elections and their role within American politics.[12]

The same is true with regard to nineteenth-century racial divisions and political differences. Black Americans faced greater obstacles than perhaps any other group in seeking a political voice. Literacy tests, poll taxes, and property requirements were just some of the barriers to registration that prevented blacks, poor whites, and immigrants from voting. Yet in that era of racial segregation and lynching of black Americans, many black women also pushed for the franchise, organized suffrage clubs, and participated in rallies and demonstrations, even though they were not able to cast a ballot.[13]

In analyzing election returns, we look at the most basic form of electoral participation—the vote. Since voting requires only a minimal expenditure of effort, it is the easiest participatory act to perform for those who are eligible. Furthermore, all other electoral activity is either geared toward garnering votes or contingent on securing election. Of course, voter participation has the added advantage of being easily measurable. Whether viewed as an indicator of the total amount of citizen involvement in electoral politics or simply as a measure of participation at the most rudimentary level, voting is the most readily available and universally useful way to measure mass participation in electoral politics.[14]

The view of mass behavior available through quantitative analysis of election returns, however, like that provided by more traditional historical sources, is not free from distortion. Scholars often question the accuracy of quantitative records, including election returns and census data. Voting is mediated through a political system controlled by a complex set of legal, institutional, and informal arrangements, which affect both the act of voting and the recording of votes. We can never know with certainty the degree to which an election was "honest," whether votes were cast willingly or not, whether coercion to vote or abstain took place, or whether ballots were miscounted or lost or the ballot box was stuffed.[15] Therefore, although working with "hard numbers," we must be sensitive to uncertainty both in those numbers and, more importantly, about their meaning. The historian can compensate in two ways: by quantitatively assessing the degree of uncertainty in election statistics and by comparing and checking quantitative measures with qualitative evidence to gain a richer picture of the meaning of those measures. Pairing quantitative analysis with more traditional historical research increases the accuracy and value of quantitative work and provides us with a fuller picture of mass politics.

I chose to analyze mass political behavior in twenty successive national elections—the last five presidential and off-year elections in the nineteenth century and the first five of each in this century. This study thus begins in 1880 after the end of Reconstruction had returned political independence to all of the states and concludes with the 1918 election, which took place as the Progressive Era drew to a close and World War I reshaped the nation's politics. In the analysis I group together the elections from 1880 to 1898 in order to describe the late-nineteenth-century electoral system and do the same with the early-twentieth-century elections from 1900 to 1918. To a certain extent, partitioning the analysis in this manner involves the use of ideal typologies.

The late-nineteenth-century and early-twentieth-century systems that are contrasted throughout are, in part, constructs that illuminate changes in the nature of mass electoral politics over the forty-year period. It is quite possible, as I hope is apparent, to see roots of early-twentieth-century changes in the 1880s and 1890s, as well as the persistence of many late-nineteenth-century trends into the second decade of the twentieth century. Nonetheless, dividing the time period into two distinct segments, and generalizing about both, enables me to uncover patterns that would be lost in the details of a chronological election-by-election narrative.

Grouping elections in this way has gained much support over the last forty years. American political history can be divided into five discrete electoral eras. These eras, or "party systems," are seen as periods of relatively stable patterns of mass voting that are separated from each other by realigning phases. Although there is much controversy about the exact nature of electoral realignments (especially whether they occur in one critical election or over a series of elections) and about the timing of the phases, there is general agreement that the late nineteenth and the early twentieth centuries were distinct political periods. The party-systems approach to American political history first developed as a way to periodize aggregate voting behavior, but it is now being interpreted much more broadly. Party systems feature not only enduring voting patterns but also a stable balance of power between the parties, consistent institutional structures, and sustained patterns of political leadership and policy outcomes. The party-systems approach thus is a way to structure analysis of mass electoral behavior and link it to a larger picture of the American political system.[16]

If we are to fully understand the meaning of electoral participation, the connections between voting and the exercise of power by the state must be explored. Ignoring this relationship has been a central weakness of much of the "new political history," which has tended to look at public policy only for its symbolic importance in electoral politics.[17] Voting is a personal act with political ramifications. In the late nineteenth century, the demands of participatory electoral politics reverberated throughout the political system and structured both the formation and the administration of public policy. In the early twentieth century, the demobilization of the mass electorate permitted the insulation of political decision making and the expansion of government power. Mass politics can and should be understood, therefore, within the context of the development of the modern American State, which it both reflected and affected.

In contrasting the late-nineteenth- and early-twentieth-century party systems, therefore, our concerns range beyond the forty years under direct consideration. The electoral system of the eighties and nineties was part of a unique mode of nineteenth-century American politics that extended back to the 1830s, whereas the period 1900 to 1918 witnessed the emergence of a distinctly twentieth-century polity. The changes in American politics during the early years of this century thus involved much more than a generational realignment of the party system. The electoral process experienced a transformation that fundamentally and irrevocably altered the nature of politics in this country. The legacy of the transformation endures to this day.[18]

To supplement my quantitative analysis of election returns, I draw on a wide variety of historical, political science, and political sociology literatures. Although both vast and rich, scholarship on American politics in the late nineteenth and early twentieth centuries is fragmented into several distinct and independent traditions, each with its own focus. Older work, which concentrates on third-party protests (especially Populism), on bosses, machines, and reformers, on the machinations of political insiders, and on the rise of interest-group politics, has been supplemented by the ethnocultural school of interpretation, a renewed interest in both the legal structure of politics and the growth of administrative government, and increasingly sophisticated work on political culture. In addition, diverse social science literatures, focusing on voting, realignment and party systems, pluralism, and political development, can be extremely useful to the historian of late-nineteenth- and early-twentieth-century American politics. I use these disparate literatures to help illuminate mass electoral politics and link electoral analysis to other facets of the political process.

My approach, then, is broadly synthetic. Quantitative analysis of aggregate voting gives an overview of mass electoral behavior during these crucial decades in American political development. I place that analysis within the larger context of the late-nineteenth- and early-twentieth-century party systems, thereby connecting popular electoral politics with the structure of government and the exercise of power. This focus can provide a unifying framework for a wide range of diverse works on American politics that are rarely drawn together. As with all syntheses, the level of generalization is high. But the goal, after all, is to explore a fundamental transformation of American politics.

PART ONE

Participatory Mass Politics

CHAPTER ONE

America Votes

A Nation of Electoral Participation

During the last twenty years of the nineteenth century, the American electorate was highly mobilized. Elections captured the attention of the voters as never before or since. Americans cast ballots for presidents, governors, legislators, judges, mayors, councilmen, coroners, sheriffs, tax collectors, and innumerable other officials. Terms of office were short and the list of elected officials long. Since elections were spread throughout the year, politics rarely died down.

For most voters, the physical act of casting a ballot was the climax of an extended period of campaign activity. Before Election Day rolled around, Americans participated in countless political meetings, barbecues, marches, rallies, parades, and bonfires. Electoral politics dominated the pages of the nation's newspapers and echoed from the pulpits of almost every denomination. As balloting approached, politics and the coming election became the primary subjects of private and public discourse. The principal purpose of all the tumultuous political activity was to turn out voters on Election Day. But participation did not begin and end on Election Day. The full scope of public involvement in a year-round process also needs to be assessed, as well as the social basis of mass participation.

Massive Voter Participation

Nationwide, a record number of eligible voters cast ballots during the 1880s and 1890s. Indeed, throughout most of the United States, nearly the entire electorate cast their votes on Election Day.[1] Even in the West, where the population was thinly spread and political organizations were young, and in the South, where voter participation laws were highly restrictive, turnout was remarkably high.

For the five presidential elections from 1880 to 1896, national voter turnout averaged 79.2 percent; in the North, an average 84.1 percent of the electorate cast ballots, as shown in table 1.1.[2] Voter participation was highest in the most populous regions of the country, including the four mid-Atlantic states—Delaware, New Jersey, New York, and Pennsylvania—and the north central region of Illinois, Indiana, Michigan, Ohio, and Wisconsin. For this entire period, presidential turnout *averaged* over 85 percent in twelve states and over 90 percent in five.[3]

Turnout figures for specific presidential elections highlight the magnitude of voter mobilization. In the various parts of the country, voting peaked in different elections. In many states 1888 produced the highest turnout; in others, participation in 1896 exceeded 1888 levels: ten states experienced the highest turnouts in their histories in 1896.[4] In the 1880 election the mid-Atlantic states averaged 89 percent turnout, in the 1888 election the midwestern states averaged 88 percent participation, and in 1896 the north central states averaged an unprecedented 96 percent.[5]

TABLE 1.1
*Mean Regional Presidential Turnout
Percentages, 1880–1896*

Region	Presidential Turnout
New England	73.3
Mid-Atlantic	85.3
North Central	91.2
Midwest	84.0
South	60.3
Border	78.4
Mountain	66.7
West	76.0
North	84.1
Nation	79.2

NOTE: See "Units of Analysis" in Appendix 1 for a complete list of states in each region.

TABLE 1.2
Presidential Turnout in States That Surpassed 90 Percent

State	1880	1884	1888	1892	1896
New Hampshire	91.6	86.8	90.2	86.1	78.2
New Jersey	96.4	88.3	90.4	89.3	87.8
New York	92.5	88.6	91.7	85.4	83.9
Illinois	89.4	85.4	85.4	88.1	96.9
Indiana	96.8	93.8	95.6	91.5	97.6
Michigan	85.2	87.0	92.7	83.7	95.3
Ohio	93.6	92.8	91.6	85.9	95.1
Wisconsin	89.7	94.0	92.7	87.3	95.5
Iowa	86.8	91.5	89.5	89.3	95.6
Kansas	79.4	89.1	96.5	87.1	87.6
Minnesota	87.2	81.8	90.2	77.4	86.0
West Virginia	82.5	86.3	94.0	89.7	93.4

It is striking that during the eighties and nineties, a dozen states experienced voter participation in excess of 90 percent, as shown in table 1.2. Nearly half of the nation's eligible voters (45 percent) lived in these states. In comparison to mid-twentieth-century voter participation, where 50 to 60 percent voter turnout is considered normal, such figures are truly extraordinary.

In order to illustrate the expanse of electoral participation during the late nineteenth century, peak presidential turnout is presented in map 1.1. In the entire band of northern states, from New York and New Jersey to Minnesota and Iowa, mass participation reached exceptional heights. The north central states had the greatest turnouts in both presidential and off-year elections, with averages over 90 percent. In the Midwest, Iowa, Kansas, Minnesota, and South Dakota also experienced strikingly high levels of participation, while Nebraska, North Dakota, and Missouri turned out over 80 percent of their voters. Among the populous mid-Atlantic states, participation exceeded 90 percent in both New Jersey and New York. Pennsylvania's turnout was lower but still averaged over 80 percent.[6] The border states of Maryland, West Virginia, and Kentucky experienced extensive voting as well. Together, these four regions contained two-thirds of the nation's eligible voters.[7] Table 1.3 provides a suggestive breakdown of these figures. Over 80 percent of the nation's voters lived in states where turnout exceeded 80 percent; over 60 percent lived where it topped 85 percent.

Although elsewhere in the nation voter turnout did not quite reach these heights, electoral politics still attracted mass participation. In New

England, where restrictive voter registration laws made participation more difficult, turnout varied considerably from state to state.[8] Presidential turnout averaged over 85 percent in both Connecticut and New Hampshire, while Maine peaked at this level. Participation was generally lower in Massachusetts, Vermont, and Maine but still averaged 70 percent.[9] Only in Rhode Island, which had especially tough legal restrictions on eligibility, were voting levels drastically below the national average.[10] Thus, although most of New England did not experience strikingly high turnouts on the same scale as the rest of the North, the vast majority of New Englanders voted.

In the sparsely populated mountain and West Coast states, turnout was related to the length of time that these states had been settled.[11] In California and Oregon, participation in the five presidential elections averaged over 75 percent; in Nevada, over 70 percent. California's turnout peaked at 81.4 percent in 1888, and Oregon's reached 85.1 percent in

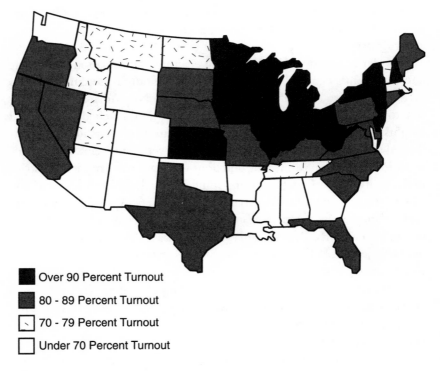

■ Over 90 Percent Turnout

■ 80 - 89 Percent Turnout

□ 70 - 79 Percent Turnout

□ Under 70 Percent Turnout

Map 1.1

TABLE 1.3
Peak Voter Turnout Percentages, 1880–1896

Turnout	Number of states	Percent of Nation's Eligible Voters in 1890	Cumulative Percent of 1890 Electorate
over 90%	12	44.4	44.4
85% to 90%	10	18.7	63.1
80% to 85%	8	17.5	80.6
70% to 80%	6	7.2	87.8
under 70%	7	12.2	100.0

1896. Among the newly and barely settled mountain states, Montana, Idaho, and Utah each turned out over 75 percent of their eligible voters in 1896. In a region where the population was thinly spread and both government and political organizations were young, we would expect turnout to be low.[12] In the face of these obstacles to electoral participation, it is remarkable that so many voters went to the polls.

Despite the fact that the lowest levels of electoral participation were in the South, the majority of the late-nineteenth-century southern electorate also voted. In every southern state except Mississippi, turnout exceeded 50 percent in at least one presidential election during the 1880s and 1890s. In seven of the ten states, turnout surpassed 65 percent.[13] In five—Florida, North Carolina, South Carolina, Texas, and Virginia—turnout peaked at over 80 percent.[14] For the five presidential elections, turnout averaged 74.9 percent in Virginia, 75.9 percent in Texas, and 83.8 percent in North Carolina.

Most southerners, both black and white, voted during the late nineteenth century until the enactment of poll taxes, literacy tests, and other restrictive legislation curtailed mass electoral participation.[15] These laws effectively eliminated black voter participation and severely curbed white voting as well. The effect on voter turnout is readily apparent. For example, in South Carolina, 83.1 percent of the eligible voters cast ballots in 1880. Following the passage of disfranchising legislation in 1882, turnout fell to 42.9 percent in 1884 and 35 percent in 1888. In Florida, 86.3 percent of the electorate went to the polls in 1880, 82.8 percent in 1884, and 78.2 percent in 1888. After the adoption of a poll tax in 1889, turnout dropped to 35.5 percent in 1892. Of the ten southern states, the five that passed restrictive legislation before 1892 all had turnout levels below 60 percent during the 1890s.[16] The five states that had not yet passed such laws all experienced voter participation above 70 percent.

The solid South, the South of minimal political participation and unchallenged Democratic dominance, did not emerge until suffrage restriction enervated southern politics.[17] Indeed, before the passage of disfranchising statutes, the evidence suggests that the South was becoming more like the rest of the United States in terms of both electoral participation and effective political opposition.[18] In several states accelerated political activity, heightened partisan intensity, and increased voter turnout accompanied the Independent and Populist challenges to the Democratic Redeemers. Thus, while the electorate in some states in the South was demobilized during the eighties and nineties, in other southern states, as in the rest of the United States, politics was participatory.

Clearly, there were significant regional differences in mass electoral behavior during the eighties and nineties. In New England, the West, and the South, turnout was more limited than in the populous mid-Atlantic, north central, and midwestern regions. Nonetheless, the extent of mass participation is striking. Throughout the nation, with only a few exceptions, Americans voted in remarkable numbers.

The Core Electorate

Turnout figures can tell more than how many Americans voted. They also reveal much about the intensity of mass participation. By comparing turnout in high profile presidential elections, which inevitably drew extensive media coverage and popular interest, with lower profile congressional and gubernatorial elections, we can assess some of the depth of popular involvement in electoral politics. Analysis of midterm turnout enables us to gauge the size of the core electorate—those voters who participated fully in electoral politics.[19]

Although turnout figures for off-year elections by themselves are useful indices of mass involvement in electoral politics, there are two common summary measures that can illustrate the depth of voter participation—roll-off and drop-off. Roll-off is a measure of the percentage of voters who fail to vote a complete ticket.[20] Drop-off, on the other hand, is an index of the percentage decrease in turnout from a presidential election to the succeeding off-year congressional election. Drop-off, therefore, measures the percentage of voters who participate only in high profile presidential elections.[21]

TABLE 1.4
*Mean Turnout Percentages in Presidential and
Off-Year Elections, 1880–1898*

Region	President	Governor off-year	Congress on-year	Congress off-year
New England	73.3	63.3	73.1	61.6
Mid-Atlantic	85.3	71.9	83.4	69.7
North Central	91.2	76.0	90.5	76.9
Midwest	84.0	74.8	82.6	73.7
South	60.3	53.5	59.1	44.9
Border	78.4	58.7	76.0	61.4
Mountain	66.7	60.4	65.7	60.6
West	76.0	72.8	73.2	69.1
North	84.1	70.3	82.8	70.6
Nation	79.2	66.6	77.9	65.3

NOTE: See "Units of Analysis" in Appendix 1 for a complete list of the states in each region.

During the late nineteenth century, massive participation was not limited to presidential elections. The vast majority of American voters participated in all elections and cast complete ballots. As table 1.4 indicates, in presidential elections, 77.9 percent of the eligible voters in the nation voted for congressional candidates. In the North, the comparable figure was 82.8 percent.[22] Each of these figures was just 1.3 percent below the figure for presidential turnout. Average state-level roll-off was only 2.8 percent in the whole country and 2.3 percent outside of the South. Most striking, in the regions with the highest turnout, the percentage of voters who voted a partial ballot was the smallest. In the mid-Atlantic states, roll-off averaged only 1.8 percent. In the north central states, a mere 0.7 percent failed to vote complete tickets. These extraordinarily low levels of roll-off are not simply an artifact of the use of party-printed ballots, which were almost always complete. Thirty-two states, including all five north central states, adopted the Australian ballot by 1892, so the continued existence of minimal roll-off suggests the predominance of core voters.[23]

Turnout figures for midterm elections provide additional evidence of the extent of mass politicization. Off-year turnout in the North for both gubernatorial and congressional races averaged just over 70 percent. In twelve states, off-year congressional turnout peaked at over 80 percent.[24] Voting levels in 1894 were the highest that this nation has ever experienced in a midterm election.[25] Indeed, turnout in late-nineteenth-century off-year elections generally exceeded normal levels of voter participation in twentieth-century presidential elections. For the whole country, drop-off averaged 18.6 percent, but outside the South it was only 13.4 percent. Thus, over 80 percent of the national voting electorate and over 85 percent of the voting electorate in the North participated fully in electoral politics. This involvement indicates the depth, and hints at the social significance, of electoral participation in the late nineteenth century. The vast majority of the electorate voted, and the vast majority of voters were core voters.

Who Voted

To understand these remarkable turnout figures, we need to explore further exactly who was voting in late-nineteenth-century America. To do so entails identifying what groups were excluded from the electorate, and therefore from voting, as well as estimating the extent of participation among various social groups that were included in the electorate. By paying close attention to the ways in which gender, ethnicity, class, occupation, age, residence, and other important social divisions affected turnout, we can develop a picture of the contours of mass electoral participation.

The primary parameter of electoral participation in the late nineteenth century was gender. Men voted and women did not. In a society characterized by a gender division of social activities, electoral politics largely belonged to men. Women were denied suffrage throughout the country in state and federal elections until the 1890s. A few women in the sparsely settled West won the franchise toward the end of the century, but the vote remained beyond the reach of the vast majority of American women.[26]

For adult men, there were few significant restrictions on either the franchise or voter participation during the eighties and nineties. Neither class, race, nor ethnicity limited legal access to the ballot. Taxpaying and most other economic prerequisites for voting had been abolished by nearly all of the states before the Civil War, and the Fifteenth Amendment to the Constitution outlawed racial limitations on suffrage. Immigrants routinely gained the vote upon naturalization, and several states even enfranchised those who had declared their intention to become citizens. Near the end of the century, states sought to curtail the franchise of blacks, immigrants, and the poor through poll taxes, literacy tests, res-

idency requirements, and voter registration; but until such laws were enacted, only a very small percentage of American men over the age of
twenty-one were not eligible to vote.[27]

Voting was nearly universal among those who were enfranchised. For
one thing, little distinction in voter turnout can be made between rural
and urban areas. Turnout was particularly robust in Indiana and Iowa,
both agrarian states, and in New York and Illinois, both of which contained large urban centers. Rural voting in Pennsylvania, for example,
exceeded urban participation, but both farming regions and cities experienced high turnouts. From 1876 to 1896, the mean turnout in presidential elections was 85.2 percent in Philadelphia County and 71.8 percent
in Allegheny County. Participation averaged 88.5 percent in eight rural
counties and 88.1 percent in four "industrial-mining" counties.[28]

A variety of other county-level studies have revealed a similar pattern
of extensive agrarian voting. In New York, rural turnout in both presidential and gubernatorial races exceeded that of urban counties by nearly
10 percent; voter participation in rural New Jersey surpassed that of the
five largest Garden State cities.[29] Throughout Indiana, voting reached
remarkable levels, with the rural counties running ahead of the urban
areas. The older, more stable farming areas had the highest participation
rates in the state.[30] These findings are significant because they run
counter to classic twentieth-century voting studies that associate rurality
with low political participation.[31] More extensive analysis of county- and
precinct-level election returns is necessary before the relative participation rates of urban and rural Americans can be ascertained. For now,
however, it is clear that in the late nineteenth century farmers voted regularly.

Voter participation also extended to the immigrants and their descendants that filled America's cities during the Gilded Age. In 1890, for example, 78 percent of Chicago's population were foreign born or of foreign stock. Impressive citywide voter turnouts make it clear that immigrants and their sons were voting on a regular basis.[32] Urban turnout was
consistently high nationwide, with inner-city immigrant wards often
turning out an even larger percentage of voters than silk-stocking
wards.[33] Using regression analysis of late-nineteenth-century county-
level data, Paul Kleppner finds that foreign-born voters, not surprisingly,
participated at lower rates than native-born voters. The turnout of
second- and third-generation Americans, however, was slightly higher
than that of the native-stock electorate.[34] Despite being handicapped by

mobility, language difficulties and long work hours, America's immigrant population regularly made it to the polling booth.

Some historians have argued that the largely unskilled and immigrant working class abstained from electoral politics, which they saw as irrelevant to their lives, and concentrated their struggle on the workplace.[35] The numbers do not support this position. The high levels of voter participation throughout the nation and in large cities necessitated a voting working class. Indeed, for the whole country, Kleppner finds no significant relationship between voter turnout and wealth.[36] This is a very important discovery since we know that in the twentieth century electoral participation is positively related to enhanced social class and increasing wealth.[37] In contrast to the modern electorate, during the late nineteenth century all economic classes were active participants in electoral politics.

Furthermore, not only were all social segments of the electorate mobilized, but new voters also were successfully incorporated into electoral participation. Participation was not limited to older voters who had personally experienced the life and death struggles of Civil War politics. As new voters came of age, they apparently went to the polls in massive numbers. From 1880 to 1896 the size of the national eligible voter population grew by over 50 percent as a result of natural increase and immigration. Yet the number of votes cast for presidential candidates more than kept pace with this expansion.[38] Although there is no way to estimate accurately the participation rates of different age cohorts from aggregate election data, the maintenance of high turnout levels over time strongly suggests that new voters were voting in large numbers.[39]

In this regard, the late-nineteenth-century electorate also differed significantly from that of the middle to late twentieth century. One of the principal findings of twentieth-century survey research is that young people participate in politics at a much lower rate than their elders.[40] American boys growing up in the late nineteenth century, however, were being socialized into a highly participatory political system, and when they came of age, they joined their fathers in voting.

Although more research is necessary before we will have a full portrait of exactly who voted in past elections, there is abundant evidence of the breadth of late-nineteenth-century voter participation. The sheer magnitude of turnouts indicates the absence of substantial age, occupational, ethnic, or socioeconomic biases in participation rates among men. This conclusion has been buttressed by detailed studies of county-level voting behavior that have invariably shown that all social segments of the electorate cast ballots.

Many forces can prevent individual voters from voting in any given election. Illness, family problems, work demands, transportation difficulties, travel, and relocation can preclude participation. Bad weather on Election Day always had the potential to reduce turnout, especially for the large rural population of the nineteenth century, which could face enormous difficulty in getting to the polls. Most important, the extensive geographic mobility of the late nineteenth century disfranchised a significant number of voters and made it much more difficult for many others to vote.[41] Considering all of these factors, it is not unreasonable to suppose that 10 to 20 percent of the eligible electorate was physically incapable of voting in any given election. If this was the case, late-nineteenth-century voter turnouts were virtually complete.

Evidence of substantially full turnouts comes from firsthand accounts of Election Day activities. Working from extensive pre-election polls, party organizers were able to keep track of voter participation throughout the day and make sure that their supporters made it to the polls. Only rarely did a voter resist partisan overtures and refuse to vote altogether.[42] Thus, we can conclude that during the eighties and nineties, practically all who were eligible to vote *and able to do so* cast their ballots.

Furthermore, although American men were fully mobilized by electoral politics in the late nineteenth century, the exclusion of women from the vote did not mean that they were uninvolved politically. As recent scholarship has made clear, a rich tradition of women's voluntarist political activity developed alongside electoral politics. Indeed, the social construction of gender in late-nineteenth-century America, which restricted women's access to electoral politics, spurred many to political action in other forms. If women were the "natural" guardians of morality and piety, as most nineteenth-century Americans believed, then they had public as well as private responsibilities. Women, black and white, mobilized themselves into a wide variety of reform organizations, benevolent associations, and other charitable enterprises. We have no hard numbers to gauge the extent of women's voluntarist politics, but the qualitative evidence of sustained widespread activity is significant.[43]

Most women, particularly of the middle and upper classes, were also involved one way or another in electoral politics. Public concerns, even nonpartisan issues of morality and charity, brought women face-to-face

with government and elected officials. Furthermore, they were cohabi-
tants in a society and culture suffused with electoral mobilization.
Women could not help but be interested and involved, even if they did
not enjoy suffrage. As we will see, women participated in the endless political activity that surrounded elections.[44] Some late-nineteenth-century
women were in fact enfranchised for a variety of local elections, usually
those relating to "women's concerns" such as schooling.[45] Full suffrage
was not unthinkable but remained a contested issue throughout the
1880s and 1890s.

Though political roles were clearly divided along gender lines, these
lines were far from impermeable. Mary Ryan has recently argued that in
terms of political history, the concept of "separate spheres" for men and
women obscures as much as it enlightens. She concludes that

> in the last quarter of the nineteenth century, under the cover of a public
> language that recognized and acclaimed the private virtues of females,
> women were entering the public carrying interests of their own and armed
> with a full stock of political tools, from the symbols of feminized politics
> (e.g., handkerchiefs) to access to the ears of legislators (e.g., as lobbyists) to
> the street weapons of the disenfranchised (e.g., brickbats) to a share of
> state power (e.g., public funds for private charities).[46]

Late-nineteenth-century women thus had their own rich world of public
political activity and a related role in electoral politics.

In uncovering the political activities of women, it is important to re-
member that denial of the vote was a fundamental limitation of nineteenth-century electoral politics. The United States had the most extensive suffrage in the world, but half of the American population was still
excluded. As a result, women were less fully incorporated into public
politics than men. Without the mobilizing forces of electoral politics,
the ability of women to act politically was often adversely affected by social circumstances. For late-nineteenth-century women, ethnicity, class,
age, level of education, and place of residence frequently militated
against political involvement.[47] Furthermore, without the vote women
had to mediate their political concerns through a male electorate and
male officeholders.

Nonetheless, in the age of popular electoral politics, women as well as
men were politicized. Participating directly in charitable and voluntary
public activities and indirectly in the spectacle of electoral politics,
women were part of the popular politics of the late nineteenth century.

Gender was a restriction but not a boundary to the ethos of mass political participation in the late nineteenth century.

The Scope of Electoral Politics

To assess the full extent of late-nineteenth-century electoral mobilization, we must look beyond the numbers and examine the role that politics played in American life. Huge voter turnouts did not simply materialize on Election Day; they were the product of year-round political activities.

To begin with, elections were much more frequent during the nineteenth century than they are today. Electoral politics seemed never to end. Morton Keller quotes an Iowa politician who complained, "We work through one campaign, take a bath and start in on the next."[48] For example, New Jersey conducted annual elections in March, April, May, and December.[49] Generally, local, county, state, and national officials were elected in separate contests. Philadelphia held municipal elections in February, whereas Pennsylvania state elections were in October and national elections in November.[50] One- and two-year terms of office were most popular, but even in states with longer terms, the terms were usually staggered so that new elections for most offices were required annually.[51]

The sheer number of elected officials was enormous. With a federal system of government, Americans elected representatives at the national, state, district, county, city or township, and ward level. To take one example, James Bryce observed the multitude of government officials chosen by ballot in cities in Ohio during the 1880s. Table 1.5 summarizes his findings and clearly illustrates the reach of the electoral system.

Election was most extensive at the local level. New York City, for example, elected a mayor, a comptroller, seventeen aldermen, twenty-four city councilmen, twelve city supervisors, a twenty-one-member board of education, a corporation counsel, and assorted other local officials, including judges.[52] Although small towns did not usually elect specialized legislative bodies, they voted for numerous administrative officers who often collectively performed legislative functions. Even the smallest townships in Illinois, for example, cast ballots for a supervisor, a clerk, an assessor, a collector, highway commissioners, justices of the peace, and constables.[53] Counties usually elected even a greater number of officials.

TABLE 1.5
Elected Offices in Ohio during the 1880s

Federal Offices:
Electors of the President of the United States, Members of the House of Representatives

State Offices:
Governor, Lieutenant-Governor, Secretary of State, Treasurer, Attorney General, State Senators, Members of the State House of Representatives, Judges of the Supreme Court, Members of the Board of Public Works, State Commissioner of Common Schools, Clerk of the Supreme Court, Auditor of the State

District Offices:
Circuit Judge, Judge of the Court of Common Pleas, Members of the State Board of Equalization

County Offices:
County Commissioner, Infirmary Directors, County Treasurer, Sheriff, Coroner, County Auditor, Recorder, Surveyor, Judge of Probate, Clerk of Court of Common Pleas, Prosecuting Attorney

City Offices:
Mayor, City Clerk, Auditor, Treasurer, Solicitor, Police Judge, Prosecuting Attorney of the Police Court, Members of the Board of Police Commissioners, Members of the Board of Infirmary Directors, Trustee of the Water Works, Clerk of Police Court, City Commissioner, Street Commissioner, Civil Engineer, Fire Surveyor, Superintendent of Markets

NOTE: Elected city offices varied; some cities chose to appoint some of these officials. Unpaid elected offices were excluded as were those that pertained only to Cincinnati and Cleveland.
SOURCE: James Bryce, *The American Commonwealth*, 2:87.

Pennsylvania counties were typical. Each elected a board of three commissioners, a sheriff, a coroner, a protonotary, a registrar of wills, a recorder of deeds, a treasurer, a surveyor, three auditors, a clerk of the court, a district attorney, and often a judge.[54] In fact, outside of urban areas, many local jurisdictions elected all of their government employees, including those that today are thought of as strictly administrative.[55] Though safe seats existed in many locales, so many offices were up for grabs in so many different contests that electoral politics was a constant presence in late-nineteenth-century America.

An extended period of political campaigning invariably preceded Election Day. In both city wards and rural townships, party caucuses or primary elections, or both, were used to nominate local candidates and to select delegates for higher-level district, city, and county nominating conventions. These conventions in turn performed the same function as local caucuses. They nominated candidates and selected delegates for even more important state and national conventions. The public process of choosing both candidates and delegates often involved a substantial segment of the electorate. In 1880, for example, New York City's parties "required 72 primary elections and 111 convention nominations to make up their tickets."[56] Similarly, on an annual basis Nebraska generally held at least two and sometimes as many as four political conventions above the county level. Almost all of them were preceded by county-level conventions.[57] At the same time and in the same manner, voters were frequently directly involved in the selection of party leaders at all levels.[58]

Even where the voters did not directly select party slates, local ratification meetings and rallies were held to endorse candidates. As gatherings of the party faithful, these served as calls to action. With public displays including speeches, singing, bell-ringing, and cannon fire, ratification meetings began the process of marshaling support for the upcoming election.[59]

Once candidates were chosen and ratified, mass participation began in earnest. Local political clubs organized to mobilize the electorate.[60] Named after presidential and gubernatorial candidates or local party leaders, clubs came together for the duration of a campaign to supplement the regular party organizations. Most were composed of all supporters of a ticket within a given geographical area, either county or ward, but some were organized by ethnic group or workplace.

> Each presidential campaign is the signal for an outburst of clubs, Republican and Democratic, of commercial travelers, of clerks of dry-goods stores, of lawyers, of merchants, of railroad employees, of workmen's clubs formed, not by wards, but by workshop, the workmen in a large factory dividing, perhaps into two clubs, the one Republican, the other Democratic; clubs of coloured men; Irish, German, Polish, Swedish clubs; even Republican or Democratic 'cyclists' brigades.[61]

Campaign clubs usually sponsored uniformed marching companies, which would publicly parade their support for the party's ticket throughout the election campaign. Presidential elections brought out the largest political displays. "By September and October," according to Michael McGerr,

> clubs and companies marched and counter-marched across the North. In small towns, each party typically had a campaign club, a marching company or two and perhaps companies of veterans, boys and blacks. There were so many marchers in cities that the parties grouped the companies together in battalions, legions, regiments, brigades and armies, whose

colonels and generals issued "battle orders" to the troops on the eve of parades.

McGerr estimates that more than one-fifth of all voters in the North played an active role in these campaign organizations.[62]

As campaigns progressed, these clubs reached out to involve virtually the entire population in the political spectacle. Rural and small-town Americans, as well as big-city residents, responded and demonstrated their support publicly, repeatedly, and enthusiastically. Among the most popular events were banner- and flag-raisings. Political clubs usually attracted large crowds to hang party banners or flags in front of campaign headquarters, in the center of town, or on a hilltop overlooking the town. Often, especially in rural areas, poles seventy or more feet high were planted to fly the banners. The parties would compete to raise the tallest pole, which was seen as a sign of upcoming victory. The poles had to be guarded throughout the campaign from partisan attempts to cut them down.[63]

In the weeks before Election Day, both the number and the variety of political events grew. Campaigns sponsored innumerable social gatherings, especially barbecues, picnics, and bonfires. Even more important were the political marches and parades that mobilized supporters time and again. "Every city and every rural district treats itself to these during the campaign," Ostrogorski observed, "and they would think themselves almost disgraced if they were deprived of them." He recognized the appeal of these colorful events:

> Fireworks, torch-light processions, cavalcades on horseback or on bicycles, ridden by hundreds or even thousands of men and women wearing a special uniform, bicycle orchestras, aquatic parades with hundreds of boats in a row, parades in the streets attended by large contingents of the followers of the party, are so many means to testifying to the enthusiasm which animates its members.[64]

By day or night, political parades drew large numbers of participants and even larger audiences, who themselves participated by cheering wildly, waving handkerchiefs and banners, and lighting fireworks. Supportive businessmen and homeowners lit up their offices and homes along the parade route, while those in opposition darkened theirs.[65]

Campaigns drew Americans to rallies as well, where they gathered to listen to political speeches. The parties blanketed the country with orators to meet the public demand.[66] The best of those speakers, the Blaines and the Bryans, attracted huge crowds of ten thousand or thirty thousand or even fifty thousand people to hear their lengthy talks. All-day orations were not uncommon, nor were all-night torchlight rallies, when crowds would listen through the night to speech after speech.[67]

The breadth of this political activity was truly astounding. At the presidential level, for example, Bryan visited twenty-seven states and spoke over six hundred times (averaging eighty thousand words each day) to an estimated five million people in 1896. Although McKinley stayed at home and ran a front porch campaign, more than three-quarters of a million supporters came to his house to hear him deliver a brief address.[68]

Late-nineteenth-century campaigns mobilized most segments of American society. Businesses distributed campaign literature to their employees, as did many unions. Government workers, including policemen and firemen, campaigned particularly vigorously. Social and cultural groups likewise took sides. Church sermons admonished parishioners not just to vote, but to vote the right way.[69] The nation's newspapers ran avowedly partisan front-page stories as well as editorials.[70]

Individuals openly displayed their political involvement. Political buttons and lapel pins adorned with portraits of the candidates or campaign slogans were proudly worn. The intensity of partisan passions found material expression also in ornate political ribbons, which were inscribed in silver and gold on brightly colored fabrics and ran up to a foot long and three inches wide.[71] Politics mattered so much that it even became a common practice to name infants after political heroes. Jackson, Clay, Harrison, and Tyler were popular first names during the nineteenth century.

In addition to sheer numbers, there is abundant descriptive evidence that a cross-section of the population involved itself in the hoopla. All levels of society, as Ostrogorski witnessed, not only attended political speeches but also actively marched in political parades: "all classes of the population are represented, from the prince of finance down to the common people; heads of business firms and members of the bar fall in, shouting themselves hoarse, in honour of the candidates of the party, just like ordinary laborers." Likewise, describing rural rallies, he found that "farmers generally come in large numbers, on horseback, in breaks, or on foot, often with their families.[72]

As campaigns reached into every corner of public life, electoral politics commanded the attention of not only the male electorate, but of women and children too. Whole families lined daytime parade routes, attended indoor speeches and outdoor rallies, and enjoyed political barbecues and other socials. Some women even rode in political parades, often as symbols of liberty, virtue, and beauty or of their state or town. Other women contributed actively to political events—cooking food, sewing banners, decorating halls, and cleaning up. Nineteenth-century gender norms limited the roles that women could play, especially since much of popular politics took place in traditional male enclaves, including saloons, livery stables, and clubhouses. Nonetheless, women were involved in a wide variety of campaign activities.[73]

Examining the material culture of late-nineteenth-century campaigns, Roger A. Fisher discovers that "a surprisingly large number of campaign mementos seem to have been wholly or primarily feminine in appeal. . . . In addition to the silk and linen handkerchiefs popular during the period, in large part as women's items, campaign objects intended solely for women included necklaces, pendants, bracelet charms, compact mirrors and pin cushions." Women were also the likely targets of decorative ceramics, glass, textiles, and household objects adorned with political portraits and symbols. The production of these political artifacts for women and women's extensive distribution is indicative of women's inclusion within the orbit of participatory electoral politics.[74]

Political enthusiasm spread down to children as well; even young boys and girls in elementary school collected and wore political buttons.[75] Passions could run deep, as the *Newark Evening News* recognized with displeasure in 1884:

> Go into any schoolhouse during a national campaign, and it will be a safe venture that you will find the great majority of children violent little partisans, ready to do valorous battle for the candidate upon whom their infantile affections are centered and firmly convinced that the diminutive adherents of the opposing factions are both conspirators in pinafores and traitors in short pantaloons.[76]

Older boys enrolled in political clubs and marching companies, providing much of the "manpower" in many uniformed marching companies.[77] Involvement in the spectacle of campaigns incorporated boys into the electoral process and prepared them to be active voters when they came of age.

The hoopla of campaign politics built up steadily as Election Day approached. From pole-raisings to barbecues to rallies, public involvement grew. Betting on elections was common, often involving public displays as well as monetary payoffs.[78] The penultimate events were the election-eve torchlight parades. Both parties tried to marshal their full forces as a demonstration of the victory to come. With the night sky aglow with bonfires and fireworks, enthusiasm reached a high pitch.[79]

When Election Day finally arrived, it was a festive holiday occasion. The actual casting of ballots was certainly not a solemn, formal process. According to Jean Baker, "[n]o one expected reverential silence; election days were noisy affairs filled with the incessant staccato of firecrackers, guns, cries and yells."[80] Most voters went to the polls on their own, as individuals rather than in groups.[81] Whole towns, however, gathered to observe and participate in the experience. In rural New York, for example, farmers and villagers would take at least half a day off from work to attend the polls. Those who left before the votes were counted would return in the evening to celebrate and settle election-day bets.[82] As boisterous celebrations, election days were the embodiment of late-nineteenth-century participatory mass politics.

Even when all the votes were counted, the winners declared, and election bets paid off, popular involvement did not end. Postelection celebrations featured much of the excitement and partisan display of pre-election rallies. Lewis Atherton describes a Democratic celebration in Monroe, Wisconsin, following Cleveland's victory:

> Again the cornet band was called into action to head a parade containing men carrying brooms marked "solid South." Others were dressed as tramps, intended as take-offs on Blaine and Logan. Mottoes and transparencies, uniformed juvenile marching clubs, fireworks and prismatics on all sides of the public square, shots from improvised cannon, Chinese lanterns everywhere in the courthouse park, speeches, and then a bonfire featured the local celebration.[83]

Sometimes whole communities gathered for postelection suppers. Whether partisan affairs or communal celebrations, men and women joined together to relish the political competition that had just concluded and to look forward to the next contest.

The Social Basis for Mass Participation

The vast scope of popular involvement in electoral politics reinforces the picture of mass participation that we derived from our analysis of electoral behavior. Extraordinary voter turnouts were the end result of participatory electoral campaigns. All segments of the public were reached, the electorate fully mobilized. The scale, extent, and intensity of political activity, moreover, provides a place to begin to understand why the public was so involved. To judge from campaign activity, electoral politics was meaningful for Americans in ways that went beyond the selection of public officials. Political participation served important social and cultural, as well as political, functions. It is this broader significance of politics in American public life that we must decipher.

To begin with, electoral politics provided public recreation and entertainment for late-nineteenth-century Americans. Political campaigns were impressive, exciting spectacles, offering ample opportunity for public involvement. Barbecues, rallies, parades, and the like enlivened people's lives and furnished much-needed breaks from daily routines. For rural Americans, political occasions provided relief from the isolation and toil of farm life; for city-dwellers, campaigns offered fellowship and escape from an environment that could be dehumanizing. It is little wonder that Americans looked forward to campaign events with eager anticipation and enjoyed them immensely.[84]

Political campaigns had much in common with other types of entertainment. Lawrence Levine demonstrates that nineteenth-century theater, concerts, and art were both participatory and largely nonhierarchical. Nineteenth-century Americans generally did not make the same distinction between high art and mass culture that twentieth-century Americans do. As a result various forms of culture intermingled, and different groups and classes found entertainment together. The line between audience and performer often blurred as a deeply engaged public interacted with performances. Of course, culture was far from uncontested: cultural occasions could be the site of much contention, particularly involving class and ethnic conflict. At stake in cultural struggles, however, were many of the same issues fought over in political campaigns. In terms of public involvement, breadth of entertainment forms, public inclusiveness, and social contentiousness, electoral campaigns were familiar to nineteenth-century Americans. They were a typical mode of amusement in a nation that had a widely shared public culture.[85]

Election campaigns were similar in form and experience to other types of nineteenth-century amusements, but they were much more available and more readily acceptable. Political recreation came at no cost to the individual voter and his family—their participation was often even subsidized. Equally important, the political nature of election campaigns imbued them with a special purpose. Electoral politics, however entertaining, could not be confused with frivolity. Quite the contrary, the seriousness of the business at hand freed Americans to fully enjoy a wide range of amusements.[86] It is understandable that the never-ending spectacle of electoral politics was a principal means of mass entertainment for the Gilded Age.

Though it was an exciting diversion from everyday life, the social aspect of electoral politics offered late-nineteenth-century Americans far more than escape. Amid all the hoopla, Americans found fellowship; they made connections with each other. As Paula Baker shows, this was especially true for men. "The right to vote," she argues, "was something important that men held in common." Parties and campaign clubs were fraternal organizations. Much of the business of politicking took place in male preserves (saloons, barbershops, and livery stables), and much of the language of politics was masculine—campaigns were organized, fought, and understood in military terms.[87] Rough and relentlessly conflicted, political campaigns brought men together in exciting and meaningful activities. Furthermore, Baker persuasively maintains that for the late nineteenth century, "participation in politics helped to define 'manhood.'" The virtues associated with political action—"integrity, self-assertion, loyalty, devotion to principle and friendship"—were widely extolled as essential male character traits. The very definition of what it meant to be a man was thus in part constructed in the public culture of electoral politics.[88] No wonder that late-nineteenth-century men relished political action and conflict.

In linking men together and providing them with fraternity, electoral politics also served to bridge class boundaries. Men from all social groups participated in campaign endeavors and voted. Politics gave rich and poor, farmers and villagers, urban workers, white-collar professionals, and business elites a common set of interests and activities. As Michael McGerr explains, it was the content of nineteenth-century campaigns, as well as the experience of campaigning, that tied the classes together: "Spectacle, played out by these groups, became an intricate dance of accommodation between candidate and people, between rich men and poor men." Examining campaign rituals, he finds that they often "underscored the power of the North's workers and farmers," repeating "age-old expressions of the pride and power of labor." At the same time, however, partisan display was also frequently paternalistic.

Wealthy men footed the bill for campaign clubs and marching companies and in the process established their generosity, importance, and status.[89] Consequently, in terms of class relations, the culture of campaigns and the experience of politicking offered mixed messages, which varied by time and place but were flexible enough to be understood differently by different segments of society. Politics brought Americans of different classes into contact with each other and served as an arena of both common action and class conflict. With a multiplicity of meanings, electoral campaigns reflected, reinforced, and indeed constructed social relations between the classes in late-nineteenth-century America.

Furthermore, the integrative role of politics extended beyond that of fraternity and interclass mediation to the entire community. American life in the nineteenth century was centered on geographic communities that were very diverse, ranging from small farming villages to rural towns to urban ethnocultural enclaves. Localism was a defining feature of all. In Robert Wiebe's words, "it was a nation of loosely connected islands."[90] This does not mean, however, that communities were isolated either physically or ideologically. Over the course of the nineteenth century, roads, railroads, and telegraph lines had linked the nation together. Urban neighborhoods became parts of citywide labor and consumer markets, and rural farms and villages were increasingly tied into regional and even national marketing networks. National news flowed into the most secluded burg. Localism, as Samuel Kernell has suggested, was thus not a culture grounded in "organic parochialism." Rather, island communities should be understood as largely self-reliant subunits of national development.[91] They adapted to social change but retained a large degree of autonomy. Throughout the century, geographic communities were the focal point of social organization and daily life.

The integrative functions performed by politics were particularly important because communities suffered from high residential mobility. As families moved again and again, they had little time to send down roots, and those who remained in one place had to live with a constantly changing set of neighbors and friends. Despite the rootlessness of the American people, however, the nineteenth century has been seen as an age of "unusual community strength."[92] The vitality of community life was due, at least in part, to the political culture. Whether they were Democrats or Republicans, Americans took their political identities with them as they moved, and these political allegiances made local life comprehensible wherever they settled.[93] Electoral politics integrated migrants into their new communities and sustained community cohesion when long-term residents departed.[94]

As varied as local communities were during the late nineteenth century, electoral politics was important to all. Politics, as we have seen, brought communities together, providing them with a public life. Churches, religious organizations, and other voluntary associations performed similar social functions, but politics alone was inclusive. Voting was open to all men; campaign activity drew the participation of the entire community. Relentlessly, indeed essentially, conflicted rather than consensual, participation in electoral politics nonetheless provided late-nineteenth-century American men with their most concrete sense of being part of a community and, in so doing, fostered community integration.

Politics was able to perform these functions because the social identities of most people coalesced. Far from being cross-pressured by conflicting forces, most Americans found that their familial, occupational, religious, ethnic, and neighborhood ties reinforced each other.[95] Electoral politics served a crucial integrative function by linking these various identities together. Americans voted as their families, friends, coreligionists, and coworkers did and in opposition to people whom they viewed as different—religiously, ethnically, and socially. As a result, partisan preferences were reinforced and active participation encouraged. These social conditions were ideal for the maintenance of a highly politicized electorate.

The integrative role of politics was most important on the local level, but elections also served to link individuals and communities to the nation. Political parties and the partisan press were the major sources of news and information about national events during the late nineteenth century. Presidential elections were national, as were the parties and the campaigns they ran. On the local level, parties worked to merge their community campaigns into the larger framework of national politics. They accomplished this goal, in part, through the use of national and patriotic symbols, as Jean Baker has found. Rather than develop their own partisan and local iconography, both parties drew upon the same set of representations: the flag, the eagle, liberty poles, and the seal of the United States. They each celebrated and harked back to the Revolution and George Washington. As a result, Baker concludes, "election campaigns brought Americans together in a highly stylized political drama that helped make their national life more coherent." It was through electoral politics that Americans learned the meaning of their national identity, and most clearly felt part of their nation.[96]

Political activity clearly had broad social and cultural significance for nineteenth-century Americans. Electoral politics was an arena for both conflict and mediation, furnishing entertainment, fellowship, fraternity, interclass linkages, a sense of community, a feeling of how people fitted into that community, and a bond to the nation as a whole. For both individuals and communities, electoral politics met a wide range of social and cultural needs and thus occupied a larger sphere of life than it would in the twentieth century. It was this greater meaning of electoral activity that underlay the full politicization of late-nineteenth-century America.

Of course, social factors by themselves do not explain late-nineteenth-century mass participation. Electoral politics had political as well as social significance; as always, politics was about power.[97] The nature of the political system had a great deal to do with political involvement. Elections were much more central to the political process than they are today, and mass organization and mobilization were the keys to electoral success. Since almost all important government officials were popularly elected, electoral politics functioned directly to manage conflict, fill public office, organize government, and thus distribute power and economic benefits. Vital political needs, therefore, motivated many Americans to vote and necessitated the mobilization of the electorate by political leaders. The closely competitive structure of partisan politics made voting all the more important.

Americans were so actively involved in electoral politics during the latter part of the last century because of a unique confluence of social, cultural, *and* political factors. The key to understanding this amalgam lies with the political parties, which helped tie together late-nineteenth-century society as they served as the chief means of political action. One must look at the parties to add depth to the picture of late-nineteenth-century mass participation.

Party Rule

The Politics of Mass Participation

Although the lowering of suffrage barriers in the late eighteenth and early nineteenth centuries was a necessary precondition for mass participation, the development of powerful political parties was the decisive factor that led to the incorporation of the American public into the electoral process.[1] Social conditions supported a political system characterized by mass participation, but neither the emergence nor the vitality of such a system was inevitable. Working in favorable social circumstances, political parties organized and mobilized the mass electorate.[2] Americans, in turn, seemed to have developed strong attachments to their party. "The vast majority of voters on both sides are partymen," Josiah Strong lamented in 1890, "who vote the same way year after year."[3]

The Voting Behavior of a Partisan Electorate

Since there were no political surveys of nineteenth-century voters, the depth of mass partisan attachments cannot be directly appraised. We can, however, evaluate voting behavior. Behavioral measures of partisanship reveal much about the role of party in electoral politics. Although not equivalent to attitudinal measures and not so robust as those we used to

TABLE 2.1
Mean Split-Ticket Voting in Presidential
Elections, 1880–1896

Region	All Elections Ticket Splitting	N (Cases)	Two-Party Ticket Splitting	N (Cases)
New England	4.0%	30	2.0%	23
Mid-Atlantic	2.2%	20	.5%	13
North Central	2.8%	25	1.1%	15
Midwest	0.5%	28	3.2%	8
South	2.2%	50	6.7%	23
Border	3.9%	20	1.0%	15
Mountain	20.5%	17	2.6%	8
West	7.4%	12	1.0%	6
North	6.9%	152	1.6%	88
Nation	8.2%	202	2.6%	111

NOTE: See "Units of Analysis" in Appendix 1 for a complete list of states each region.

look at participation, behavioral measures of electoral partisanship can be a starting point for examining the significance of party for late-nineteenth-century Americans.[4] As we assess the role that party played in mass voting, it is important to keep in mind the third-party challenges that were so prevalent during this period and relate these to our understanding of mass partisanship.

Analysis of returns can be used to measure the partisanship of an electorate both in any given election and over time. Assuming that partisan allegiance is expressed on Election Day by the casting of a straight party ticket, we can estimate the extent of party loyalty in the mass electorate. I constructed an index of split-ticket voting to measure the percentage of voters who did not vote a consistent party line on a particular ballot (see table 2.1).[5] As a way to assess the impact of third-party challenges, two different split-ticket voting averages were calculated—one including all presidential elections in each state and one including only those elections that were predominantly two-party contests on the state level. The latter approach excluded all races in which minor-party candidates received more than 6 percent of the total vote.[6]

The populous northern states experienced minimal ticket splitting in presidential, gubernatorial, and congressional races. Aggregate split-ticket voting averaged 4 percent or less in the New England, mid-Atlantic, and north central states. In the midwestern, mountain, and western states, as well as in the South, however, ticket splitting was a significant phenomenon. It is important to recognize that these were the regions where Populism made its strongest inroads. The vast majority of split-ticket voting occurred in precisely those elections that involved substantial third-party voting.

In elections without important minor-party challenges, ticket splitting averaged only 2.6 percent in the entire country and 1.6 percent in the North.[7] In two-party contests, mean split-ticket voting was 2 percent or less in the New England, mid-Atlantic, north central, border, and western regions. Not surprisingly, the figures for the midwestern and mountain states were slightly higher, reflecting some breakdown in party loyalty because of continual third-party activity. The South alone experienced a considerable amount of ticket splitting in two-party elections, but this was largely the result of gubernatorial elections in which Democratic candidates ran unopposed.[8] As a measure of aggregate party loyalty, figures for split-ticket voting indicate that when given a choice between only Democratic and Republican candidates for major offices, few voters in the late nineteenth century split their votes.

Below federal and state-level offices, ticket splitting was more common. Analyzing district-level election returns for a plethora of offices in New York and New Jersey, John F. Reynolds and Richard L. McCormick found substantially more split-ticket voting than state-level analysis reveals. Most of this ticket splitting, however, was caused by intraparty factionalism on the local level. During the late nineteenth century, partisan loyalty apparently guided voter behavior at the top of the ticket, but local squabbles within each party disrupted partisan voting for lower offices.[9]

Straight ticket voting was facilitated by the use of a party-strip balloting system during most of the nineteenth century. As long as party-printed tickets were used on Election Day, it was difficult to vote for candidates from different parties.[10] But the low level of ticket splitting during the late nineteenth century was not simply an artifact of this balloting system. Ticket splitting remained low in most states after the introduction of the Australian ballot. By 1892 thirty-two states had eliminated party-strip balloting, and by 1896 another seven had followed suit.[11]

Mean split-ticket voting in predominantly two-party contests in these states was only 1.2 percent in 1892 and 2.9 percent in 1896. From 1880 to 1896 ticket splitting in two-party presidential elections averaged only 2.3 percent in states that utilized a reformed ballot. This figure is actually slightly lower than the national average in all two-party presidential

TABLE 2.2

Pearson Product-Moment Correlations (r) for State-Level Partisan Voting in Presidential Elections Nationwide, 1880–1896

	Republican Vote				Democratic Vote			
	1884	1888	1892	1896	1884	1888	1892	1896
1880	.88	.85	.73	.67	.90	.87	.63	.62
1884		.94	.69	.58		.93	.68	.61
1888			.79	.68			.77	.63
1892				.77				.08*

NOTE: The starred correlation is not significant at .05.

contests (2.6 percent). Although ballot reform made it easier for voters to cast a split ticket by giving them—for the first time—the opportunity to vote for candidates from different parties on the same ballot, most voters still did not split their tickets.[12] Regardless of the type of ballot in use, split-ticket voting in the North during the 1880s and 1890s was minimal where there was little third-party activity.

Measures of partisan stability over time indicate a similar pattern of voter loyalty. Correlation analysis of state-level election returns reveals an underlying continuity in partisan voting throughout this period (see table 2.2).[13] The correlations in the table for both the Democratic and Republican parties are all significant and of moderate strength, with the single exception of the Democratic vote in 1896. The magnitudes of these correlations are not simply an artifact of the use of state-level election returns. Paul Kleppner's analysis of county-level data produced correlation coefficients of similar magnitude.[14] Although these figures indicate consistency in aggregate voting behavior, they also suggest a degree of instability in party voting, especially in the 1890s when electoral politics was so tumultuous. There is little doubt that much of this instability was due to third-party challenges, but it is impossible statistically to separate out the effects of minor-party activity with correlation analysis.

Correlation analysis can be supplemented by a measure of partisan swing over time. Using an index of party-vote instability that averages the partisan swing for both the Democratic and Republican parties from one election to the next, table 2.3 presents the mean state-level party-vote instability percentages for each region.[15] Nationally, party-vote instability averaged only 7.3 percent in presidential elections and 7.5 percent in congressional elections. Figures for the North alone were comparable: 7.2 percent in presidential elections and 6.8 percent in congressional ones. Party-vote instability averaged under 4 percent in the mid-Atlantic states, under 3.5 percent in the border states and under 3 percent in the five north central states.[16] These figures indicate that aggregate partisan voting was basically stable from election to election during the 1880s and 1890s.

Partisan loyalty over time was most evident in two-party states. Table 2.4 lists the mean party-vote instability percentages for both presidential and congressional races in those states that did not experience significant third-party activity. Any state in which minor parties averaged over 6 percent of the total votes cast for presidential or congressional

TABLE 2.3
Mean State-Level Presidential and Congressional Party-Vote Instability, 1882–1896

Region	Presidential Party-Vote Instability	N (Cases)	Congressional Party-Vote Instability	N (Cases)
New England	6.0%	24	4.5%	48
Mid-Atlantic	3.8%	16	6.0%	32
North Central	2.9%	20	4.5%	40
Midwest	8.6%	22	9.9%	48
South	7.6%	40	9.7%	80
Border	3.4%	16	3.9%	32
Mountain	25.6%	11	12.6%	26
West	7.3%	9	7.3%	20
North	7.2%	118	6.8%	246
Nation	7.3%	158	7.5%	326

NOTE: See "Units of Analysis" in Appendix 1 for a complete list of states in each region.

TABLE 2.4
Mean Party-Vote Instability in Two-Party States, 1882–1896

Region	Presidential Party-Vote Instability	N (States)	Congressional Party-Vote Instability	N (States)
New England	6.0%	6	4.1%	5
Mid-Atlantic	3.8%	4	3.4%	2
North Central	2.8%	4	3.0%	2
Other Northern States	3.4%	7	4.6%	4
North	4.1%	21	3.9%	13
South	7.3%	8	7.5%	1

NOTE: See "Units of Analysis" in Appendix 1 for a complete list of states in each region.

candidates during this period was excluded from the calculations of these means.[17] In twenty-one northern states, containing two-thirds of the nation's 1890 electorate, party-vote instability for these five presidential elections averaged only 4.2 percent.[18] Only in the South did aggregate partisan voting evidence much instability in two-party states. In the North, where voters had a choice only between the Democratic and Republican parties, they consistently voted for the same party, election after election.[19]

The stability in partisan ties in this period is even more striking when one considers both the nature of the electorate and the volatility of politics in the 1890s. In the first place, the electorate was growing at a phenomenal rate—over 50 percent from 1880 to 1896. Population expansion and geographic mobility meant that the composition of local electorates changed dramatically from election to election. Even more remarkable, the 1890s witnessed two huge shifts in partisan fortunes. The Democratic party's stock soared in 1890, only to plummet four years later. Despite these portentous changes, partisanship dominated the nation's voting behavior in the 1890s as it had throughout much of the century. Quantitative analysis of aggregate election returns clearly indicates that few late-nineteenth-century voters switched from one major party to the other, and even fewer split their allegiance during any single election year. Americans voted repeatedly for their political party, voting complete party tickets again and again.

The fact that most of the instability in the eighties and nineties occurred in elections characterized by third-party challenges can be seen as a further indication of the partisanship of American voters. Minor parties served as a safety valve for the partisan electorate. Unwilling to switch to the opposing camp, disillusioned late-nineteenth-century Democrats and Republicans turned to third parties. Where they emerged, third parties added a significant amount of volatility to partisan politics, but they did not disrupt the underlying patterns of loyalty.[20]

Although partisanship characterized voting behavior during the 1880s and 1890s, party politics was tumultuous. Competition between the parties was intense and relentless. Equally important, internal competition within both major parties was extensive at nearly every level. Intraparty conflict—although usually hidden in the final vote by stability in each party's base of support—was continuous. Bitter intraparty rivalries testified to the importance that voters placed on every choice their party made.[21] Late-nineteenth-century electoral politics was characterized by strong partisan loyalty on Election Day and stability in party voting over time, but it was nonetheless contentious and vibrant.

A Partisan Electoral System and Press

To understand the partisanship of the mass electorate, we need to look directly at the parties and their role within the electoral process. To begin with, the parties dominated at every stage of electoral politics. Among other things, they registered voters; printed, distributed, and counted ballots; nominated candidates; financed and ran campaigns; and controlled the distribution of political information through an overwhelmingly partisan press. Political parties functioned as both the gatekeepers to electoral politics and the agents of collective action in the electoral arena: they brought electoral politics to the American public and led a partisan electorate to the ballot box in unprecedented numbers.

In the late nineteenth century, the parties directly controlled the actual electoral machinery. Partisan considerations were a decisive factor in the conduct of elections. Always looking for an added advantage, the parties constantly contested election laws. Each party pressed for changes in the timing and place of elections, the size and location of election districts, voter eligibility requirements, and campaign regulations.[22] Partisan considerations even controlled the admission of new states. When Republicans regained control of both houses and the presidency in 1888, they moved quickly to admit six predominantly Republican western states to the Union. Two Democratic states, Arizona and New Mexico, on the other hand, were not admitted until 1912. Similarly, on the local and state level, relentless gerrymandering followed each shift in partisan fortunes and added considerably to the volatility of Gilded Age politics.[23] From a broader perspective, all of this tinkering, though designed to help one party or the other, served to accentuate the partisanship of the electoral system.[24] Regardless of the changes made, the mechanics of running elections always remained firmly in the hands of party officials.

Partisan control over the electoral process began with the qualification of voters. Party officials did the actual work of enrolling voters. In areas where voter registration was required, party canvassers kept track of registration lists and made sure that all prospective supporters were included. The parties went the farthest in qualifying new immigrants.

Party men guided them through naturalization, often, as Ostrogorski reported, paying the costs involved:

> Along with registration, the party Organizations devote themselves, in much the same way, to the naturalization of aliens likely to increase their electoral contingents. In the cities each large party committee has a permanent sub-committee in charge of the naturalization of immigrants. . . . The Organizations make them go through all the necessary formalities, pay the naturalization fees for them, and keep them warm, so to speak, for the coming elections.[25]

This helps explain why registration and active participation rapidly followed the granting of citizenship in the late nineteenth century. From the very first steps in the electoral process, the parties facilitated voting and guided Americans through the process.

Parties also were responsible for actually conducting elections.[26] Representatives from each recognized party—usually only the Democratic and Republican parties—set up polling places, policed the casting of ballots, and counted votes. On Election Day, party officials were clearly in charge. Bipartisanship, rather than nonpartisanship, was supposed to safeguard the public interest.[27]

For most of the nineteenth century, the parties even printed the ballots. Each party distributed its own ballot, listing only that party's candidates. The actual act of casting a ballot, in effect, involved voting for a party ticket rather than for individual candidates. This was most transparent in presidential elections since the names of presidential candidates often did not even appear on the ballots. Party strips usually listed only nominees for a party's electoral college electors.[28] In effect, voting involved casting one's lot with a particular party.

As long as the parties printed the ballots, such a declaration of support was generally public. Party-strip ballots differed from each other in color and shape. Partisan election officials could observe which ticket was dropped into the ballot box.[29] The system was far from monolithic, since interparty competition, as well as intraparty factionalism, made party-strip voting a contentious process. Discontented local partisans could and did distribute both their own tickets and "pasters" containing the name of a single candidate to be glued over a name on the regular party ticket.[30] Nonetheless, when the parties printed the ballots, they dominated the process of voting.

Toward the end of the nineteenth century, the position of the parties within the electoral process began to change. In a brief span of five years from 1887 to 1892, thirty-eight of the forty-four states adopted Australian ballot legislation, which provided for an official, state-printed, consolidated ballot.[31] Ballot reform was the first of many efforts to strip parties of their control over the conduct of elections. As we will see, these efforts had a significant impact on political behavior during the Progressive Era.[32] By itself, however, ballot reform had only a slight effect on late-nineteenth-century elections.

Few states adopted the Australian ballot before the 1890s, and even then, the type of reformed ballot that most states implemented continued to make it easy to vote a straight party line.[33] The parties were so firmly in command that they scarcely saw ballot reform as a threat and in many cases facilitated its rapid enactment. The use of a state-printed ballot, after all, saved parties the significant expense of printing their own ballots. Equally important, a single, standardized state-printed ballot could also help partisan leaders maintain control over dissident factions that lost the ability to distribute their own tickets or pasters.[34]

Regardless of which ballot form was used, late-nineteenth-century political parties controlled access to electoral office through a near monopoly over the nomination of candidates. Almost all elections were partisan, with the parties directly determining who ran for office under their name.[35] In most states a pyramid of partisan conventions selected candidates. Local conventions directly chose party nominees for local offices and delegates to congressional district, legislative district, or state conventions. These conventions, in turn, selected candidates and delegates for the next level of conventions. Conventions, of course, were composed mostly of the most active partymen. Under this system the selection of candidates was within the dominion of the party cadre.[36]

In conjunction with conventions and caucuses, parties also used primary meetings and elections to designate candidates. Late-nineteenth-century primaries, like conventions, were party-run affairs.[37] Only party members could run in primaries and only party members could vote. Though the party cadre did not retain as much control over nominations as they did with a convention system, support of the party organization generally remained the key to nomination by primary election.[38] With both the convention and the primary systems, political parties determined who stood for office.

Having chosen the candidates, parties then dominated political campaigning. Unlike those of the twentieth century, late-nineteenth-century campaigns did not focus on individual candidates. Parties often did not nominate their candidates for statewide offices until a month or two before an election and frequently waited until the last week to name local hopefuls.[39] Some candidates, especially on the local level, actively campaigned, but many more remained in the background. Openly canvassing for votes was still seen by some as a display of unseemly political ambition.[40] Under these circumstances, candidate-centered campaigns were impossible.

Party leaders, rather than individual candidates, organized the campaigns for their entire ticket. John Reynolds describes the extent of party control over campaigns in New Jersey:

> At the conclusion of the nominating process, the parties' state executive committees took responsibility for managing the campaign. They mapped out strategy, raised money, and made decisions about what resources (speakers, literature, or cash) would go where. The state committees also appointed their county-level counterparts, which printed up party tickets and took responsibility for selecting ward or township committees.[41]

In other states, party committees were elected or chosen at conventions, but in all they ran the campaigns. Purse strings, as always, were a key means of control. Individual candidates (as well as those seeking patronage positions) were generally required to contribute to the campaign, but party committees managed the dispersal of funds.[42] What they paid for, as we have seen, was partisan spectacle. A seemingly endless stream of rallies, parades, barbecues, pole-raisings, bonfires, and the like was organized to celebrate the party and marshal support for the entire ticket. With the focus always on the party and its entire slate of nominees, individual candidates were thoroughly beholden to their party for election.[43]

Even at the presidential level, the parties superseded the candidates. Unlike many of their predecessors, late-nineteenth-century presidential candidates were no longer restricted to silence by republican suspicion of ambitious politicians. Increasingly active in their campaigns, some presidential nominees even undertook speaking tours. Whether campaigns were run from the stump or the front porch, however, respect for the dignity and decorum of the office still circumscribed the candidate's role. Party, rather than personality, remained the focus. Not until the very end of the century did individual candidates, first William Jennings Bryan and then Theodore Roosevelt, become the focus of the national campaigns.[44]

The predominance of party in political campaigns rested not only on partisan mastery over the machinery of elections, but also on the partisanship of the press. In an age before electronic communication, newspapers played the central role in the spread of political information. Political news, particularly on the national level, was the lifeline of the fourth estate and was almost always delivered with a partisan slant.[45]

The overwhelming majority of papers in the country, urban and rural, big and small, avidly supported either the Democratic or the Republican party. Surveying the mid-nineteenth-century press, Richard Jensen finds that there were 1,620 partisan newspapers in 1850 with a combined daily circulation of over two million (nearly one copy for every voter). In contrast, there were 83 "independent" papers with a total circulation of only three hundred thousand, concentrated in Philadelphia, Boston, and New York.[46]

During the last two decades of the century, both the number of newspapers and their total circulation increased enormously. Some of this growth was due to the proliferation of urban mass dailies, but most of it was in small, local papers, some of which were in foreign languages. The parties subsidized many of these community papers directly or indirectly with party and government printing contracts. Almost all of the local newspapers were, of course, intensely partisan. They regularly carried political inserts supplied by the parties and routinely distributed partisan campaign literature as elections approached.[47]

Party allegiance was proudly proclaimed on mastheads and editorial pages throughout the nation. "Republican in everything, independent in nothing," declared the *Chicago Inter Ocean*, and the *LaCrosse (Wisconsin) Democrat* announced itself to be "Democratic at all times and under all circumstances."[48] Partisanship extended to every corner of the paper: little distinction was made between editorials and news stories.

> The papers place at their disposal, for the advocacy of the candidates and the policy of the party, not only the pens of their editors, but also their columns by inserting this or that communication or article which the committees supply them with. For this purpose there are, at the head-quarters of the parties, and often also attached to State committees, press bureaus which prepare copy for the newspapers in the form of telegraphic dispatches, editorials, correspondence, etc.[49]

The partisan slant was anything but subtle. As national elections approached, "the chief journals," James Bryce observed, "have for two or three months a daily leading article recommending their own and assailing the hostile candidate, with a swarm of minor editorial paragraphs bearing on the election."[50] From his study, Jensen concludes that year-round "the party line was inherent in every line of newscopy not to mention the long authoritative editorials. The stupidity of the enemy and the triumphs of the party were chronicled in every issue."[51] Without a doubt, a partisan press enabled political parties to structure the dissemination of political information to the electorate.

Toward the end of the century, the tight bond between press and party began to loosen.[52] Increasing numbers of urban newspapers, both elite papers and sensationalist dailies, were independent of direct party control. Pioneering the "new journalism," Joseph Pulitzer declared, "we serve no party but the people."[53] Financial success for these papers depended not on party largesse but on circulation and advertising revenue. Though most papers retained their partisan ties, the decline in affiliation was significant. Looking at the press in the North, Mike McGerr finds that "by 1890, 25 percent of the more than 9000 Northern weeklies stood before the public as independent papers; 24 percent of the region's 1300 dailies claimed independence as well."[54]

Independence from party affiliation, however, did not generally mean nonpartisanship. Almost all newspapers retained a strong partisan perspective. Papers that had become "independent" continued to take editorial positions in partisan politics. Equally important, the partisan framing of news reporting may have become more subtle but no less real. The *St. Louis Post and Dispatch*, for example, became even more ardently Democratic in Pulitzer's hands.[55] Throughout the eighties and nineties, the old-style party press still dominated as over three-quarters of the nation's papers continued to be officially aligned with a party. Even with the new journalism, partisanship remained a strong filter through which news was delivered. The late-nineteenth-century electorate, for the most part, received its political information through the lens of party.

Partisan control over the election process and the spread of political information meant that the parties played principal roles at nearly every point where individual citizens came in contact with the political system. The parties controlled the arenas and set the rules of politics. The dominant position of the parties helps explain the partisanship of the mass electorate. When Americans participated so extensively in electoral politics in the late nineteenth century, they were engaging in party politics.

Party Organization

Late-nineteenth-century parties occupied a commanding position in the electoral system, but they were far from monolithic organizations. As Woodrow Wilson observed in 1885, they had a "curious, conglomerate character."[56] Gilded Age parties were fragmented, decentralized, and perpetually conflicted, both internally and externally.[57] Of all the resources that parties possessed, the most important was the extensive network of powerful, contentious local party organizations. The potency of partisan politics was based on precinct, ward, and county bodies and on the community leaders who directed them.[58]

During the late nineteenth century, political parties scarcely existed as national organizations. Neither party had a permanent national presence. The Democratic and Republican national committees, generally consisting of one member from each state or territory, were chosen every four years at the national convention. The committees' responsibilities focused on the conduct of the presidential election. Once the campaign was over, the Democratic and Republican national committees fell "into a state of suspended animation."[59] Not only were they largely inactive between presidential elections, but their role within electoral campaigns was also organizationally circumscribed. The national committees distributed literature, supplied speakers, and (most importantly) funneled money to doubtful states, but the activity of electioneering took place at the local level. Campaigns were communal events in which the national party played only a tangential role.[60]

The national parties were dependent on state and local organizations and had little influence over them. The Republican party was "a congeries of state and local organizations, each of which named candidates, raised funds, conducted campaigns, distributed patronage and favors, and governed or sniped at the opposition scarcely disturbed from outside their immediate jurisdictions."[61] Even more fractured than the Republicans, "the Democratic party was a random collection of local interests and leaders," as H. Wayne Morgan noted in his detailed account of Gilded Age political struggles.[62]

At the state level as well, decentralism characterized both parties. Often precariously balanced among competing factions, state parties were coalitions rather than cohesive organizations. For example, a close look at one of the nation's most influential state organizations, the dominant Republican organization in Pennsylvania (the Cameron-Quay-Penrose machine), reveals that it was continually caught up in conflicts among and within strong organizations in Philadelphia, Pittsburgh, and the rural counties. The state "machine" was, in the words of two Pennsylvania historians, "a confederation of local party chieftains."[63]

In such a fractured system, U.S. senators played a crucial role at the center of state politics. Elected by state legislatures, their office depended on their ability to manufacture and maintain support among various party factions. Senators, by virtue of their power in Washington, were often able to link party organizations within their state to national politics and bring federal resources, particularly patronage, under the control of the state party. As intermediaries in a decentralized system, U.S. senators provided some degree of integration for the majority party in each state; the minority party, devoid of this vital resource, often remained divided.

Below the state level, partisan politics was relentlessly contentious, and local party leaders had to struggle to maintain control. Even the most entrenched big-city political machines faced challenges both from within their ranks and from other party organizations. Indeed, a machine is a poor metaphor to describe party organizations in the late nineteenth century.[64] These organizations were anything but smoothly running, efficient mechanical devices. None of them, not even the strongest in New York, Boston, Philadelphia, and Chicago, were able to monopolize the nomination of party candidates over an extended period of time, much less guarantee the election of their party's nominees. Not even Tammany Hall, reputedly the most powerful urban machine in the country, had a secure hold on its local party (the New York City Democratic party) during the late nineteenth century. Tammany was just one of many organized factions within the Democratic party and was often internally divided. Likewise, in Boston, Philadelphia, Chicago, Jersey City, and other urban centers, "bosses" faced opposition from within their own organizations and parties.[65] The same was generally true in smaller cities and towns, where factions were even more fluid and personalist.[66]

In contrast to national politics, however, both major parties were highly organized on the local levels. Although contentious, local party organizations were permanent institutions; elections came and went, but party committees endured. Both parties contained a myriad of organizations that reached from the state level down through the county, city and township, ward and precinct levels. There was, of course, significant variation in the strength and extent of party organizations in different parts of the country. The more newly and sparsely settled states in the northern midwestern, mountain, and western regions lacked fully developed parties.[67] The overwhelming majority of Americans, however, lived in states where both major parties were highly organized.

Local party organizations, in terms both of structure and of numbers of people involved, was complex and, in the case of cities, exceptionally large. City and county central committees reigned over a system that included numerous county and city subcommittees and ward, district, and precinct committees, each with their own captains, leaders, and organizers. In such cases as New York City, there may have been as many as one party worker for every fifteen voters. The central committee of Tammany Hall itself had over fourteen hundred members.[68] Even in small towns and rural farming areas, local organizations did a remarkable job of blanketing entire counties. Nationwide, Ostrogorski estimated that eight to nine hundred thousand men served on local party committees, with at least fifty thousand participating above the local level.[69]

Intraparty factionalism had much to do with the vitality of local party organizations. In the tumultuous, competitive world of late-nineteenth-century partisan politics, party leaders had to work diligently to maintain their base of support. Ward, city, and county leaders controlled their parties only by securing the support of low-level local organizations and leaders.[70] Local organizations, in turn, had every incentive to mobilize voter support since their standing within the state party, including the number of seats allocated at state conventions, was directly based on the number of votes they drew.[71] As a result, both parties concentrated their resources and energy on building and maintaining strong local organizations—organizations that to a large extent were the key to voter mobilization and electoral success.

Parties were strong and active, then, at the community level, where American life was focused. Since local parties were relatively independent of centralized direction, they were free to concentrate their resources on parochial issues and needs. Parties thus established themselves at the center of community life and consequently maximized their capacity for effective voter mobilization.

The Mobilization of Individual Voters

On the local level, late-nineteenth-century party organizations forged strong links to individual voters. Here, partisan politics was personal, immediate, and concrete. Partymen in both rural and urban areas knew each voter individually, and party politics was closely tied to daily life, providing a wide range of social activities. More important, local party leaders and their organizations devoted their resources and energy to servicing their constituencies. These services, together with the personal attention and social opportunities that local politics provided, were a major factor in establishing and sustaining close ties between individual voters and their party.

Because most local party activities were informal, private, and routine, the relationship between parties and voters, forged on the block and in the neighborhood, is difficult for the historian to uncover. Outside of urban areas, information is particularly scanty, so we know far more about the machinations of Gilded Age national politicians than about the activities of local power brokers. Newer political histories have focused both on the ethnocultural roots of partisanship and the cultural significance of partisan activities, but they largely neglect local politics and its constituent functions.[72] This is unfortunate, for the intense partisanship of the late nineteenth century and the consequent ability of the parties to mobilize the electorate fully was as much rooted in the day-to-day personal side of politics as in its social and symbolic importance.

The attention that the parties devoted to individual voters is readily apparent in their pre-election activities. In much of the country, the parties could and did contact virtually every single voter in house-to-house canvassing. Jeremiah Jenks, a late-nineteenth-century political scientist, described the extent of pre-election polling:

> Before the election, arrangements are made by each local committee to canvass thoroughly the voters in the locality; to make a list containing all their names, with the parties to which they belong; to mention who are doubtful and who, in consequence, are open to persuasion of any kind; and to give any other information regarding individual voters that will be of use in the coming election. For use at the time of election other books are ordinarily prepared containing the name of every voter who needs to be looked after by the committee on or before election day.

Polling played a central role in getting out the vote:

> It may be necessary to send a carriage to bring the voter to the polls; it may
> be necessary to get his employer to bring influence to bear to secure the
> vote; it may be wise to get his friend to change his opinions by argument; it
> may be sufficient to see that on election day he is offered a certain sum of
> money. . . . It is not too much to say that in important elections in doubtful
> states every voter is individually looked after by local committees. [73]

The breadth of local organization necessary to conduct such polling was
enormous; the value for the parties of such a focus on individual voters is
self-evident.

The personal approach was so important that party organizers did not
limit contact with voters to political occasions. Far from it, partymen
made sure that they were intimately involved in the daily life of their
constituents throughout the year. They rarely missed a wedding, a fu-
neral, a christening, a housewarming, or a barbecue.[74] "I know every
man, woman, and child in the fifteenth district," George Washington
Plunkitt, Tammany Hall's most famous ward heeler, reminisced, "except
them that's been born this summer and I know some of them too. I know
what they are strong in and what they are weak in and I can reach them
by approachin' at the right side."[75] Precinct, district, and county leaders
such as Plunkitt made partisan politics personal and concrete for voters,
thereby integrating them into the electoral system.

Neighborhood institutions, particularly saloons, were sites for much
politicking. Before the turn of the century, there were over two hundred
thousand licensed saloons in the country and at least fifty thousand unli-
censed drinking establishments. In a city like Chicago, saloons outnum-
bered the total number of groceries, meat markets, and dry goods stores
combined. Many drinking spots, particularly those that catered to groups
of workers or to neighborhood ethnic groups, were busy throughout the
day. They teemed with activity, serving bracers before work and free
lunches with nickel beers, providing free toilets and newspapers throughout the day, cashing checks, doubling as convenience stores and message
centers, and dispensing fellowship all evening long.[76] Locating himself in a
neighborhood saloon, the partyman was available to his constituents, ready
to hear their needs and concerns and, as was often necessary, stand them a
drink.[77]

In many instances, the parties themselves opened and maintained clubs and clubhouses for their supporters.[78] In addition to the excitement engendered by innumerable campaign events, these centers also sponsored picnics, parades, glee clubs, softball teams, clambakes, dances, fireworks, and many other purely recreational activities.[79] Such activities provided a measure of social integration for rural and urban communities and, thus, served as a counterbalance to the massive immigration and rapid geographic mobility of the age. In so doing, they also linked voters and their families with a partisan electoral system.

Beyond social activities, the parties provided jobs, social welfare, and innumerable direct services for their constituents. Through patronage, government contractors, and other connections, party officials were able to find work for many voters. In return, the voter was expected to be a loyal party supporter. Plunkitt bragged that he could "always get a job for a deservin' man." He kept track of available work and often interceded with employers to arrange jobs for his constituents.[80]

The number and types of jobs at the direct disposal of politicians were often quite large. In Chicago Jane Addams reported that the alderman of her ward (the nineteenth) could "boast" that he had as many as twenty-six hundred constituents on the public payroll, including day laborers.[81] The Republican party organization in Philadelphia controlled an estimated fifteen to twenty thousand jobs. The Gas Works alone employed over two thousand political appointees.[82] In New York City perhaps as many as one out of twelve household heads had a public position.[83] Patronage and minor elective offices provided employment for vast numbers of loyal partisans in rural areas as well. In upstate New York in the 1890s, for example, the local Republican organizations elected and appointed over three hundred county, three thousand village, and thirteen hundred town officials.[84]

Federal patronage, too, was an enormously useful source of jobs and money. The federal government alone provided nearly one position for every hundred voters.[85] The federal bureaucracy grew from roughly 51,000 employees in 1871 to 100,000 in 1880 to 130,000 in 1884 to 190,000 in 1896. The enactment of the Pendleton Act in 1883, which created a classified civil service on the federal level for the first time, did little to limit party patronage. Civil Service coverage was left to presidential discretion and was expanded only slowly during the eighties and nineties. Neither party, after all, was willing to see valuable positions removed from partisan control. As a result the parties had as many federal patronage positions available to them in 1900 as they had in 1883.[86]

Federal patronage, like lower-level positions, was largely under the command of state and local party leaders. Possession of the White House was crucial, because the president made all federal appointments.[87] Presidents, however, with few exceptions, allowed senators of their own party free rein in making patronage appointments in their own states. Senators had full control in congressional districts represented by members of the opposing party. By custom, congressmen of the same party were generally conceded the right to nominate postmasters in their hometown and to be consulted by senators on postal appointments elsewhere in their district. Such power and influence were significant because a congressman often received control of more than two hundred postal appointments alone.[88]

Federal postmasterships were particularly valuable patronage positions. When the Republicans recaptured the White House in 1888, 427 of the 437 presidential postmasters replaced were Democrats, and 510 of the 513 new appointees were Republicans.[89] Not all postal positions paid well, but their worth to the parties was nonetheless substantial. By 1896 there were 78,500 patronage positions in the postal service, 76,000 of which were part-time fourth-class postmasterships paying less than fifteen hundred dollars annually.[90] Fourth-class postmasterships were plum jobs: the work was rarely demanding, and the position carried much local influence, especially in smaller towns and rural areas. In the age before rural free mail delivery, farmers and citizens of small towns traveled to the postmaster to get their mail, so the postmaster was at the center of a town's communication network.[91] "The fate of the party and the administration lies in the crossroads post-offices," the *Washington Post* reported on June 16, 1882. Likewise, according to the *New York Tribune*, "[e]ach country post office is the center of news, and around its stove each winter night assembles a convention wherein the political opinions of the mature are strengthened or modified, and those of the young are formed."[92] The politicization of the small-town post office, like that of the urban saloon, helped to keep the parties at the center of late-nineteenth-century life.

The ability to provide employment was an extremely valuable party resource. Not only did these jobs tie many voters and their families to their local party, but they also secured the active participation of most of the men in party activities. Among other things, patronage appointees were expected to contribute a portion of their salary to their party. ("They would be ingrates," Plunkitt declared, "if they didn't contribute to the organizations that put them in office.")[93] Since political parties raised a significant amount of their financial resources in this way, patronage to a large extent supported the vast local political organizations of the late nineteenth century.[94] At every level, patronage helped to sustain the party in power and, in the closely competitive system, to motivate the party that was out of power.

Although patronage was central to the operation of late-nineteenth-century parties, providing jobs was only one of the many ways in which politicians took care of their supporters. Over the course of the year, local parties furnished many direct and immediate services that provided their constituents with significant assistance.[95] Many of these constituent services, including providing bail, getting charges, fines, and taxes reduced, and aiding immigrants in obtaining citizenship, were of major importance to the people they helped. Others, such as arranging for street lights to be repaired and obtaining permits to open fire hydrants in the summer, improved the lives of constituents in smaller ways. But whether their problems were large or small, Americans often turned to local politicians for personal assistance.[96] Congressmen and senators, likewise, were endlessly called upon by individual voters to assist in personal matters.[97] Sometimes the exchange relationship between party leaders and their supporters was a direct quid pro quo. Voters were often paid a few dollars or bought a drink at the local pub after they cast their ballot.[98] More often than not, however, party services were called upon when needed by voters who demonstrated their loyalty regularly at the ballot box.

A focus on the daily, concrete concerns of constituents was also apparent in the actions of elected politicians in both legislative and executive offices. The issues that dominated party politics at the local level were, for the most part, direct, immediate, and practical. Questions of zoning, of where to build streetcar lines and parks, battles over street lighting and gas services, debates about liquor sales, public school curricula, and Sunday observances—these were at the heart of local politics. Americans in the late nineteenth century looked to politics to settle a wide range of economic and cultural conflicts. Politicians, in formal as well as informal ways, concentrated their attention on their constituents' parochial concerns. This occurred at all levels of politics. Most state and national politicians devoted a large percentage of their resources and time to servicing their constituents back home.[99]

The ability of politicians to address many different local concerns was a major factor in integrating the American public into the political system. This assimilation was particularly important for the poor, the foreign born, urban dwellers, and the inhabitants of rural America, for whom social conditions weighed against political participation.[100] By providing welfare services (however primitive) and personal attention, as well as a variety of social opportunities, parties were able to mitigate social disadvantages and at the same time involve all Americans in political activity.[101]

For the parties, then, devoting most of their attention and resources to individual and community needs made enormous sense. Constituent services built a strong bond between individuals and their party that was reflected in voting behavior. Jane Addams, an outspoken critic of this type of politics, well understood how the system worked. After detailing the vast array of services that the alderman in her district procured for his constituents, she lamented that "the Alderman is really elected because he is a good friend and neighbor."[102] Party leaders, through their actions and words, made it clear that particularist politics secured the support of voters. "What tells in holdin' your grip on your district is to go right down among the poor families and help them in the different ways when they need it." Plunkitt declared, "It's philanthropy, but its good politics, too—mighty good politics."[103]

The Social Basis of Partisanship

Parties also mobilized voters as members of social groups, as Catholics, Baptists, Italians, laborers, and so on. By establishing a link between party affiliation and social identities that were central in American life, political parties wove themselves into the social fabric and partisanship was constantly reinforced. It was the combination of social linkages and personal ties that explains why the parties were so phenomenally successful in mobilizing voters.

The social roots of party identification are readily apparent in late-nineteenth-century voting behavior. Regional and ethnocultural differences underlay the partisan division of the vote during the eighties and nineties. Nearly every study of partisan voting behavior undertaken during the last thirty years has revealed two main cultural fault lines dividing the electorate.[104]

One cleavage, reflecting the divisions of the Civil War and Reconstruction, split voters along sectional and racial lines. In the southern and border states, the Republican party generally attracted most of its votes from blacks and up-country whites, whereas the Democratic party maintained its prewar base of support.[105] A similar division was clearly evident in those parts of the North that had experienced significant immigration from the South. In Illinois, Indiana, and elsewhere, most white ex-southerners voted Democratic, whereas blacks throughout the North cast their votes for Republican candidates.[106] In virtually every area of the North, from Colorado mining camps to New York City Jewish neighborhoods, sectional nativity was reflected in voting behavior.[107] Throughout the North, Republicans continued to wave the "bloody shirt," cloaking themselves in the Union cause in order to activate Civil War loyalties.[108] Nationally, a strong sectional cleavage was apparent in partisan voting. The Democratic party drew most of its strength from the South; the Republican party, from the North and the West.[109]

Within the North, however, a second cultural cleavage was also reflected in partisan voting. The Democratic and Republican parties had distinct ethnic and religious bases of support. The northern Republican party's stronghold was in the pietist denominations—Quaker, Congregational, Presbyterian, Methodist, and Baptist—predominantly old-stock Americans. In contrast, most of the Democratic party's votes came from the newer, immigrant groups, many of which were Catholic; it also had supporters among German Lutherans, Episcopalians, and other liturgical sects.[110]

As critics have pointed out, serious methodological problems have plagued the quantitative analysis of the social roots of voting behavior. These conundrums derive from reliance on relatively homogeneous units of analysis, looseness of definitions of ethnic and religious groupings, inadequate understanding of the relationship between economic and cultural variables, the inability to deal with the religiously unaffiliated segment of the population, overdependence on analysis of politics in only one part of the country (the north central states), and—most serious—the difficulties inherent in making inferences about individual behavior from ecological data.[111] Nonetheless, despite these problems, the weight of quantitative evidence, using many different methodologies, makes it clear that ethnocultural divisions were an important dimension of mass partisanship. Though these divisions were not the only significant determinant of mass partisanship, as some have implied, they were certainly an important factor.

Not surprisingly, the most hard fought and long-lasting political battles revolved around political issues rooted in cultural differences. Throughout the North, state and local politics divided most bitterly on temperance, women's suffrage, Sunday observances, public and private schooling, parks and recreational services, and gambling. Identifying drinking as a sin and the source of many social problems, temperance reformers and prohibitionists looked to alcohol reform to instill social discipline in the working habits and family behavior of immigrants and laborers. To Catholics and many immigrant groups, alcohol reform seemed an attack on their cultural, communal, and even religious values, and the right to consume alcohol became an issue of self-determination.

As the home of most pietists, the Republican party frequently supported restrictions and prohibitions on alcohol use, while the Democratic party sought to protect its constituents' right to imbibe. The record is clear: during the middle and late eighties the Republican party endorsed prohibition in twenty-seven states and opposed it only in California, whereas the Democratic party opposed prohibition nationally and in every midwestern state.[112]

Partisan conflicts over schooling also erupted repeatedly: in Wisconsin, Illinois, and elsewhere, old-stock Republicans sought to pass legislation mandating English-language school instruction. German Americans, both Catholic and Lutheran, used the Democratic party to defend their right to continue instruction in German within their own schools.[113] In New York City the parties continually skirmished over the proper use of Central Park; in New Jersey bitter fights were fought over racetrack gambling. At stake in these and other urban areas were different cultural conceptions of public space, private and public ownership of land, economic morality, and leisure.[114]

Time and again, the electorate divided when pietists in the Republican party and various minor parties tried to make use of coercive government power to solve cultural problems. In the North, Democrats resisted attempts to legislate mores and behavior. These impassioned conflicts engendered strong partisan passions in voters and contributed to the polarization of the party system. In this context the depth of partisan loyalty and the stability of party voting during the late nineteenth century are understandable.

Virtually all social, ethnic, and religious groups were mobilized by the cultural politics of the eighties and nineties. Whether or not religious

and social organizations formally took an active part in political contro-
versies—and many denominations and ethnic organizations were directly involved in specific political battles—these groups became central
reference points in the party system.[115] Voters exhibited both positive
and negative reference group behaviors, uniting with their community
against opposing social and cultural groups.[116]

Although partisan division throughout the North had much in common, local variation was significant. In a community-based system, the
nature of local social divisions greatly affected partisanship. To take the
most prominent example, in areas with large Catholic populations, German Lutherans, who had a long history of squabbling with German
Catholics, generally voted Republican, whereas Catholics voted Democratic. However, in areas where pietists dominated and pushed forward
aggressive reform programs, German Lutherans often turned to the Democratic party and an alliance with Catholic voters in order to defend
their right to drink alcohol and run German-language schools.[117]

Looking closely at New Jersey, Reynolds has discovered substantial
evidence of negative reference group behavior affecting partisan loyalties
on a local level. In areas with a large concentration of black voters, the
New Jersey Democratic party's appeal on sectional and racist lines attracted additional white Protestant voters, while in areas with a substantial immigrant population, the nativist rhetoric of the Garden State's Republican party garnered the support of additional native-born voters.[118]
Partisan preferences also varied with residence: urban, suburban, town,
and rural farm voters responded differently to campaigns.[119] In many
ways local variation added to the intensity of partisan ties—ethnocultural
groups and the voters within them responded politically to the social divisions and cultural conflicts within their own community.

There was also a decided class cast to many of the cultural conflicts of
the late nineteenth century. The working class and the poor bore the
brunt of temperance, Sunday blue laws, restrictions on leisure, and other
attempts to legislate behavior. The pietist denominations, which voted
Republican, generally attracted a higher percentage of businessmen and
professionals than the liturgical churches. The newer immigrants and
southern migrants, who were the bedrock of the Democratic party in the
North, were more likely to be laborers and poorer than the Republican
old-stock voters.[120]

Unfortunately, most quantitative scholarship on nineteenth-century
voting behavior has focused on distinguishing between different social

factors that underlay partisanship rather than on the conjunction of various elements. In particular, much of the work that reveals the ethnocultural basis of party ties simultaneously denies the relevancy of economic divisions. "Party divisions in voting patterns," Samuel Hayes concluded, "were cultural, not economic, in nature."[121] Kleppner also insists that "partisan affiliations were not rooted in economic class distinctions. They were political expressions of shared values derived from the voter's membership in, and commitment to, ethnic and religious groups."[122] Problematic assumptions underlie the quantitative work upon which these conclusions are based. Privileging ethnicity over class, these historians control for ethnocultural factors in their statistical analysis of socioeconomic factors, causing the link between partisanship and economic status to decline in significance. These quantitative historians therefore dismiss findings that socioeconomic status was associated with partisan divisions as spurious by-products of ethnocultural divisions.[123] They miss the fundamental point that economic and cultural factors were intertwined.

It was the confounding of various social factors, rather than their relative importance, that was the most significant feature of late-nineteenth-century political divisions. The evidence suggests that more often than not, regional, religious, ethnic, economic, and political cleavages divided the population along similar lines. They lived, worked, prayed, played, and voted with people of the same ethnic, religious, economic, and political groups. Churches, lodges, benevolent societies, social clubs, and other cultural and social associations were relatively homogeneous. Partisan affiliation was part of a shared community culture. Group association and activity continually reinforced a partisanship that was grounded in community values and lifestyles.[124]

Both Democratic and Republican parties worked hard to maintain the ties between group membership and partisanship. Careful to balance their tickets and their campaign appeals among their various ethnic, religious, and regional supporters, the parties paid close attention to the various sociocultural components of their coalitions and tailored their appeals to the concerns of each group.[125] At all levels of politics, elaborate sets of symbols and images were used to exploit these linkages. Each party nurtured its own style and character to connect state and national politics and local concerns.[126] "Democrat" and "Republican" were important labels that provided voters with a frame of reference for understanding politics and making electoral decisions.

In effect, parties placed parochial community identities and concerns in a larger context. Tying together individuals and social groups on the local level, they also linked local communities with a broader framework of state and national politics.[127] In so doing, they helped to integrate a fragmented, mobile, heterogeneous society.[128] In nineteenth-century America, political parties were the only social institutions that had the resources and organization to unite a widely disparate electorate. Parties, Hays wrote, were "massive federations of associational activity to bring people together. . . . [They] translated the community of ethnicity and religion into larger institutions at a time when alternative social relationships had not emerged."[129] The political parties melded the diverse American people into one body politic.

Thus, party politics was more than the sum of its parts, more than just a series of campaigns and elections; the parties were at the center of community life. For most Americans political identity was firmly rooted in their social life and was therefore tangible. Partisanship was not merely a reflection of other social identities—it was important in and of itself. "The bonds of party are many and strong," Tom Patterson, a leading Colorado politician, recognized in 1892. For either a Democrat or a Republican, "his party is to him much like a home. It develops fascinations and affections that are difficult to surrender."[130] Throughout the country, men proudly identified themselves as Democrats or Republicans. Although there were no voter surveys in the 1880s and 1890s,[131] the political behavior of the electorate suggests that partisan ties were exceptionally strong and stable. Party allegiance—cultivated by diligent partisan organization and reinforced by community associations—was a lifelong commitment for most voters, and one that they passed on to their children.

Understandably, partisan passions were intense, since the issues of culture, morality, and behavior imbued politics with a special salience. Partisan passions baptized in Civil War blood, moreover, did not yield easily. As a result the psychological distance from Democrat to Republican could be enormous. For example, political orators such as Senator John J. Ingalls of Kansas pictured campaigns in military terms: "The Republican and Democrat are as irreconcilably opposed to each other as were Grant and Lee in the wilderness. They use ballots instead of guns, but the struggle is as unrelenting and desperate and the result sought the same."[132] In this climate, most Americans regarded party loyalty as a virtue. Partisan politicians and nonpartisan reformers alike agreed— most voters were intensely loyal to their party.

Partisanship and Politics

Late-nineteenth-century partisan loyalty can be understood, therefore, in several different ways. For voters, partisanship had a sociopsychological quality, rooted in ethnocultural, religious, regional, and economic identities; it was taught from father to son, from the pulpit, in the lodge, and in the workplace and reinforced by lifelong participation in the spectacle of partisan politics. Loyalty to party was a standing decision predisposing voters to cast a ballot for their party. For many men, being a Democrat or a Republican was a central part of their character.[133]

Yet if mass partisanship is understood simply as a reflection of sociological group ties and individual psychological predilections, it loses its political content. Partisanship, as Morris Fiorina explains, "is *not* something learned at mommy's knee and never questioned thereafter." Fiorina argues that voters, in effect, keep a "running tally" of subjective evaluations of party performances. Voting decisions are made retrospectively, using past performance as a guide to future action. "The cumulation of these evaluations," he suggests, "is the basis of the long-term partisan predisposition known as party identification." Partisan identification thus develops and changes over time, "in accord with [the individual's] perceptions of societal conditions, political events and the performance of incumbent officeholders."[134]

This conceptualization of partisanship allows for a variety of party identifiers. At one extreme are those voters who so strongly favor one party that it would take a monumental change for them to alter their stance. At the other extreme are voters whose partisanship simply reflects their current vote intention. At different times in our political history, the distribution of voters along this continuum has varied significantly.[135]

An understanding of partisanship as the sum of past political evaluations can be profitably applied to the late nineteenth century. The intense partisan passions of the age reflected the fact that voters observed a great deal of difference between the parties. Repeatedly called upon to vote, people generally had little trouble deciding between the two parties. From experience, they knew which party represented their cultural interests and offered them, their families, and their community, a steady flow of goods and services.

Late-nineteenth-century voters did not enter the electorate a blank slate; they brought with them the cumulative affect of their preadult political socialization in a deeply partisan political culture. Nonetheless, partisanship also needs to be understood as the end product of the mobilizing activities of parties. Voters did not develop political connections out of thin air; partisanship was cultivated and nurtured by political parties.

The legal-institutional framework of American politics greatly facilitated party politics. The parties possessed a wide array of resources, giving them the ability to structure and shape the dissemination of political information and, in the process, mold public attitudes. Extensive party organization, particularly at the grassroots level, brought politicians into direct contact with voters on a daily basis. They assiduously crafted voter support by routinely providing constituents with goods and services. Equally important, responsiveness to collective concerns, particularly cultural concerns, enabled the party workers to link up with central social groups. As a result parties were extremely successful at mobilizing voters both as individuals and as groups. Party identification was built and sustained, and constituents voted regularly, consistently, and in record numbers. Mass partisanship went hand in hand with mass participation.

To fully understand the connection between participation and partisanship, it is necessary to explore further the political dimension of power in late-nineteenth-century America. Whereas favorable social circumstances enabled the parties to mobilize the electorate, political conditions necessitated that they devote most of their resources to this task. In particular, close competitive elections made it imperative to maintain the loyalty of their supporters and get their voters to the polls. The heart of the political system in the late nineteenth century was the link between mass participation, partisan loyalty, and electoral competition.

CHAPTER THREE

Electoral Competition

The Dynamics of the Late-Nineteenth-Century Party System

To say that the late-nineteenth-century electoral system was characterized by stability in both voter participation and partisan attachments is not to say that mass politics was placid. With extensive party organizations relentlessly working to mobilize voters and with the outcome of elections dependent on their success, campaigns had an intensity that is hard to recapture. Contentiousness within each party added to the tumult of the electoral contests. Repeated third-party challenges likewise enlivened politics throughout the eighties and nineties. It was fierce competition between the parties, however, that was responsible more than anything else for the vibrancy, indeed the volatility, of the electoral system.

Electoral Competition

To measure the closeness of elections, I constructed an index of electoral competitiveness, which equals the percentage of the total vote that separated the Democratic and Republican parties subtracted from 100.[1] A score of 100 indicates full competition; as the gap between the two parties widens, the index score declines. Generally, scholars consider electoral politics competitive if the average margin of victory is less than 10 percent of the total vote, which translates into a score of 90 or above on this index.[2]

TABLE 3.1
Mean State-Level Competitiveness Scores, 1880–1896

Region	Presidential Elections	Gubernatorial Elections	Congressional Elections
New England	79.9	82.4	81.8
Mid-Atlantic	92.5	88.7	89.8
North Central	94.3	92.0	92.7
Midwest	82.4	82.1	77.2
South	66.9	44.8	56.1
Border	92.6	88.6	90.5
Mountain	68.1	83.6	81.5
West	93.5	91.9	88.4
North	85.8	85.5	85.3
Nation	81.1	75.5	78.2

NOTE: See "Units of Analysis" in Appendix 1 for a complete list of states in each region.

Sometimes elections are more hard fought than final vote totals indicate, as was the case in the eighties and nineties when third parties garnered a significant percentage of the vote. Consequently, it is important to pair analysis of electoral competition with an examination of third-party activity. In particular, discovering when and where third-party challenges approached or exceeded the margin of votes that separated the two major parties can enhance the evaluation of electoral competitiveness.

Table 3.1 regionalizes the mean state-level competitiveness scores for presidential, gubernatorial, and congressional elections from 1880 to 1896. Nationally, state-level competitiveness averaged only 81.1 in presidential contests, 75.5 in gubernatorial races, and 78.2 in congressional elections. On the average, the margin of victory between the two major parties was around 20 percent. In the North, however, elections were generally tighter. Competitiveness averages were over 85 in presidential, gubernatorial, and congressional races. Even more striking, in those regions where there was little third-party activity, competition between the Democratic and Republican parties was consistently close. In presidential elections the mean competitiveness scores in the mid-Atlantic, north central, border, and western regions were 92.5, 94.3, 92.6, and 93.5, respectively. Over half of the nation's eligible voters lived in eighteen states, where competitiveness averaged over 90 for the five presidential elections between 1880 and 1896.[3]

The use of average figures partially hides the full extent of electoral competition.[4] Since the number of elections analyzed is small, averages were greatly affected by exceptional cases. One or two noncompetitive contests drastically lowered a state's mean competitiveness rating. In many parts of the country, the evaporation of electoral competitiveness, particularly in 1896, had this effect.

Looking directly at the competitiveness of the northern states in each presidential election, it is clear that most contests were exceedingly close,

TABLE 3.2
Presidential Competition in the Settled Northern States, 1880–1896

State	1880	1884	1888	1892	1896	Mean 1880–1892	Mean 1880–1896
Connecticut	98.0	99.1	99.8	96.8	69.3	98.4	92.6
Maine	93.9	84.6	81.9	87.2	61.3	86.9	81.8
Massachusetts	81.2	92.0	90.6	93.4	56.8	89.3	82.8
New Hampshire	95.3	95.2	97.4	96.0	57.2	96.0	88.2
Rhode Island	74.6	79.8	89.1	95.0	58.1	84.6	79.3
Vermont	58.1	62.7	55.3	61.2	36.6	59.3	54.8
New England	83.5	85.5	85.7	88.3	56.5	85.7	79.9
Delaware	96.5	86.6	88.4	98.6	89.9	92.5	92.0
New Jersey	99.2	98.4	97.6	95.6	76.4	97.7	93.4
New York	98.1	99.9	98.9	96.6	81.2	98.4	94.9
Pennsylvania	95.7	91.3	92.0	93.7	75.3	93.2	89.6
Mid-Atlantic	97.4	94.1	94.2	96.1	80.7	95.4	92.5
Illinois	93.5	96.3	97.0	96.9	87.0	95.9	94.1
Indiana	98.6	98.7	99.6	98.7	97.1	98.9	98.5
Michigan	84.8	89.4	95.2	95.7	91.0	91.2	91.2
Ohio	95.3	95.9	97.6	99.9	95.2	97.2	96.8
Wisconsin	88.9	95.4	94.0	98.3	77.1	94.1	90.7
North Central	92.2	95.1	96.7	97.9	89.5	95.5	94.3
Iowa	75.9	94.8	92.2	94.7	87.4	89.4	89.0
Kansas	69.3	75.8	75.8	51.8	96.0	68.2	73.7
Minnesota	73.1	78.1	85.5	91.9	84.3	82.1	82.6
Missouri	86.2	92.5	95.1	92.5	91.3	91.6	91.5
Nebraska	69.7	83.2	86.3	68.9	94.3	77.0	80.5
Midwest	74.8	84.9	87.0	79.9	90.7	83.5	81.7
Kentucky	84.1	87.6	91.7	88.3	99.9	87.9	90.3
Maryland	91.2	94.0	97.1	90.1	86.9	93.1	91.8
Tennessee	91.0	96.3	93.5	86.5	94.2	91.8	92.3
West Virginia	90.1	96.8	99.7	97.6	94.6	96.0	95.8
Border	89.1	93.7	95.5	90.6	93.9	92.2	92.6
Colorado	94.8	87.4	85.6	58.9	28.9	81.7	71.1
Nevada	95.2	87.5	84.7	80.5	37.7	87.0	77.1
California	99.9	93.4	97.2	100	99.4	97.6	98.0
Oregon	98.4	95.7	89.1	73.5	98.0	89.2	90.9
Mountain/ Western	97.1	91.0	88.1	78.2	66.0	86.4	84.3
Totals	88.2	90.3	91.0	88.5	78.7	87.3	89.5

even tighter than the five-election averages might have led us to believe. In table 3.2 the competitiveness scores for the settled northern states indicate that competition in the North reached exceptionally high levels. In every state except Vermont, competitiveness ratings exceeded 90 in at least one election. Twenty-four states scored over 94 in at least one election, and eleven scored over 98. In key states, the division of the presidential vote between the two major parties was almost equal. Presidential elections, in effect, were decided in New Jersey, New York, Illinois, Indiana, and Ohio, where the normal division of the vote was dead even. Control over the White House rested on small pluralities in these hotly contested states.[5]

Meaningful electoral competition extended beyond the national level to state and local races.[6] In many states, gubernatorial and congressional races were even more hard fought than presidential contests. To illustrate the full extent of state-level competition, peak gubernatorial competitiveness levels are presented in map 3.1. In every northern state except Maine, Vermont, and Maryland, competitiveness scores surpassed 94 in at least one gubernatorial election.[7] Even more striking, the most populous states experienced statehouse contests that were decided by less

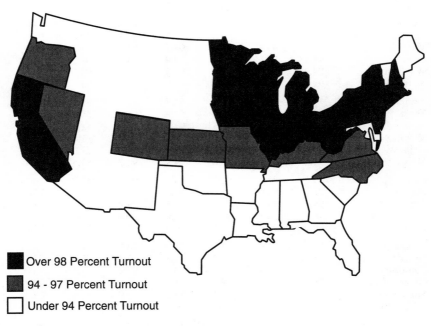

■ Over 98 Percent Turnout

▨ 94 - 97 Percent Turnout

□ Under 94 Percent Turnout

Map 3.1

TABLE 3.3
Mean State-Level Third-Party Voting
Percentages, 1880–1896

Region	Presidential Elections	Gubernatorial Elections	Congressional Elections
New England	3.3	5.7	4.2
Mid-Atlantic	2.7	7.1	7.2
North Central	4.4	7.5	6.4
Midwest	10.8	18.5	18.4
South	4.7	13.3	13.9
Border	3.1	11.7	4.7
Mountain	15.5	18.4	18.6
West	7.3	11.4	11.2
North	6.5	11.1	10.0
Nation	6.1	11.6	10.9

NOTE: See "Units of Analysis" in Appendix 1 for a complete list of states in each region.

than 2 percent of the total vote. Massachusetts, New Jersey, New York, Pennsylvania, Illinois, Indiana, Michigan, Ohio, and Wisconsin all scored over 98 on the competitiveness index at least once in gubernatorial elections.[8] During the 1880s and 1890s, the opposition party had a good chance of winning power in every northern state outside of New England.

Congressional races were equally tight, with eleven states averaging over 90 during the 1880s and 1890s.[9] Again, the largest states experienced the most competition. Congressional elections were consistently close in New Jersey, New York, Pennsylvania, Illinois, Indiana, and Ohio. As a result their congressional delegations were often narrowly split between the two parties.[10]

Electoral competitiveness between the two major parties alone does not tell the whole story of political competition. Throughout this period various minor parties, particularly the Prohibitionist party and a wide array of farmer-labor organizations, challenged the Democratic and Republican parties. In many states third parties and splinter tickets attracted a significant number of votes, especially in state and local races. Table 3.3 lists the mean state-level, minor-party voting percentages for each region.[11] From 1880 to 1896, third-party candidates accounted for over 6 percent of the vote in presidential elections and over 10 percent of the vote in gubernatorial and congressional elections. With so many votes at stake, third parties had a significant impact on the outcome of

TABLE 3.4
Pearson Product-Moment Correlations (r) between
Electoral Competitiveness and Minor-Party
Voting, 1880–1896

	Presidential Elections	Gubernatorial Elections	Congressional Elections
North	-.35	-.57	-.48
Nation	-.26	-.26	-.37

NOTE: All are significant at .001.

many elections. Fluctuations in minor-party voting inevitably affected competition between the two major parties.

In most parts of the country, the two major parties were generally less closely matched in races where third parties won a share of the vote. In table 3.4 the correlations for presidential, gubernatorial, and congressional elections, all significant and of moderate strength, indicate an inverse relationship between minor-party voting and electoral competitiveness. Third-party candidates, including Prohibitionists and Populists, tended to draw their support disproportionately from one or the other of the two major parties.[12] Consequently, when they were effective at the polls, third parties usually undercut the competitive balance between the major parties.

It is worth noting that the correlations between minor-party voting and electoral competitiveness are stronger for the North than for the nation as a whole. In the South the adoption of disfranchising legislation virtually eliminated all meaningful opposition to the Democratic party in state after state. The constituency for both the Republican party and third-party opposition movements lost access to the ballot. Third-party challenges thus largely vanished, and with them went the ability of the Republicans to seriously contest elections.[13]

Elsewhere, minor parties nationwide added volatility to electoral politics. In an age of massive turnouts and stable partisan ties, third-party voters provided an important pool of available voters, which both the Democratic and the Republican parties worked hard to woo. Even when the major parties failed to win these voters directly, they could secure minor-party support by entering into a fusion arrangement. Such alliances were an ever-present possibility in the late nineteenth century.[14]

With party-printed balloting, two or more parties could agree on a single ticket at any time before Election Day. Parties could also fuse par-

tially, supporting the same candidates for some offices and different candidates for others. The adoption of the Australian ballot, which took
control of the ballot out of the hands of the parties, made such strategies
more difficult but far from impossible.[15] Prominent temporary alliances
included Democrats with Greenbacks, Populists with various labor parties in the North, Republicans with Populists and Independents in the
South, and Greenbacks with Prohibitionists throughout the North.
These alliances enabled both Democratic and Republican candidates to
win the support of disaffected voters, whose votes were particularly valuable in an age when voters would not normally defect from one major
party to the other.[16]

Fusion arrangements often determined the outcome of elections.
With the two parties closely competitive in most states, minor parties
frequently held the balance of power. From 1880 to 1896, minor parties
in the North held the balance of power in over one-third of all elections
(see table 3.5).[17] Third-party challenges affected gubernatorial contests
most frequently, but they also played important roles in presidential and
congressional races.

The actual pattern of electoral competition and third-party activity
differed from state to state and region to region. The mid-Atlantic,
north central, border, and western states experienced the most constant
competition. In many of these states only a few percentage points separated the two parties in nearly every election, although in the mid-

TABLE 3.5
Percentage of State Elections in Which Minor Parties
Held the Balance of Power, 1880–1896

Region	Presidential Elections	Gubernatorial Elections	Congressional Elections
New England	10	22	22
Mid-Atlantic	35	38	39
North Central	52	62	47
Midwest	27	54	33
South	4	7	7
Border	15	36	19
Mountain	24	36	34
West	50	50	44
North	29	40	33
Nation	23	32	26

NOTE: See "Units of Analysis" in Appendix 1 for a complete list of
states in each region.

Atlantic and north central regions competition fell off somewhat in 1896. Minor-party activity varied considerably, however, throughout these four regions. In the western states, third-party voting was quite extensive, and minor parties held the balance of power in almost one-half of all elections. In the mid-Atlantic and north central states, the two parties split the vote so evenly that even small third parties often held the balance of power.[18] On the other hand, minor parties in the border states did not draw enough support to be a significant factor in most elections despite close, two-party competition.[19] In all four regions, the effect of minor-party challenges was to heighten partisan competition and to guarantee that no state was safe for either party.

Although elections were not so consistently close elsewhere in the North, the two parties were still competitive. In New England, the Democrats and Republicans were most closely matched in Connecticut and New Hampshire, but every state in the region except Vermont experienced some tight elections. Since minor parties attracted few votes in New England, they rarely had a significant effect on elections. Two-party competition evaporated throughout the region in 1896 with the decline of the Democratic party.[20]

The pattern of competition in the midwestern and the mountain states was strikingly different. As in the rest of the North, every midwestern and mountain state experienced some close elections during the eighties and nineties. But in these regions extensive minor-party activity disrupted two-party competition. Three-way contests among Democrats, Republicans, and Populists were rarely close, but the possibility of fusion made political contests much more uncertain than final vote totals suggest. Where fusion did occur, as in Kansas and Nebraska in 1896, election returns reveal an intensely competitive political environment.[21]

Some southern states also experienced close electoral contests. Virginia and North Carolina were consistently competitive, as was Florida before it passed disfranchising legislation in 1891. In all three states the margin of victory was generally less than 10 percent.[22] Some races were also hard fought in Louisiana and Arkansas, although competition there was more sporadic.[23] In fact, during the eighties and nineties every southern state except Georgia, South Carolina, and Texas possessed a viable opposition party,[24] since insurgency within the Democratic party in the 1880s and Populism in the 1890s greatly increased political competition.[25] Only with the enactment of restrictive legislation did electoral competition disappear from the southern states.

Thus, control over government was always contested, frequently divided, and never secure. On the national level, no president from Grant to McKinley garnered a majority of votes. The presidency changed party hands in every election from 1880 to 1896, and neither party controlled both houses of Congress for more than two years in a row. Control of Congress was split for eight of those sixteen years; for two years the party that controlled Congress did not hold the presidency. In the individual states also, the parties frequently alternated in office and divided control over the government.[26]

The turnover in political office, consequently, was rapid. In every session during the nineteenth century, freshmen held between 30 and 60 percent of the seats in Congress, and the average length of service hovered around five years.[27] Recognizing this relentless rotation in office, James Bryce did not exaggerate when he observed that "a member of the House can seldom feel safe in the saddle."[28] At the state level, too, holding office could be a tenuous proposition: the annual turnover rate in some state legislatures averaged 75 percent. For example, between 80 and 90 percent of Nebraska's state legislators were newcomers each term; less than 4 percent of the legislators in Iowa, Illinois, and Wisconsin served three consecutive terms.[29]

The volatility in office at both the state and the federal level was accentuated by political maneuvering by parties to maximize their position in a competitive environment. When parties gained control over state governments, they frequently used their power to redistrict, creating majorities for themselves in as many districts as possible. The intent of most late-nineteenth-century gerrymandering was not to create safe seats with large partisan majorities, but to position one's party to win the most seats in the future.[30] In the process, they minimized their party's marginal advantage in individual districts, with the result that the loss of a few votes often translated into a large turnover in office. Such shifts were quite common, in part because it was easier to run for office as a challenger than as an incumbent. Opposition parties usually restricted intraparty bickering and coalesced to contest for office. The prospects of gaining access to the resources of government often gave challengers a greater ability to raise campaign money. In contrast, factional disputes, especially over the distribution of patronage, frequently plagued the party in power.[31] With incumbents consequently vulnerable, few men stayed in office for long.

Over the course of the late nineteenth century, electoral volatility increased, and the national equilibrium between the two parties became

TABLE 3.6
Congressional Partisan Divisions, 1881–1899

Congress		House			Senate		
Session	Years	Rep.	Dem.	Other	Rep.	Dem.	Other
47	1881–83	147	135	11	37	37	1
48	1883–85	118	197	10	38	36	2
49	1885–87	183	140	2	43	34	0
50	1887–89	152	169	4	39	37	0
51	1889–91	166	159	0	39	37	0
52	1891–93	88	235	9	47	39	0
53	1893–95	127	218	11	38	44	3
54	1895–97	244	105	7	43	39	6
55	1897–99	204	113	40	47	34	7

SOURCE: Congressional Quarterly, Guide to U.S. Elections, 928.

less stable (see table 3.6).[32] With regard to the composition of Congress, small fluctuations in partisan voting resulted in two major swings in political fortunes: the Democrats broke the balance in the early nineties, winning sweeping control of the House in 1890 and the Senate and the presidency in 1892, only to be swamped by a move back to the Republicans in 1894 and 1896. The dimensions of these shifts in Congress were truly extraordinary. The Republicans lost 78 seats in the House in 1890, including 6 in Wisconsin, 7 in Illinois, 4 in Iowa, 6 in Michigan, 9 in Ohio, and 5 in Kansas. Just four years later, the Democrats lost 113 seats. In 1894, twenty-four states did not elect a single Democratic congressman and six elected only one Democratic representative. In all of New England, only one Democratic congressman was elected; in the Midwest, the Democrats won only 3 seats out of 89.[33]

As these large fluctuations in party fortunes indicate, both the Republicans and the Democrats faced severe challenges during the eighties and nineties. The Republican party's hold on the North became increasingly tenuous as expanded European immigration and population growth among predominantly Democratic social groups gradually changed the ethnocultural composition of the electorate.[34] During the nineties, Populism also threatened the Republicans with the loss of important midwestern states. Agrarian insurgency posed an even bigger problem to the Democratic party, first from within the party and then from outside.[35] Populism severely undermined the Democratic party's stronghold in the South, thus imperiling its national position. In the end, the Democrats fractured between a conservative wing that backed Grover Cleveland and an agrarian faction that demanded reform.

Meanwhile, intraparty factionalism continued to divide both parties. Schisms over local issues, especially cultural concerns, services, and party leadership, repeatedly erupted. Inevitably, internal competition within each party had an impact on national politics, since neither party was able to gain a secure hold over more than a few states. As a result American politics in the 1890s was so tumultuous that control over the government on all levels was literally up for grabs.

Electoral Competition, Partisanship, and Participation

For elections to have democratic significance, voters must have meaningful choices that possess realistic prospects for success at the polls. As we have seen, this was clearly the case in late-nineteenth-century America. Mass participation was extremely high because voters saw significant differences between the Democratic and Republican parties. Intense competition between the two parties provided the political basis for the mobilization of the electorate.

A comparison of electoral politics throughout the United States illustrates the strong connection between mass participation, partisan voting, and electoral competitiveness. The most competitive regions experienced the highest levels of voter participation and the most stable partisan voting patterns: close elections, stable party voting, and huge turnouts characterized politics in the north central and mid-Atlantic states. On the state level, ten states—Indiana, Illinois, Ohio, Wisconsin, New Jersey, New York, Connecticut, New Hampshire, Iowa, and West Virginia—led all others in participation, partisan stability, and electoral competitiveness. In contrast, in the southern and mountain states, where electoral politics was the least competitive, voter turnouts were lower and party voting less stable.

Correlation analysis can enable us to evaluate quantitatively the relationship among electoral competition, partisan voting, and voter turnout. Table 3.7 presents the Pearson product-moment correlation coefficients (r) among the different political variables that we have examined. The correlation matrix was calculated on the basis of state-level figures for the entire country from 1880 to 1896. All the correlations are in the right direction, of moderate strength, and significant. Electoral competitiveness and voter turnout were positively related in presidential, gubernatorial, and congressional elections. Partisan instability, as represented

TABLE 3.7

*Pearson Product-Moment Correlations (r) for the Entire Nation
for Presidential Elections, 1880–1896*

	GTO	CTO	PCOM	GCOM	CCOM	STV	PPVI	CPVI
PTO	.90	.99	.66	.65	.62	-.23	-.21	-.22
GTO		.89	.60	.59	.49	-.17	-.21*	-.15*
CTO			.66	.58	.61	-.17	-.24	-.19
PCOM				.67	.81	-.42	-.53	-.48
GCOM					.73	-.44	-.30	-.31
CCOM						-.28	-.35	-.37
STV							.50	.31
PPVI								.68

ABBREVIATIONS: PTO, Presidential Turnout; GTO, Gubernatorial Turnout; CTO, Congressional Turnout; PCOM, Presidential Competitiveness; GCOM, Gubernatorial Competitiveness; CCOM, Congressional Competitiveness; STV, Split-Ticket Voting; PPVI, Presidential Party-Vote Instability; CPVI, Congressional Party-Vote Instability
NOTE: All Correlations except starred ones are significant at .001. Starred correlations are significant at .05.

TABLE 3.8

*Pearson Product-Moment Correlations (r) for the North
for Presidential Elections, 1880–1896*

	GTO	CTO	PCOM	GCOM	CCOM	STV	PPVI	CPVI
PTO	.92	.97	.43	.33	.28	-.14*	-.29	-.26
GTO		.94	.46	.22	.24	NS	-.27	NS
CTO			.43	.27	.22	NS	-.36	-.16*
PCOM				.71	.72	-.43	-.68	-.45
GCOM					.67	-.43	-.58	-.48
CCOM						-.28	-.53	-.48
STV							.59	.33
PPVI								.76

ABBREVIATIONS: PTO, Presidential Turnout; GTO, Gubernatorial Turnout; CTO, Congressional Turnout; PCOM, Presidential Competitiveness; GCOM, Gubernatorial Competitiveness; CCOM, Congressional Competitiveness; STV, Split-Ticket Voting; PPVI, Presidential Party-Vote Instability; CPVI, Congressional Party-Vote Instability
NOTE: All listed correlations except starred ones are significant at .001. Starred correlations are significant at .05. NS indicates correlations that are not significant.

by split-ticket voting and party-vote instability, had a moderately negative correlation with competitiveness and a slightly negative correlation with turnout.[36] In other words, party voting was less stable in less competitive, less participatory elections.

The inclusion of the 1896 election reduced the magnitude of each of the correlation coefficients in table 3.7.[37] This election was a turning point between nineteenth- and twentieth-century electoral behavior: although turnout remained very high in 1896, electoral politics in many parts of the country did not feature the same degree of partisan competition and stability that had characterized earlier elections. Nonetheless, even with the 1896 election included, the relationships among participation, partisan voting, and competitiveness are all statistically significant.

These correlations are not simply a by-product of the vast sectional differences in voting behavior between the North, where competitiveness and turnout were high, and the South, where both were relatively low. Table 3.8 illustrates that the same relationships hold true when the North is analyzed separately. The correlations among voter turnout and electoral competitiveness in the North are all statistically significant, but of a smaller order. The lower levels of correlation can be explained by the small variation in both turnout figures and electoral competitiveness scores in the northern states.[38] As for partisan voting, the correlations between partisan stability and electoral competition again are stronger than between partisanship and participation.[39]

These relationships existed throughout the eighties and nineties. In every single election, voter participation and electoral competitiveness were positively related. The correlations were all significant, with coefficients ranging from a high of .80 in 1888 to a low of .56 in 1880. The relationships among both competitiveness and turnout and our measures of partisan stability were significant for the elections of 1888 and 1892, the only two elections in which these factors varied enough to permit effective use of correlation analysis on the small number of cases involved in cross-sectional analysis.[40]

Despite the limitations on correlation analysis caused by the small number of cases and the modest variations in the variables considered, both cross-time and cross-sectional analysis confirm that there were significant connections among political participation, partisan stability, and electoral competitiveness throughout the eighties and nineties. From these interrelationships, a late-nineteenth-century electoral "system" emerges. If we can specify the system's specific linkages, our understanding of Gilded Age electoral politics becomes clearer.

To begin with, electoral competition functioned to stimulate voter participation both directly and indirectly.[41] As rational political actors, late-nineteenth-century voters were more likely to go to the polls when their ballot had importance. Thus, the closer voters perceived an election to be, the more motivated they were to vote.[42] Moreover, such close competition motivated parties to make voter participation a top priority. Victory (and the resultant rewards) or defeat in a partisan, competitive electoral system depended on getting out the vote. Political parties thus devoted their substantial resources to that task.[43]

Political parties directed their mobilization efforts at their normal supporters, magnifying the importance of the social networks that sustained mass partisanship. In the heat of close-fought contests, the linkages between parties and ethnocultural, religious, family, occupational, and peer groups intensified; consequently, the closer an election was perceived to be, the less likely voters were to change their party preference.

The relationship between mass participation and partisanship was both robust and reciprocal. Voters with strong and stable partisan preferences were more likely to vote regularly, and the parties labored to ensure that they did just that. Furthermore participation in frequent elections sustained partisan stability. Since there was no surplus pool of potential voters in the eighties and nineties, party activity was aimed at maintaining existing partisan preferences rather than at attracting new supporters; as voters responded to party appeals in election after election, partisanship was continually reinforced. Large turnouts and stable partisan voting also helped sustain close political competition. Since almost all eligible voters cast ballots regularly and consistently for the same party, competitive election followed competitive election.

These strong interrelationships among voter participation, partisan stability and electoral competitiveness imbued the late-nineteenth-century electoral system with great vitality. Political conditions, specifically a strong, competitive party system, as well as social conditions, provided the basis for mass political participation.[44] The basic contours of American electoral behavior therefore remained strikingly consistent throughout the eighties and nineties.

Participatory Politics and Party Government

The dynamics of the late-nineteenth-century electoral system reverberated throughout American politics. The political parties, responding to the relentless demands for voter mobilization, were very successful, as we have seen, in performing important elective and integrative functions. Specifically, parties excelled in informing, mobilizing, and socializing the American public; organizing the electoral system; electing officeholders; and distributing goods and services. The responsibilities of the parties, however, extended beyond the electoral arena. A full picture of electoral politics must also consider government and the exercise of public power.[45]

The command that the parties exercised over electoral politics during the eighties and nineties put them in a predominant position within government. The vast majority of public officials were elected in partisan contests or appointed by partisan officeholders. Both elected officials and patronage appointees were dependent on continued party support. The parties, with dominion over access to office, were thus in a position to organize and direct the operation of government.[46] Contemporary observers—partymen and critics alike—recognized the centrality of the party in Gilded Age government. No one was more eloquent and more critical in describing the importance of party than James Bryce:

> The spirit and force of party in America has been as essential to the action of the machinery of government as steam is to a locomotive engine; or, to vary the simile, party association and organization are to the organs of government almost what the motor nerves are to the muscles, sinews, and bones of the human body. They transmit the motive power, they determine the directions in which the organs act.[47]

For better or worse, the parties dominated electoral politics, and so too did they control late-nineteenth-century government.

At the national level, party leaders organized both houses of Congress, controlled the internal distribution of power among members, and structured the flow of legislation.[48] With congressional leadership firmly in partisan hands, party caucuses worked to ensure that legislative behavior adhered to the party line. "The caucus is the drilling ground of party," Woodrow Wilson observed. "There its discipline is renewed and strengthened, its uniformity of step and gesture regained."[49] On contested issues, partisanship seems to have guided congressional voting. Party certainly was the major axis that divided senators and congressmen on most close votes.[50] Party control over individual legislators was less formal and complete than in European parliamentary systems, but party nonetheless shaped the actions of most congressmen and senators.

Parties played an equally important role in state legislatures, where party leadership and legislative authority invariably lay in the hands of the same men. Most legislators followed party lines when voting on contested issues. In Iowa, Illinois, and Wisconsin, for example, the majority of both Democratic and Republican legislators opposed each other on over two-thirds of all disputed roll call votes. On nearly one-third of these votes, 80 percent of each party was on the opposite side from that of the other party.[51] The vitality of parties at the local level likewise ensured that city councils were guided by partisan concerns, particularly in areas of strong intra- and interparty competition.

Partisanship also characterized the judiciary, many of whose members were directly elected in partisan contests. With partisan considerations also guiding appointments to the bench at all levels, the judicial system remained an integral part of party politics.[52]

The executive branch was perhaps the most partisan of all. Control over patronage and other valuable government resources made city hall, the governors' mansion, and the White House the largest prizes in late-nineteenth-century electoral politics. Partisan concerns dominated the construction of administrations. Presidents, governors, mayors, and county executives faithfully devoted their offices to rewarding supporters.[53] With partisanship deeply entrenched in all areas of the state, late-nineteenth-century government can be fairly characterized as party government.

Among other things, the dominance of party meant that all supplicants had to work within the bounds of a partisan system. Individual claimants, corporate interests, organized interest groups, and their lobbyists pressed their claims upon party leaders and through partisan channels. Parties controlled the public arena; interest groups came to them when they wanted public action.[54]

Not surprisingly, party government was deeply attuned to the needs of a highly competitive electoral arena. The need to maintain coalitions and continually mobilize supporters was reflected in both the formulation and implementation of public policy. In particular, the parties were strongly attracted to risk-free programs that rewarded supporters. Because virtually the entire electorate was mobilized and partisan, there were few unattached voters available to be won over by policy initiatives. The loss of even a small number of votes, on the other hand, could spell defeat for the party in power. The calculus of winning elections therefore dictated that the parties avoid divisive issues and focus on actions that reinforced partisan support.

Distributive economic policies thus seemed ideal. Providing goods, services, and privileges facilitated economic development and built voter support. "The riches that governments bestowed were various indeed," Richard McCormick writes. First and foremost was land, but also important were tariff protection; tax exemptions; pensions; charters and franchises to deliver public services; the use of eminent domain; the right to dam and channel waterways, fence property, and construct roads; and the use of public lands to graze animals, trap, log, and transport goods. Equally significant was government subsidization and construction of the nation's transportation and communication infrastructure, including roads, canals, railways, bridges, harbors, and telegraph lines.[55] Political concerns were far from the only factors predisposing nineteenth-century government to pursue distributive policies. In the developing economy, the economic value of government assistance to individuals and groups seeking to harness the nation's abundant resources was enormous. Nonetheless, the correspondence between late-nineteenth-century distributive policies and the needs of party government dependent on a participatory electoral system is striking.

All levels of government, from Washington, D.C., down to the smallest township, concentrated on distributive policies and actions. At the federal level many of the most basic policy issues, particularly those having to do with land use, transportation, and economic development, involved the use of the national government to aid particular interests. Nothing attracted more congressional attention throughout the Gilded Age than tariff legislation, which was explicitly designed to benefit the widest possible range of economic concerns.[56] Congress also devoted a great deal of time and energy to private demands, including pensions, war claims, patents, and patronage. A seemingly infinite variety of particularist projects planned to benefit the constituency of individual congressmen and senators also found their way into legislation.[57]

Equally important, most of the day-to-day activities of the federal government were service-oriented. Outside of the military, the most active branches of the national government were the post office, the land office, and the customs bureau. The national government seemed far less involved in legislating and governing than in distributing goods and services.[58] The focus on distributive policies was confirmed in ruling after ruling by a federal judiciary committed to economic development.[59]

State governments were no less preoccupied with meeting the parochial concerns of constituents. On the policy level, state governments throughout the country pursued "mercantilist-style policy"—land grants, cash subsidies, tax exemptions, and the like—to promote economic development.[60] "Rival claimants for state favoritism," Ballard Campbell shows, besieged state legislatures in the north central states. Much legislative time was spent on passing fencing and licensing laws, setting bounties and subsidies, and locating asylums, orphans' and veterans' homes, and schools.[61] The same was true in Colorado, where fencing laws and agricultural rights received the greatest attention.[62] State governments tried to disburse benefits widely to gain the maximum political advantage. During the 1890s in New York, for example, the Republican legislature paired expensive improvements on the Erie Canal with aid for macadam roads in other areas of the state.[63] Such policies enabled ambitious politicians to build strong state-level political organizations. Men like Matthew Quay of Pennsylvania and Thomas Platt of New York were masters at distributing government goods and services to supporters.[64]

This type of distributive politics was, if anything, even more important on the local level. Local governments, after all, were responsible for providing Americans with water, gas, light, public transportation, fire and police protection, welfare aid, education, recreational facilities, and much more. This meant that local governments had franchises, licenses, privileges, tax credits, and jobs to distribute.

As individuals and various groups vied for the best deals from local, state, and federal governments, political conflict erupted over specific distributive policies. Economic resources, however, were abundant, almost infinitely divisible (so that the bounty was spread around), and additive. Tariff protection, for example, was ideal for the purposes of party government. Protection for one commodity did not preclude protection for another. Furthermore, tariff protection, like land sales, transportation improvements, and most other distributive policies, was widely available year after year. Though the political bickering over government aid seemed relentless to politicians, these policies were generally not socially divisive. The losers in distributive politics were not broad-based economic, ethnocultural, or sectional groups, but individuals or small groups of individuals. Since those who did not get what they wanted were encouraged to try again, distributive politics did not have much of a downside for the parties at the polls.[65]

Without a doubt, distributive policies were subject to much abuse. Government services all too often were sold to the highest bidder, and public needs were sacrificed for private gain. Government contracts, franchises, and licenses made a few men very rich. Public lands were given away at an unprecedented rate, and public money was spent for development that profited private enterprise. Large corporations, especially the railroads, gave huge sums of money in campaign donations and direct bribes to ensure favorable public policies.

Nonetheless, a broad range of the population received benefits from distributive public policies. Responding in some way to almost all demands for goods and services, party government was able to aggregate the interests of a very heterogeneous and mobile nation. On the local level, this system of universal payoffs was the only way that heterogeneous, decentralized, and rapidly growing cities could be successfully governed in the late nineteenth century. In New York and many other urban centers, regardless of abuses, distributive economic policies fostered development and a modicum of government planning while delivering vital services.[66] The responsiveness of both parties to their supporters ensured that rural and small-town residents also received a share of government aid.[67] On the state and national levels, distributive policies facilitated the exploitation of America's abundant resources and provided the services necessary for rapid economic development. The aggregation of particularist demands into broad distributive policies was thus a major achievement of party government.[68]

Although party government assisted economic growth with distributive politics, the need for government to regulate development grew. At the local and state levels, state supervision of public services had always been considered a basic function of government. During the late nineteenth century, technological change, economic development, and explosive growth necessitated increased government intervention. States, for example, passed laws requiring that all urban electric, telephone, and telegraph lines be placed underground and setting standards for natural gas pipes. States and localities nationwide responded to development with new regulations.[69]

The limits of this response, however, are important to recognize.[70] Most of the new regulations adopted were narrow in scope and technical in nature. Designed to spur development, not restrict it, local and state regulatory legislation was weak and enforcement even weaker. In fact, party government barely addressed the enormous regulatory problems posed by rapidly expanding cities, industrial development, and the increasingly interdependent market economy.[71]

The history of railroad regulation best illuminates the limitations of late-nineteenth-century regulatory politics.[72] At the center of economic development, transforming the nation into one national market as they grew to unprecedented size and accumulated enormous capital and power, the railroads prompted calls for regulation from all directions. Local boosters, producers, shippers, consumers, and the railroads themselves all sought the aid of government for various and conflicting reasons.[73] In some states, especially in the midwestern, mountain, and western states, the virtual unanimity of interests within the state concerning the railroads led party leaders to champion regulatory legislation.[74] Nonetheless, state regulation invariably proved inadequate, because legislation inevitably limited both funding and enforcement authority.[75] Moreover, from the mid-1880s on, the federal courts began to strike down state regulations and taxation because they restricted the flow of commerce.[76] Most important, the economic scale of the industry far exceeded the reach of state governments. The demands for effective railroad regulation thus inevitably came to focus on the federal government.

Faced with fundamentally conflicting interests, it took Congress "nine years and a hundred legislative proposals" to fashion the Interstate Commerce Act (1887). In the end Congress applied the principles of distributive policies to railroad regulation and included something for everyone. According to one congressman, the result was "a bill that practically no one wants and yet everyone will vote for; that practically no one is satisfied with and yet they are ready to accept it; a bill that no one knows what it means and yet all propose to try the remedy provided therein."[77] The act settled none of the issues at stake in railroad regulation. "Congress," Stephen Skowronek concludes, "had not transformed the conflicts within society into a coherent regulatory policy but had merely translated those conflicts into governmental policy and shifted them to other institutions."[78] When the Interstate Commerce Commission actually tried to regulate the railroads, the Supreme Court responded by overturning most of its decisions, thereby reducing "the ICC to a mere statistics-gathering agency." Late-nineteenth-century courts, like Congress, were unable to reconcile themselves to effective regulatory government.[79]

Political ideology cannot explain the reluctance of nineteenth-century politicians to enact meaningful regulatory policies. Nineteenth-century liberalism did not preclude government involvement in the economy. Far from it, party government on all levels intervened actively and repeatedly in the economy during this period; government was deeply involved in promoting economic development and distributing economic goods. Distributive and regulatory policies differed only to the extent that distributive policies promoted economic activities and regulatory policies restricted them.[80] For the most part, however, late-nineteenth-century proponents argued that regulatory policies were necessary for economic development. In terms of government intervention in the economy, the distinction between distributive and regulatory policies was as much a difference in magnitude as in kind.

Nonetheless, with respect to late-nineteenth-century politics, the gulf between the two types of economic policies was huge. Whereas distributive policies enabled the parties to service all of their supporters, regulatory policies almost always alienated some voters. Since the predominant partisan cleavages in this period were ethnocultural and regional rather than functional, supporters of both parties were found on all sides of regulatory issues. The late-nineteenth-century party system, therefore, did not encourage the expression of regulatory economic policies: with the Democratic and Republican parties so evenly matched, neither could risk losing support by implementing government controls. As a result, what regulation did occur was almost invariably, like the railroad regulation, of a symbolic nature. Because the political climate was characterized by full participation and stable partisanship, both parties had little to gain, but much to lose, by engaging in regulatory politics.

The political considerations that structured late-nineteenth-century economic policy, both distributive and regulatory, also helped to shape the way party government handled class conflict. The parties, especially in urban areas and industrialized towns, could not afford to ignore workers' grievances. Too many votes were at stake. Party leaders therefore responded to working-class voters, as they did to all voters, with individualized distributive goods and services.[81] The collective concerns of workers, likewise, were injected into partisan politics. In many small towns and cities, mayors, city councils, and the police forces that they controlled were attuned to the needs of their constituents even when their constituents were engaged in labor conflicts.[82] Moreover, in some places during the eighties and nineties, explicitly prolabor tickets gained control of local governments through the ballot box and reshaped public policy.[83]

Nonetheless, electoral politics for the most part proved an inhospitable arena for class-based activism. Although there was a socioeconomic component to late-nineteenth-century partisan cleavages, both parties depended on the support of a wide spectrum of voters. As coalitions that transcended class boundaries, the parties could not afford to appeal to voters strictly along economic lines. The incorporation of class concerns into electoral politics necessarily involved accommodations to the demands of coalition politics. With party rather than economics governing electoral mobilization, class concerns were subordinated to partisanship.[84] Thus, the political expression of class conflict was limited and party government never dealt directly with the basic issues of industrial control.

Though the dynamics of the late-nineteenth-century electoral system militated against the full expression of class conflict, cultural concerns were given wide play. Party alignments, as we have seen, readily facilitated the political expression of cultural concerns. Conflicts over temperance, Sunday observances, schooling, and recreation, however, proved impervious to political solution. The basic social and cultural divisions that split American society could not be resolved by attempts to legislate behavior. In fact, the ease with which the party system translated cultural conflicts into political battles only exacerbated tensions while freezing partisan divisions along cultural lines.[85]

Party ties were intensified by the politicization of cultural conflict, but leaders in both parties recognized that they had much to lose from social politics. On cultural issues, it was impossible to aggregate diverse interests and craft positions to satisfy all sides. These were all-or-nothing questions. Although the Democratic and Republican parties each had clear ethnocultural bases of support, both were still coalition parties with diverse constituencies. In the highly competitive electoral environment, cultural politics could cost both parties, but particularly Republicans, crucial votes. When Republican candidates supported attempts to legislate behavior, they lost the backing of voters who did not share these cultural convictions. But when the party did not actively endorse these efforts, other votes were lost to minor parties, which focused on cultural reforms. As a result, many Republican party leaders and organizers, including William McKinley and Mark Hanna, concluded that the only way to restore stability to their party was to remove cultural issues from partisan politics altogether. Given the repeated failure of party government to resolve cultural conflict, this would prove to be an attractive solution.[86]

Party government thus had certain obvious strengths and weaknesses when it attempted to formulate public policy. Although partisan leaders were successful at aggregating the interests of their constituents and shaping policies that included something for everyone, they were unwilling and unable to formulate policies that produced clear winners and losers. Since they were responsive to voters, parties were often forced to deal with economic and cultural issues that they would have preferred to leave alone. Party government, nonetheless, remained generally unsuccessful in handling all economic and cultural issues that could not be resolved by aggregating interests.

Policy formation was not the only weakness of late-nineteenth-century government. The administrative capacities of party government were also extremely limited. Given the rapid turnover in office, elected officials were generally inexperienced and transient. Administrative support for officeholders was weak. At the turn of the century, for example, the entire presidential staff in the White House consisted of a secretary, two assistant secretaries, two executive clerks, four lesser clerks or telegraphers, and a few doorkeepers and messengers.[87]

Government at all levels was marked by an absence of professional administration. Civil Service regulations covered less than one-half of all federal appointments in 1890, and most of these were low-level jobs. Below the federal level, few states or localities used the merit system at all. Since most government employees got their jobs through partisan patronage, government bureaucracy was unstable and subject to the vicissitudes of partisan politics.

The very structure of party government precluded effective public administration. The parties were well organized on the local level but scarcely existed as state and national organizations. With the voters tied into the political system at the grassroots level, election to higher office was dependent on coalition politics. Late-nineteenth-century political alliances were always fragile and subject to change, so political power at one level could rarely be translated into power at another level.[88] Government power was therefore fragmented. Without a professional bureaucracy, experienced government officials, and a centralized party system, the capacity of party government to regulate and administer was severely limited. Recognizing this, Stephen Skowronek concludes that the American state was "unique" in the nineteenth century because it was characterized by "a highly developed democratic politics without a concentrated governing capacity."[89]

In the end the limitations of party government undermined the stability of the late-nineteenth-century electoral system. Party government accumulated its critics. The growing economy, suffering through the pains associated with rapid industrialization and urbanization, prompted extensive demands for increased government regulation and administration. All levels of government in the 1880s and 1890s experienced concerted campaigns for public regulation of transportation, utilities, insurance, banking, and other industries, as well as for Civil Service reform.[90] Reformers also attacked abuses in the distribution of government goods and services, calling for an end to corruption.[91] At the same time, agrarian discontent with the economic system fostered urgent calls for more radical reforms to establish public regulation of the corporate economy.[92]

Both reformers and agrarian radicals found the major parties largely unreceptive to their demands and thus were forced to look elsewhere for vehicles to express their concerns. Agrarian radicals turned to third-party politics and filled the ranks of the Populist party. Many late-nineteenth-century reformers, in contrast, turned away from partisan politics altogether. Nonpartisan reformers rejected party politics as a forum for resolving political conflicts and pushed instead for the creation of nonpartisan administrative bodies capable of providing government regulation of the economy.[93] In so doing, they were assaulting the basic tenets of participatory politics.

During the 1890s these third-party and nonpartisan challenges shook the foundations of the late-nineteenth-century party system. Populism posed a serious threat to both major parties and contributed to the disruption of the national electoral balance. The principal impact of nonpartisan reform in the 1890s was in large cities, where partisan political organizations faced severe challenges from "independent" reform movements. Although reformers won an election or two in many cities, party organizations invariably regained control.[94] With deep roots in the mass electorate, the two major parties emerged triumphant in the 1890s from their struggles with both the Populists and the nonpartisan reformers. The issues raised by those who sought fundamental change would not, however, go away.[95]

Late-nineteenth-century electoral politics certainly had its limitations and abuses, but it is important to recognize that these were predominantly the weaknesses of a highly participatory system. The American public was heavily politicized, mobilized, and active in electoral politics. The party system was well organized and elections were closely contested. Government policy was determined by elected officials who were responsive to their constituents. For all its failings, the late-nineteenth-century electoral system offered the American people the potential for democratic control.

PART TWO

New Politics for a Changing Society

CHAPTER FOUR

America Stops Voting

The Demobilization of the Mass Electorate

A dramatic decline in mass electoral participation fundamentally transformed the American political system during the early twentieth century. From late-nineteenth-century heights, voter turnout fell sharply and repeatedly. As the size of the active electorate contracted, the demographic composition of the voting public became increasingly skewed along socioeconomic, regional, racial, ethnic, and age lines. The structure of democratic elections through which Americans chose their leaders and influenced the distribution of public power remained largely unchanged, but the nature and extent of public involvement in the process was permanently altered.

The Decline in Voting

Voter participation fell throughout the country during the early years of the twentieth century. National turnout from 1900 to 1916 averaged only 65 percent for the first five presidential elections in the twentieth century, as compared to 79.2 percent for the last five presidential elections in the nineteenth century (see table 4.1). The drop was most severe in the South, but participation decreased in every region of the country. In both the mid-Atlantic and north central regions, voting declined by

TABLE 4.1
*Mean Regional Presidential Turnout
Percentages, 1880–1916*

Region	1880–1896	1900–1916
New England	73.3	65.5
Mid-Atlantic	85.3	75.1
North Central	91.2	80.9
Midwest	84.0	76.6
South	60.3	30.6
Border	78.4	69.9
Mountain	66.7	66.1
West	76.0	57.1
North	84.1	73.5
Nation	79.2	65.0

NOTE: See "Units of Analysis" in Appendix 1 for a complete list of states in each region.

more than 10 percent. In the northern states as a whole, the mean early-twentieth-century turnout was 73.5 percent, down from 84.1 percent.

Since turnout continued to fall throughout the two decades following 1900, the full extent of the decline in electoral participation was even larger than is indicated by these mean figures. As table 4.2 shows, by 1912 and 1916 national voter participation hovered near 60 percent, while in the North only slightly more than two out of three eligible voters continued to cast ballots. In only twenty years—from 1896 to 1916—voter participation plummeted 14.4 percent in the midwestern states, 14.8 percent in the mid-Atlantic states, 17 percent in the border states, 18.1 percent in the western states, and 21.2 percent in the north central states.

The era when almost every eligible and able voter went to the polls had clearly ended. Participation fell off most sharply, in fact, in those states where turnout had been most complete during the late nineteenth century. Whereas voter turnout in a dozen states exceeded 90 percent during the 1880s and 1890s, only three states (Indiana, Wisconsin, and West Virginia) surpassed this level in 1900.[1] Indiana alone exceeded 90 percent in 1904 and 1908.[2] Since then, no state has turned out 90 percent of its eligible voters. Never again have the peak levels of the nineteenth century been approached.

The shape of the decline in voting is as remarkable as its extent. Although some scholars have portrayed this falloff as a sharp, short-lived occurrence,[3] voter participation diminished over an extended period of time. Turnout did not decrease in every election, nor was the process identical in every part of the country (see table 4.2), but in every region except New England, the erosion in voter participation levels was a cumulative process.[4]

Both the shape and the extent of the falloff in voting can be brought into sharper focus with the help of regression analysis. By using turnout as the dependent variable and time as the independent variable, this approach to data reveals trends in turnout over time, the magnitude of those trends, and whether or not they are statistically significant (see table 4.3)[5] Regression analysis confirms that there was a strong secular decline in voter participation in most of the country from 1896 to 1916.

TABLE 4.2
Regional Presidential Turnout Percentages, 1896–1916

Region	1896	1900	1904	1908	1912	1916
New England	69.7	66.0	65.5	64.0	65.2	66.8
Mid-Atlantic	83.7	80.9	79.7	76.9	68.9	68.9
North Central	96.1	90.4	82.9	83.7	74.8	72.9
Midwest	88.0	85.0	74.7	77.8	72.0	73.6
South	55.6	41.7	26.7	28.7	25.8	30.0
Border	84.0	78.2	68.8	70.6	63.3	67.0
Mountain	71.2	74.3	67.7	65.2	58.5	64.6
West	74.9	67.9	58.0	55.4	47.4	56.8
North	85.8	81.8	75.5	75.0	66.8	68.8
Nation	79.7	73.6	65.4	65.5	58.8	61.9

NOTE: See "Units of Analysis" in Appendix 1 for a complete list of states in each region.

TABLE 4.3
Regional Regression Coefficients for State-Level Presidential Turnout over Time, 1880–1896 and 1896–1916

Region	1880 to 1896 B	R^2	F	1896 to 1916 B	R^2	F
New England	-.42*	.04	1.0	-.32*	.00	.0
Mid-Atlantic	-.32*	.06	1.2	-.57	.33	10.8
North Central	.19*	.06	1.4	-1.11	.69	61.9
Midwest	.10*	.07	1.5	-.69	.32	19.1
South	-1.04	.08	4.0	-1.02	.17	12.4
Border	.45*	.03	1.6	-.93	.18	5.4
Mountain	-.12*	.00	.1	-.48	.10	4.1
West	-.20*	.03	.3	-.98	.52	17.0
North	-.15*	.01	.8	-.66	.13	32.9
Nation	-.30*	.01	1.8	-.70	.05	15.2

NOTE: Starred correlations are not significant at .05. See "Units of Analysis" in Appendix 1 for a complete list of states in each region.

Regression coefficients are negative and significant except for New England. The coefficients range from -.48 in the mountain region to -1.11 in the north central region, meaning that outside of New England, turnout, on average, fell by from .5 percent to 1.1 percent of eligible voters each year from 1896 to 1916.[6] The average annual national drop was .7 percent, with the north central region exhibiting the sharpest decline, over 1 percent per year and 4 percent per election.[7]

This decline in electoral participation can be illustrated by graphing the change in voter turnout over time. State-level turnout for each region of the country from 1880 to 1916 is shown in figures 4.1 to 4.8. Tables 4.4 and 4.5 summarize the information in these graphs by listing both the absolute change in turnout for each state and the slope of that change for three time periods: 1880 to 1916, 1880 to 1896, and 1896 to 1916.[8] Although the results vary by state, a basic pattern is apparent: in most of the United States, presidential turnout fluctuated at high levels in the 1880s and 1890s and then fell repeatedly after 1896.

Turnout in the populous north central states exhibited this pattern most clearly (fig. 4.3). In each north central state, participation dropped between 1900 and 1916 from late-nineteenth-century peaks. In four of the five states, voting levels recovered slightly in 1916 from 1912 lows,[9] but the overall picture is of a continuous early-twentieth-century decline. The size of these downturns, ranging from 12.7 percent in Indiana to 28.7 percent in Illinois, is striking.[10] Moreover, the slopes of these twenty-year declines are all substantial and significant. From 1896 to 1916, turnout fell off at an annual rate of .8 percent in Indiana, 1.1 percent in Ohio, 1.4 percent in Michigan, and nearly 1.5 percent in Illinois and Wisconsin. These sharp declines indicate a strong break with late-nineteenth-century participation patterns in all five states.[11]

The erosion of mass electoral participation was similar in the midwestern, border, mountain, and western regions (figs. 4.4, 4.6, 4.7, and 4.8). In most of these states as well, turnout dropped sharply and continuously from 1900 to 1912.[12] Many states experienced a slight increase in voting in 1916, but participation then was considerably below late-nineteenth-century levels. The timing of the decline varied a little from region to region: voter turnout dropped dramatically after 1896 in most border and western states but did not fall in the Midwest until after 1900,[13] when the decline was just as pronounced elsewhere.[14]

The shape and timing of the falloff in voting were somewhat different in the New England and mid-Atlantic states (figs. 4.1 and 4.2). Between

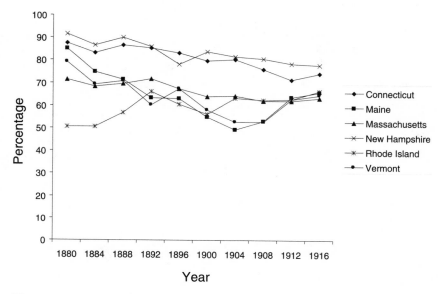

Figure 4.1

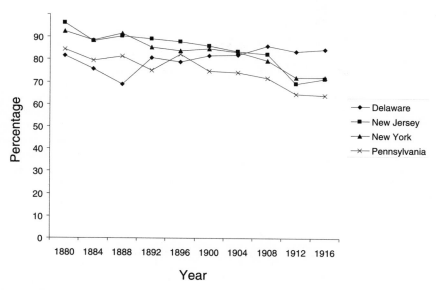

Figure 4.2

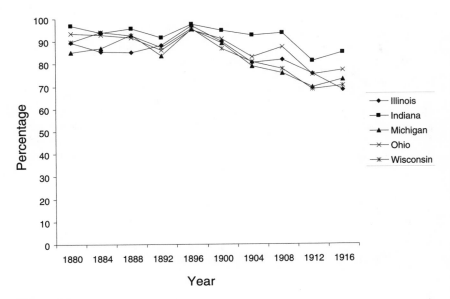

Figure 4.3

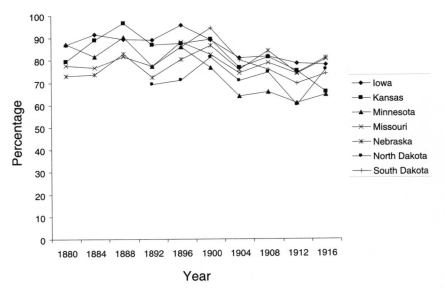

Figure 4.4

94

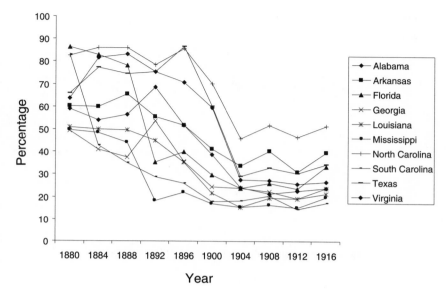

Figure 4.5

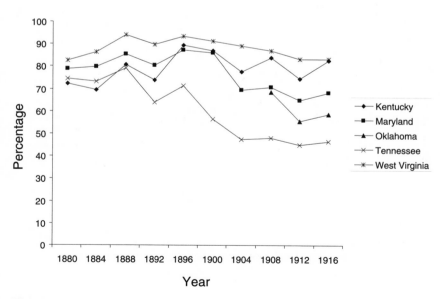

Figure 4.6

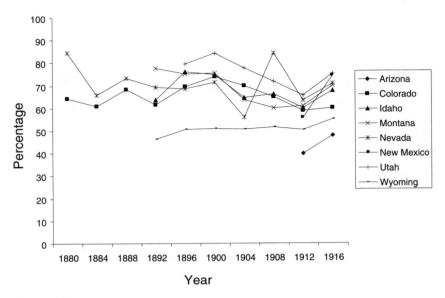

Figure 4.7

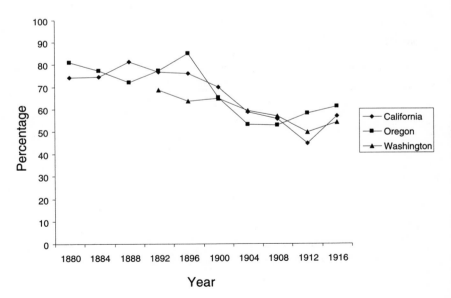

Figure 4.8

96

1880 and 1916, turnout fell in each of these states except Rhode Island and Delaware. The decline in New England ranged from 8 percent in Massachusetts to 19 percent in Maine, whereas the falloff in the three mid-Atlantic states—New York, New Jersey, and Pennsylvania—was between 20 percent and 25 percent. Voter participation in these regions, however, began to erode during the late nineteenth century. From 1880 to 1896, turnout fell in every eastern state except Rhode Island, which had never experienced extensive electoral participation.[15] The demobilization of a substantial portion of the electorate in these states thus appears to have begun slightly earlier, from 1892 to 1896, than it did

TABLE 4.4
Change in Presidential Turnout in the Settled Northern States

State	1880–1916		1880–1896		1896–1916	
	Total Change	Annual Decline (Slope)	Total Change	Annual Decline (Slope)	Total Change	Annual Decline (Slope)
Connecticut	-13.5	-.4	-4.4	-.0*	-9.1	-.6
Maine	-19.3	-.6	-22.2	-1.6	2.8	.4*
Massachusetts	-8.2	-.3	-4.3	-.2*	-4.0	-.2
New Hampshire	-13.5	-.4	-13.3	-.8	-.1	-.1*
Rhode Island	15.9	.4	9.8	2.1	6.1	.4*
Vermont	-14.5	-.5	-11.7	-.9	-2.9	0*
Delaware	2.8	.3	-2.8	0*	5.6	.3*
New Jersey	-25.0	-.6	-8.6	-.5*	-16.4	-1.3
New York	-20.5	-.6	-8.6	-.6	-11.9	-.8
Pennsylvania	-20.5	-.5	-2.2	-.3*	-18.3	-1.0
Illinois	-21.1	-.5	7.5	.5*	-28.6	-1.5
Indiana	-11.8	-.3	.1	0*	-12.7	-.8
Michigan	-12.2	-.5	10.1	.5*	-22.3	-1.4
Ohio	-16.5	-.5	1.5	-.1*	-18.0	-1.1
Wisconsin	-19.4	-.7	5.8	.1*	-25.3	-1.5
Iowa	-8.9	-.4	8.8	.4*	-17.7	-1.0
Kansas	-13.4	-.5	8.3	.4*	-21.7	-1.2
Minnesota	-22.5	-.8	-1.2	-.2*	-21.3	-1.2
Missouri	2.9	0	10.6	.6*	-7.7	-.5*
Nebraska	8.2	.2	7.6	.4*	.6	-.2
Kentucky	10.1	.2*	16.8	1.1	-6.8	-.5*
Maryland	-10.5	-.5	8.5	.5*	-19.0	-1.3
Tennessee	-27.7	-1.0	-3.0	-.4*	-24.7	-1.3
West Virginia	.6	-.1*	10.8	.7	-10.2	-.6
Colorado	-4.3	-.1*	5.4	.3*	-9.7	-.8
Nevada	-13.8	-.2*	-15.8	-.8*	2.0	.1*
California	-17.5	-.8	1.8	.2*	-19.3	-1.4
Oregon	-20.0	-.8	4.0	.2*	-23.9	-1.1

NOTE: Starred slopes are not significant at .05.

TABLE 4.5
Change in Presidential Turnout in the Southern States

State	1880–1916		1880–1896		1896–1916	
	Total Change	Annual Decline (Slope)	Total Change	Annual Decline (Slope)	Total Change	Annual Decline (Slope)
Alabama	-34.9	-1.3	-7.1	0*	-27.9	-1.5
Arkansas	-20.3	-.9	-8.4	-.6*	-11.9	-.7*
Florida	-52.9	-1.8	-46.3	-4.0	-6.6	-.4*
Georgia	-25.4	-.8	-13.8	-.4*	-11.6	-.6*
Louisiana	-29.4	-1.1	-15.4	-1.0	-14.0	-.6
Mississippi	-29.9	-1.0	-27.7	-2.5	-2.2	.1*
North Carolina	-31.1	-1.3	3.1	0*	-34.2	-1.9
South Carolina	-65.6	-1.4	-56.9	-3.7	-8.7	-.4
Texas	-31.3	-1.5	20.9	1.2	-53.2	-2.8
Virginia	-37.0	-1.8	7.2	.2*	-44.2	-2.6

NOTE: Starred slopes are not significant at .05.

elsewhere in the North.[16] In terms of overall effect, however, both regions experienced substantial reductions in electoral participation from late-nineteenth-century heights. In New England, the decline in voter turnout was largely complete by 1900, whereas in the mid-Atlantic states, as in the rest of the North, the falloff continued throughout the first two decades of the new century.[17]

Nowhere was the decline in voting more extensive and dramatic than in the South. Turnout there dropped precipitously following the enactment of disfranchising legislation (fig. 4.5).[18] In most of these states, the break from mass electoral participation occurred before 1896, but turnout continued to diminish in subsequent elections, and it fell in every southern state between 1900 and 1916.[19] The falloff in the South was much more abrupt than in the North, and participation bottomed out at a much lower level, but the general downward pattern was comparable.[20] The South, like the rest of the country, experienced repeated, cumulative declines in voting.

Both the magnitude and the shape of the early-twentieth-century falloff in voter participation were extraordinary. This was not a minor adjustment limited in size and scope; nor was it a one-time reaction to a discrete event. The drop in voting was nationwide, substantial, and cumulative. It was also unprecedented, both in American history, which until 1896 had been marked by more than a century of suffrage expansion and increased electoral participation, and in comparison to the political experience of other Western democracies.[21]

Most important, the dramatic falloff in mass electoral participation in this country proved to be an enduring phenomenon. Although voting rates have fluctuated over the twentieth century—falling in the twenties, recovering in the thirties, leveling off after World War II, and then dropping again after 1960—they have never risen much above pre–World War I levels.[22] In terms of mass participation, the 1916 electorate rather closely resembled that of the middle and late twentieth century. The decline in voting during the early twentieth century fundamentally and irrevocably changed American politics.

Demobilization and the Core Electorate

The depth of mass electoral participation declined with the fall in voter turnout. As the number of nonvoters increased, the core electorate also shrunk.[23] Fewer people were sufficiently interested in electoral politics to cast ballots in off-year elections or for less prestigious offices. The demobilization of voters thus altered the character as well as the extent of voter participation.[24]

The contraction of the core electorate was apparent in off-year voter participation, as table 4.6 shows. During the early twentieth century, turnout for midterm congressional elections averaged only 53.6 percent. The virtual absence of electoral participation in the South, where off-

TABLE 4.6
Mean Regional Turnout Percentages in
Off-Year Elections, 1880–1896

Region	1882–1894		1898–1918	
	Congress	Governor	Congress	Governor
New England	61.6	63.3	57.7	59.5
Mid-Atlantic	69.7	71.9	61.2	62.6
North Central	76.9	76.0	63.7	62.1
Midwest	73.7	74.8	61.8	63.4
South	44.9	53.5	20.2	24.7
Border	61.4	58.7	50.8	40.4
Mountain	60.6	60.4	52.8	52.4
West	69.1	72.8	49.0	53.3
North	70.6	70.3	59.1	59.7
Nation	65.3	66.6	51.4	53.8

NOTE: See "Units of Analysis" in Appendix 1 for a complete list of states in each region.

year congressional elections attracted only 20.2 percent, considerably reduced the national mean. But even in the North, less than 60 percent of those eligible went to the polls in midterm congressional elections. In the most populous regions, where nearly three-quarters of the electorate previously had participated in all elections, off-year turnout declined dramatically.

The midterm falloff was similar in size and shape to the decline in presidential turnout. On the state level, results of regression analysis on off-year turnout figures substantially parallel those on presidential turnout. In every region except the New England and mountain states, the regression slopes for voting in both congressional and gubernatorial off-year elections from 1898 to 1918 were negative and significant.[25] In the mid-Atlantic region, the decline in off-year voting was demonstrably steeper than the falloff in presidential turnout. In the other regions, however, the declines were comparable to presidential elections.

Using presidential and off-year election returns, the electorate can be partitioned into three categories: core voters, marginal voters, and nonvoters. Figures 4.9 through 4.14 divide eligible voters along these lines in order to illustrate the changes in the composition of the national, northern, and southern electorates from the late nineteenth century through the early twentieth century.[26] As is evident from all three sets of figures, the principal change during the early twentieth century was the large growth in the percentage of nonvoters and the corresponding drop in the proportion of core voters.

In the nation as a whole, the nonvoting segment of the electorate grew from just over one-fifth to over one-third while core voters fell from nearly two-thirds of all voters to just over one-half. In the North nonvoters increased from 15.9 to 26.5 percent of all eligible voters, and the core electorate shrank by a similar amount. In the South, the number of nonvoters rose from 39.7 to 69.4 percent while core voters decreased to barely one-fifth of the total electorate.[27] Nationwide, the percentage of marginal voters remained relatively constant. They increased slightly in the North and declined by nearly one-third in the South, but these shifts were minor compared to the constriction of the core electorate that accompanied the early-twentieth-century falloff in voter participation. The erosion of core voting is vivid evidence of the extent of political disengagement during the early twentieth century. One would have expected that when turnout decreased, peripheral voters would have been the first to drop out.[28] In terms of aggregate electoral behavior,

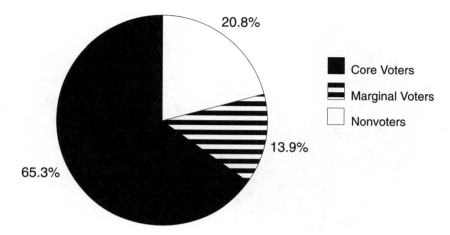

Figure 4.9

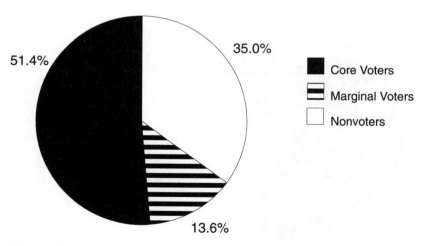

Figure 4.10

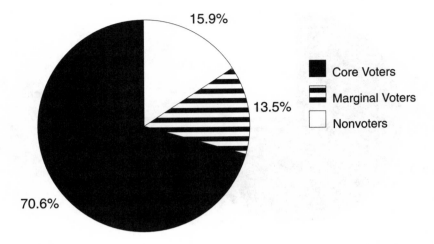

Figure 4.11

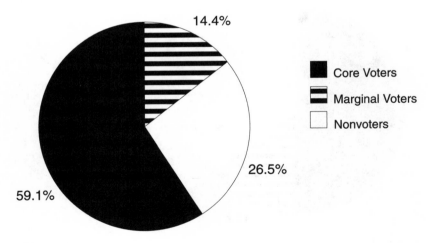

Figure 4.12

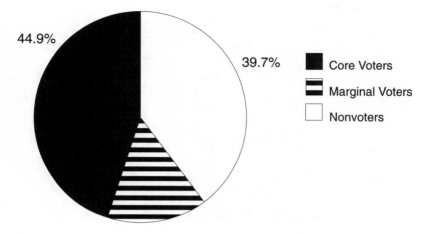

Figure 4.13

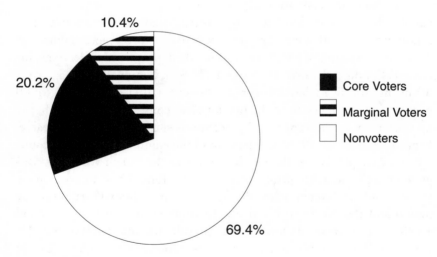

Figure 4.14

TABLE 4.7
Mean State-Level Drop-Off and Roll-Off

Region	Drop-Off 1882–1894	Drop-Off 1898–1918	Roll-Off 1880–1896	Roll-Off 1900–1916
New England	18.6	10.2	1.3	-1.6
Mid-Atlantic	14.8	18.6	1.8	4.5
North Central	14.4	24.5	.7	1.0
Midwest	10.4	21.2	2.0	3.9
South	31.0	47.5	4.7	8.4
Border	18.5	27.3	2.7	6.3
Mountain	2.4	18.2	5.3	2.6
West	6.6	20.9	4.1	4.5
North	13.4	19.7	2.3	2.8
Nation	18.6	25.7	2.9	4.0

NOTE: See "Units of Analysis" in Appendix 1 for a complete list of states in each region.

however, this was not so: the size of the marginal electorate did not decline as turnout fell off.

This disengagement from electoral politics becomes even more apparent when we look directly at the voting behavior of the active electorate. Both roll-off, a measure of those who cast incomplete ballots, and drop-off, a measure of people who vote only in presidential elections, increased significantly after 1896 (see table 4.7). Nationally, average roll-off in the first five twentieth-century presidential elections grew to 4.0 percent from 2.9 percent in the previous five contests. In the North, the increase from 2.3 percent to 2.8 percent was smaller but still noticeable. From 1900 through 1918, 62.9 percent of the eligible voters in the country and 71.1 percent of the eligible voters in the North voted for congressional candidates in presidential-year elections. These figures are 2.1 percent and 2.4 percent below the figures for presidential turnout in the nation and the North, respectively. In contrast, during the 1880s and 1890s congressional vote totals trailed presidential vote totals by only 1.3 percent in both the North and the entire nation.[29] Every region except New England and the mountain states experienced a growth in average roll-off after 1896.[30] The largest rise outside of the South was in the mid-Atlantic, midwestern, and border states.

The increase in roll-off reflected, in part, the nationwide adoption of the Australian ballot.[31] Ballot reform made it more difficult to cast a complete ballot, since voters could no longer simply deposit a party-printed ticket. In many states voters were required to mark their ballot separately for each office.[32] Still, regardless of the cause, the rise in roll-off indicates a change in voter behavior, albeit one that involved only a small portion of the electorate. In the early twentieth century, a larger percentage of voters cast incomplete ballots.

Far more significant, however, was the dramatic increase after 1896 in drop-off from presidential to off-year elections.[33] In the North, on average, nearly 20 percent of the voters who cast ballots in presidential elections between 1896 and 1916 failed to vote in the succeeding off-year election. The drop-off from high profile to low profile elections expanded in every region except New England. In the north central states, drop-off rose from under 15 percent to nearly 25 percent. In the midwestern, mountain, and western regions, drop-off more than doubled. Fully a quarter of the active national electorate during the early twentieth century was not sufficiently involved in politics to participate in off-year elections.[34]

The most extreme drop-off of voters was in the South, where nearly 50 percent of the active electorate failed to vote in off-year elections. The South also exhibited the nation's highest levels of roll-off. These signs of low political involvement are significant because they indicate that political participation fell off in the South even among those voters who were not disfranchised. Although the enactment of strong restrictive legislation made southern electoral politics exceptional, the region nonetheless shared in the nationwide demobilization of the mass electorate.

Who Did Not Vote

Both the size of the mass electorate and the extent of its involvement in electoral politics declined nationwide, but not all segments of American society were equally affected. Voter demobilization was much more extensive in some geographic areas than in others. Differentiation also occurred by gender, class, race, occupation, and age. As a result the composition of the active electorate was fundamentally altered.

One of the most striking features of the decline in electoral participation is that it occurred before most women gained the right to vote. Only a few states, mostly in the western and mountain regions, permitted women to vote prior to the enactment of the Nineteenth Amendment in 1920. In addition to Wyoming, Colorado, Utah, and Idaho, where women won the vote in the 1890s, women were enfranchised in California and Washington in 1911; in Arkansas, Kansas, and Oregon in 1913; in Illinois in 1913 (presidential elections only); in Montana and Nebraska in 1914; and in New York in 1917.[35] In 1896, 1 percent of American women lived in states where they were eligible to vote for president; twenty years later, in 1916, only 16.5 percent of women had secured this basic right. In the early twentieth century, as in the late nineteenth, women were the single largest group of nonvoters in the country. Their exclusion from electoral participation, however, did not affect voter turnout levels as discussed here, since my calculations are based on the number of eligible voters.[36] This restriction therefore had no impact on the falloff in voting between 1900 and 1918.

Some scholars argue that it was the extension of suffrage to women rather than their exclusion that depressed turnout percentages. According to John Stucker, the addition of women, almost all of whom lacked electoral experience, was responsible for most of the falloff in turnout from 1904 to 1916, as well as for the continued decline in voting through the 1920s. He argues that women originally voted at much lower rates than men. Furthermore, their participation rose only slowly in the years following suffrage as they were socialized into the political system and as young women who had been raised with the expectation of voting entered the electorate.[37] Using a variety of statistical techniques comparing turnout levels across time and across states, Stucker estimates that women's suffrage depressed voter turnout in the North by approximately 10 percent.[38]

Although there is little doubt that the enfranchisement of women did decrease the rate of turnout in the short run, the size of the effect was not nearly so large as Stucker suggests. Before-and-after analyses are problematic because the effect of women's suffrage is confounded with the downward secular trend in voting. Likewise, cross-state analyses are flawed because women were first enfranchised in the mountain and western states, regions where turnout was generally low.[39] As a result of these problems, Stucker overestimates the effect of women's suffrage on early-twentieth-century turnout. Not only was women's suffrage insufficiently widespread to account for much of the national decline in voting, but also turnout fell off just as sharply in the states that did not enfranchise women as in the states that did. In states where women could not vote, turnout dropped from 79.9 percent in 1896 to 61.3 percent in 1916.

Even if the South is excluded, turnout in this period still fell from 86.2 percent to 71.6 percent in pre-women's-suffrage states.

Yet, women did most likely vote at lower rates than men, because most women had not been socialized into electoral politics. Voting had long belonged almost exclusively to the male realm of American culture. Although the suffrage movement, temperance, and other reform campaigns brought many women into the arena of electoral politics, many others remained uninvolved.[40] But there was another factor besides the political socialization of women: underlying political conditions at the time of enfranchisement greatly affected the likelihood of women voting.[41] Except in a few mountain states, women entered the electorate at a time of decreasing voter participation. Because most women gained the vote during a political age that did not favor voter mobilization, their inexperience with electoral participation and, consequently, their relatively weak ties to the political parties weighed particularly heavily against their active participation.[42] Women's suffrage did not precipitate the early-twentieth-century decline in turnout; rather it was the broader demobilization of the mass electorate that was at least partially responsible for lower voting rates among newly enfranchised women.

Gender was just one of many social factors that greatly affected voter participation rates during the early twentieth century. Turnout varied dramatically among the various regions in the country, and within those regions, racial, ethnic, and socioeconomic groups voted at significantly different rates. In the South, where demobilization was most severe among black voters, less than one-third of the adult male citizens voted during the period. In every southern state except Mississippi and Georgia, the majority of black adult males cast ballots in 1880. By 1910 southern blacks were completely excluded from political participation.[43] Blacks were not the only southern voters who were demobilized, though: from 1900 to 1910, less than half of the eligible white voters went to the polls.[44] Moreover, among southern white voters, participation varied sharply by class. Using ecological regression analysis, J. Morgan Kousser finds a strong connection between wealth and electoral participation. During the early twentieth century, southern turnout was lowest among "socio-economically deprived groups"—white as well as black.[45]

Even within the North, voter participation varied appreciably by region, although those differences were not nearly so dramatic as the ones between the North and the South. On the average, nearly two-thirds of the eligible northern electorate cast ballots in presidential elections during the early twentieth century. As before the turn of the century, turnout was lowest in the mountain and western states and in New England. The gap in turnout between these regions and the mid-Atlantic, north central, and midwestern regions narrowed, however, because voting fell off most sharply in those states where participation previously had been highest. As a result by 1916 nonvoters comprised 26.4 percent of the electorate in the Midwest, 27.1 percent in the north central states, 31.1 percent in the mid-Atlantic region, 33 percent in the border states, 33.2 percent in New England, 35.4 percent in the mountain region, and 43.2 percent in the West.[46] Throughout the North significant portions of the mass electorate had withdrawn from electoral politics.

In the North, just as in the South, turnout dropped most sharply among lower socioeconomic groups. Consequently, with the demobilization of a large segment of the northern electorate, a severe socioeconomic differential developed in voter participation. Using ecological regression analysis on county-level data, Paul Kleppner finds that voting in the early twentieth century, unlike that in the late nineteenth century, was strongly related to economic wealth.[47] This is an important finding, since research on voting in the middle and late twentieth century indicates that social status and education are the best predictors of political participation.[48] The enduring relationship in America between socioeconomic class and voter participation is an important by-product of the early-twentieth-century erosion in mass electoral participation.

Closely related to the emergent class bias in participation was the growth of large differentials in turnout between native-born white voters and relatively poorer blacks and immigrants. Although 90 percent of the nation's black population that lived in the South was totally demobilized, northern blacks, most of whom lived in large cities, continued to vote, but in much smaller numbers than they had during the late nineteenth century. In New Jersey, for example, black turnout fell from 74 percent in 1888 to 42.1 percent in 1916.[49] By 1920 fewer blacks in both the North and the South participated in electoral politics than at any time since the passage of the Fifteenth Amendment.

Electoral participation also fell among immigrants and their descendants. During the late nineteenth century, some immigrants who had declared their intention to become citizens had been able to vote even before the naturalization process was complete. From the mid-1890s on, noncitizen immigrants were disfranchised as state after state made citizenship a prerequisite for voting. By 1925 noncitizens were completely barred from the polls.[50] Though noncitizens could not vote, their exclusion, like that of women, did not affect turnout levels, which were based on the number of eligible voters.

The electorate did include, particularly in the North, a large number of naturalized immigrants and their American-born descendants, who participated in electoral politics at a significantly lower rate than white, native-stock Americans.[51] Detailed analysis of electoral participation in New Jersey can illuminate the falloff in immigrant voting. John Reynolds estimates that only 54.2 percent of foreign-born voters cast ballots in 1916, as compared with 73.0 percent in 1896.[52] Among second-generation immigrants, those with naturalized parents voted at slightly higher rates (69.8 percent in 1912 and 1916), but those with noncitizen parents had the lowest voter participation rates (22.3 percent in 1912 and 1916) of any social group in New Jersey. Thus, increased immigration from eastern and southern Europe, which resulted in an early-twentieth-century decline in naturalization rates, had political repercussions for the second generation, which was not socialized into American electoral politics.[53]

With the demobilization of immigrant, black, and poorer voters, electoral participation fell sharply in cities. In New York, rural turnout greatly exceeded urban figures; the voting decline in cities was three times as large as that in rural areas.[54] New York may not have been typical, however. In most of the nation, rural turnout also eroded considerably from its late-nineteenth-century pinnacle. In both New Jersey and Pennsylvania, for example, the drop in voting in rural counties was comparable to the decline in urban areas.[55] Nationwide, voting fell off as sharply in rural states like Iowa, Kansas, and Minnesota as it did in urban ones.

Much more extensive analysis of county-level and ward-level election returns is necessary before the relative participation rates of different social groups can be estimated with confidence.[56] These decades witnessed the emergence of socioeconomic stratification in American voter participation, but we have only the broadest outline of the biases that developed. Immigrants, blacks, the poor, city dwellers, and probably farmers all experienced extensive demobilization, but the question of "how much" still needs to be explored. In addressing this issue, we need to keep in mind that the turnout of all social groups varied extensively throughout the nation in response to vast local differences in electoral regulations and party strength.[57] Lower participation rates among certain segments of the population, therefore, did not reflect the intrinsic characteristics of these voters (after all, the entire electorate had been highly mobilized during the late nineteenth century), but rather resulted from a confluence of social change and political action that, as we will see, thoroughly restructured American electoral politics.[58]

Although participation certainly fell most sharply among some social groups, it is important not to lose sight of the pervasiveness of the decline. The socioeconomic stratification of the electorate explains only part of the drop.[59] Voting rates decreased among men as well as women, northerners as well as southerners, native-born Americans as well as immigrants, farmers as well as workers, the middle class as well as the poor, and rural as well as urban voters. Parts of American society were more severely affected than others, but demobilization occurred throughout the mass electorate.

One key to understanding the breadth of the voting decline lies with the new voters of the early twentieth century.[60] Both the magnitude and the shape of the falloff suggest that social developments sustained the process. With the passage of time, younger, less motivated cohorts were replacing highly mobilized cohorts in the electorate.[61] The effect of this age-cohort replacement process on electoral participation was gradual, cumulative, and enduring.

There is reason to believe that older voters continued to vote in large numbers during the early twentieth century, whereas voters coming of age in those years went to the polls at a much lower rate. The prior generation of voters remained motivated by Civil War allegiances, among other things, throughout their political lives. During the 1880s and 1890s, those voters had been deeply involved in electoral battles. Their sons, who came of age in that highly charged political atmosphere, were rapidly integrated into the late-nineteenth-century party system. In contrast, the new voters in the period 1900–1918 entered the electorate at a time of decreasing electoral involvement and weakening partisan allegiances and thus were not subject to the same mobilizing forces. Unfortunately, it is very difficult to estimate the participation rates of different cohorts on the basis of aggregate election returns. Ecological regression analysis is not a very effective technique to measure age-based turnout, since age structure varies only slightly across geographical boundaries. Nonetheless, regression analysis suggests a significant negative relationship between youth and turnout during the early twentieth century.[62]

Although there were no surveys of voters during this period that would provide individual-level data to compare with these results, some support can be drawn from two local studies done in the early 1920s. Ben Arneson's 1924 survey of voters in Delaware, Ohio, found a strong relationship between voter participation and age,[63] as did a study by Charles Merriam and Harold Gosnell of Chicago's mayoral race of 1923.[64] In Chicago over one-third of all voters aged 21–29 were "habitual nonvoters" as compared with just over one-quarter of voters aged 30–39, less than one-fifth of voters aged 40–49, and just over one-tenth of voters aged 50–59 and older. Participation rates were biased by age for native-born, foreign-born, and black voters. In all social categories, the most dramatic difference in participation occurred between those who came of age before or after the mid-1890s. Though the overall voter participation rate in the 1923 Chicago election was barely 50 percent, the turnout of eligible voters who had come of age before 1894 was nearly 90 percent.[65]

To some extent, the lower participation rates of young voters during the early twentieth century represented the behavior of a particular generation of voters. Not only did this cohort vote less frequently during those years, but their turnout also did not rise appreciably as they aged. Aggregate turnout levels suggest that the mobilization of this generation never approached that of earlier political generations.[66]

The development of an electorate stratified by age, however, had ramifications that went beyond the behavior of this particular generation of voters. Since the beginning of the twentieth century, American electoral politics has been characterized by a life-cycle pattern in which electoral participation rises only slowly with age.[67] This pattern of lower participation among younger voters is not inevitable; it was not at all characteristic of nineteenth-century political behavior. In comparison to the 1880s and 1890s, twentieth-century voters have been integrated into politics at a much slower rate and to a much lesser degree.

The Erosion of Participatory Electoral Politics

The early-twentieth-century falloff in turnout reflected a far-reaching disengagement of the American public from electoral politics. As mass interest diminished, the spectacular participatory campaigns, which had once served to mobilize the nation, were gradually transformed into merchandising campaigns that did not require the active participation of voters.

To begin with, elections themselves gradually became a less pervasive element in American life. During the early twentieth century, the number of elected officials dropped sharply as appointment or competitive examination filled more government jobs. This was especially true at the local level, which had been so central to the vitality of nineteenth-century politics. Whereas a multitude of local officials once held elective posts, commonly only a handful did so by 1916. For example, looking at California, H. S. Gilbertson, assistant secretary of the National Short Ballot Organization, explained that "the old notion that every officer must be elected [has been] abandoned."[68] With a shorter ballot, longer terms of office, and the consolidation of individual elections, the frequency of elections diminished considerably.[69]

In most parts of the country, lulls emerged between electoral contests. Not only were campaigns less frequent, but public involvement also eroded dramatically. The endless array of participatory campaign activities—ratification meetings, pole-raisings, parades, marches, barbecues, rallies, and bonfires—that had so successfully mobilized the nineteenth-century electorate in the weeks and days before elections rapidly fell into disuse during the first decade of the twentieth century.[70]

Ratification ceremonies, which seemed superfluous with the increased use of direct primaries to nominate candidates, no longer attracted popular interest and were largely abandoned.[71] During the late nineteenth century, ratification conventions brought loyal supporters together, united them behind a ticket, and kicked off a season of campaigning. The unity and enthusiasm produced by such occasions stood in contrast to the divisiveness that often remained after primary elections. Without ratification meetings, the ability of the party cadres to work together and mobilize mass support lessened considerably.

Once campaigns got under way, the role of mass participation was increasingly limited. By 1908 the parties had largely abandoned efforts to assemble campaign clubs such as those that had been responsible for funneling public activism into nineteenth-century campaigns. Both the Republicans and the Democrats organized a few marching companies during 1900–1918, but these were hardly visible. The remnants of some nineteenth-century clubs remained, albeit in diminishing numbers, and a few new clubs emerged around charismatic figures (especially Teddy

Roosevelt), but the extensive network of local-level clubs that had reached out to virtually every late-nineteenth-century voter was a thing of the past.[72]

Without the club system, huge mass spectaculars were impossible to organize. The daytime processions and torchlight extravaganzas that had enlivened nineteenth-century campaigns required vast organization and manpower. Likewise, country pole-raisings and urban banner-raisings were soon abandoned. All-day rallies faded into memory, as did many smaller events at schoolhouses and county crossroads.[73] Of course, the parties retained many of the same forms of campaign activity, but parades and rallies during the early twentieth century were a pale shadow of their former selves, like the campaign buttons that continued to be produced but were rarely displayed. Drained of mass participation and enthusiasm, participatory campaign activity had lost most of its symbolic importance and mobilizing power.

Politicians increasingly focused their campaigns and concentrated their finances on activities that did not require the active participation of voters except on Election Day. Money and energy were spent on advertising through the mass media rather than on mass mobilization. By the 1920s, radio broadcasts had replaced mass meetings and all-day orations; twentieth-century candidates in turn were sold to voters in the same way that other merchandise was sold to consumers. As the role of voters became increasingly passive, it is little wonder that their enthusiasm for electoral politics waned.[74]

Contemporary commentators recognized the decline in popular political passions. During election after election, early-twentieth-century newspapers reported on popular disengagement from politics; campaigns were described as "listless," "dull," "exceedingly quiet," and "apathetic beyond all previous description."[75] Some editorialists decried the lack of enthusiasm that made elections events to be endured rather than enjoyed; others celebrated the cooling of political passions.[76] Regardless of how they felt about it, however, it was clear that the nature of public involvement in electoral politics was changing. Robert and Helen Lynd documented the results of these changes in 1924 when they studied Muncie, Indiana, which they called "Middletown": "Great as are Middletown's emotional and financial stakes in politics, elections are no longer the lively centers of public interest they were in the nineties. In 1890 Middletown gave itself over for weeks to the bitter hilarious joy of conflict."[77] The Lynds concluded, "not only the election preliminaries but the actual choice of candidates fails to arouse today the interest it did in the nineties."[78]

This decline in public involvement in electoral politics was directly related to the falloff in voting. Merriam and Gosnell's survey of nonvoters in Chicago, for example, found "general indifference" to be the major cause of nonvoting.[79] Electoral politics, the evidence suggests, was simply less important to twentieth-century Americans than to their fathers and grandfathers.

The Social Roots of Mass Demobilization

For most nineteenth-century men, electoral participation was firmly grounded in the social fabric of their daily lives; their twentieth-century children and grandchildren, however, grew up at a time when electoral politics was losing many of its social functions. One of the effects of the profound social changes wrought by large-scale industrialization, urbanization, and immigration was erosion of the social basis of mass participation in politics.[80] As local communities ceased to circumscribe American life, both culture and society were increasingly organized along functional rather than geographic lines.[81] Although new voters—who had never experienced late-nineteenth-century, community-based, participatory politics—were most affected, participation of all voters was undercut as electoral politics lost much of its broader significance.

The decreasing salience of electoral politics can be attributed at least in part to a narrowing of the role politics played in daily life. For one thing, elections lost much of their entertainment value during the early twentieth century as other recreational activities proliferated.[82] Americans could now choose from a growing variety and number of leisure-time pursuits: spectator sports (especially professional baseball, high school basketball, and boxing), amusement parks, vaudeville and melodrama theaters, dance halls, three-ring circuses, and bicycling clubs.[83] With the multiplication of recreational outlets, none of which were linked to political participation, twentieth-century Americans did not need to look to politics for escape.

Because electoral campaigns had to compete for public attention, it is little wonder that the parties rapidly abandoned nineteenth-century-style participatory campaigning. In the process, however, they forsook many of the mobilizing tools that had successfully incorporated the mass public into the electoral system. With the eclipse of spectacle-style campaigns, the opportunity for public participation in politics lessened, and apparently so did much of the pleasure that Americans derived from political occasions.

The increasing diversity of American culture also undermined the strong linkages between partisan politics and the press, which had played a major role in keeping the electorate passionately involved in nineteenth-century electoral politics.[84] The shift toward an independent press began in the late nineteenth century and accelerated during the following years as more and more papers declared their political independence. Not only did partisan affiliation wane, but newspapers also ceased to focus most of their attention on electoral politics. The large urban dailies recognized the shift in peoples' leisure pursuits by adding sports sections, women's pages, lifestyle articles, comics, and more features.[85] Increasingly, partisan politics was relegated to a few pages in one section of the paper, where column space waxed and waned in rhythm with campaign activity. In this way the press both reflected and reinforced the decreasing role that electoral politics played in early-twentieth-century culture.

As the cultural role of electoral politics contracted, party politics no longer offered men the same degree of fraternity and fellowship.[86] The marching companies and campaign clubs, which brought nineteenth-century men together in masculine political activism, gave way to twentieth-century merchandising campaigns, which treated all voters as consumers. Furthermore, the communal centers of nineteenth-century politicking—the saloon, the livery stable, and the post office—gradually lost their hold on most men. Temperance crusades closed many saloons, and free mail delivery sapped post offices of their political significance.[87] Both parties continued to maintain local clubhouses, but these appealed to fewer men than before, and they gradually fell into disuse outside of inner-city wards. Of course, the opportunity to find fellowship in political action did not vanish altogether, especially for party activists. But for the most part, twentieth-century men found fellowship with other men elsewhere, often at sporting events or in an increasing number of service clubs such as the Rotary and Kiwanis.[88]

As political activism lost its appeal and social significance, the close linkages between the people and politics that had fueled late-nineteenth-century participatory politics also began to unravel. "Individual involvement in the dense network of ethnoreligious associations no longer functioned as it had earlier to reinforce partisan identifications and stimulate individual participation." Young voters were most affected by the severing of "subculture-with-partisanship-with-participation linkages," since "most older voters probably continued to participate and vote their memories."[89] Paul Kleppner argues that this displaced congruence between ethnocultural cleavages and partisanship was the main reason that voters coming of age after 1896 were not fully socialized into the political system and hence that many of them failed to vote.[90]

The erosion of the connection between ethnocultural group membership and political affiliation was part of a larger process in which politics lost its central integrative role.[91] The early years of this century witnessed a transformation in the social base of political participation. In the late nineteenth century, when socioeconomic, ethnocultural, geographic, and political cleavages had divided the American population along roughly similar lines, partisan affiliation linked together an individual's various social identities, integrating both individuals and social groups into larger communities and the nation as a whole. The result was a distinctive mode of mass electoral politics that functioned at the center of community life. Under the late-nineteenth-century system, virtually all public concerns were addressed in the electoral arena through partisan politics. This holistic political system fractured at the end of the century.

During the early twentieth century, many Americans found that partisan affiliation did not reflect the full array of their concerns. More and more of those concerns found expression through special interest groups outside of the electoral arena.[92] Interest groups, of course, were not new, but whereas they had mediated their concerns through partisan politics during the nineteenth century, now they were increasingly independent and began to usurp many of the functions previously performed by the parties.

The virtual explosion of occupation-based organizations in the Progressive Era most clearly demonstrates the increasing significance of occupational ties. Robert Wiebe suggests that "joining an occupation was a defining as well as an identifying act. Just as a political party had once done, now the occupational association supplied many answers, hopes, and enemies far beyond the range of their immediate experience."[93] A plethora of ethnic, religious, and cultural associations also sprang up during the first two decades of the new century. These cultural organizations, like the occupational groups, represented the highly specialized concerns of their constituents while providing them with many services.

The emergence of a wide variety of specialized political associations organized along particularistic rather than geographic and partisan lines altered the landscape of American politics. In contrast to the late nineteenth century, when all of a person's social ties tended to reinforce his political affiliation, many voters found themselves cross-pressured by conflicting forces. But even for those who were not cross-pressured, political parties had become just one of many types of organizations through which Americans could relate to their government and to politics in general.[94]

In the early years of the twentieth century, geographic communities and local concerns no longer circumscribed American life. The participatory politics of the nineteenth century had been grounded in local community life, but as the nation's culture diversified and new social alternatives emerged, Americans began to look beyond their immediate locale to develop different and varied connections. The parties lost their ability to tie American society together and therefore surrendered their central place in American culture.[95] As political parties and electoral politics moved off center stage, voting became less important. For most twentieth-century Americans, voting involved the election of public officials and little else. They could not understand the vast social and cultural significance that the previous century had attached to electoral participation.

The erosion of the social basis of mass political participation can be brought into sharper focus by looking directly at political parties, the heart of late-nineteenth-century participatory politics. Voter participation fell when the parties could no longer fully mobilize the American public. But social change only partly explains this failure; parties were also under concerted attack in the political arena during the Progressive Era. To understand the decline in mass participation after 1896, we must examine the political as well as the social forces that transformed the American electoral system.

Electoral Reform and the Political Parties

The Politics of Declining Participation

During the early twentieth century, political parties lost their dominance over American electoral politics. Partisan control over key political resources eroded so dramatically that parties found it increasingly difficult to organize and mobilize the electorate. The extended decline in voter participation reflected the inability of the parties to continue to integrate the American public into electoral politics.

Neither the enervation of political parties nor the dramatic decline in mass participation was the inevitable result of modernizing social forces. Although western European countries underwent many of the same social changes as America, European political parties remained powerful mass-based organizations, and European electoral participation did not fall. To a large extent, the key to understanding the transformation of American politics lies in how political parties responded and adapted to the social changes that were remaking American society. Although these changes were well under way in the 1880s and 1890s, late-nineteenth-century political parties had the ability and incentive to involve the mass electorate in electoral politics.

Twentieth-century electoral reforms, however, deprived parties of key resources while increasing the costs of political participation. At the same time, the post-1896 evaporation of political competition removed much of the pressure for parties to maintain a highly active electorate.[1] Weakened by reform legislation and lacking strong incentives to mobilize voters, American political parties adapted themselves to a politics of decreasing participation.

Partisan Voting in the Progressive Era

The voting behavior of the American electorate during the early twentieth century was somewhat less partisan than it had been during the 1880s and 1890s. Analysis of aggregate election returns indicates a decrease in both partisan loyalty (more voters split their votes between candidates from opposing parties) and partisan stability (more voters switched parties between elections). But the drop in voter partisanship was not nearly so dramatic as the falloff in mass participation. Although in general mass voting became less partisan after 1896, party loyalty and stability continued to be a dominant feature of early-twentieth-century electoral politics.[2]

That a considerable degree of the partisanship persisted is not surprising given that most voters in the early twentieth century previously had been staunch party supporters. Socialized into politics within a party-centered electoral system and accustomed to favoring a party ticket election after election, late-nineteenth-century voters tended to retain their partisan commitments well into the twentieth century.[3] Since new twentieth-century voters were integrated so slowly into the active electorate, aggregate election returns continued to reflect the behavior of older, more partisan voters.[4] Consequently, there was a time lag before less partisan voting patterns became clearly apparent.[5] Over the course of the twentieth century, party voting became far less stable.

Aggregate election returns for 1900–1918 offer the first hints of the erosion of partisan loyalty. Split-ticket voting, which is a measure of the percentage of voters who do not cast a straight party ballot, began to rise in much of the North after 1896. In contrast to the 1880s and 1890s, when almost all partisan instability was associated with third-party activity, ticket splitting increased dramatically in two-party elections. Table 5.1 reveals that in two-party contests, ticket splitting rose in every region of the country. The national average for split-ticket voting in two-party elections nearly doubled, going from 2.6 to 4.9 percent, while the average in the North jumped from 1.6 to 4.1 percent.

TABLE 5.1
*Mean State-Level Split-Ticket Voting in Two-Party
Presidential Elections, 1880–1896*

Region	1880–1896 Ticket Splitting	N (Cases)	1900–1916 Ticket Splitting	N (Cases)
New England	2.0	23	6.2	21
Mid-Atlantic	.5	13	1.7	11
North Central	1.1	15	4.2	15
Midwest	3.2	8	5.6	18
South	6.7	23	7.9	27
Border	1.0	15	1.9	16
Mountain	2.6	8	3.3	10
West	1.0	6	2.0	2
North	1.6	88	4.1	92
Nation	2.6	111	4.9	119

NOTE: See "Units of Analysis" in Appendix 1 for a complete list of
states in each region.

Whereas late-nineteenth-century voters had invariably remained loyal
to their party when presented with a choice between candidates from
the two major parties, a small but growing number of early-twentieth-
century voters divided their votes.

Our analysis reveals a significant change in aggregate voting behavior.[6] We do not know the exact relationship between this change in aggregate voting and any shifts in the voting habits of individual voters, but
it is clear that the major parties were no longer able to attract the same
number of votes for all of their candidates. In head-to-head contests, as
well as in three-way races, the major parties no longer controlled the
votes they previously had taken for granted. Although ticket splitting was
still at relatively low levels during the early years of the century, the un-
mistakable first signs of a shift toward less partisan voting behavior are
visible.

The movement becomes clearer when we look at an index of party-
vote instability that measures partisan swing between elections.[7] Table
5.2 presents the state-level, party-vote instability averages in both presidential and congressional elections for each region. In the midwestern,
southern, and mountain regions, where Populism had disrupted late-
nineteenth-century party voting, there was less partisan instability in
congressional elections after 1896. In the rest of the nation, however,
party-vote instability increased in congressional elections.

The increase in party-vote instability was most dramatic in presidential elections. The national average partisan swing in presidential elections was 10.2 percent during the early twentieth century, as compared with 7.3 percent during the late nineteenth century. In the North, average party-vote instability rose by over 50 percent, from 7.2 to 11.2 percent. Party-vote instability increased in every region of the North except the mountain states.

Only part of this increase in partisan instability was due to the 1912 split in the Republican party. Excluding those presidential elections where party voting was disrupted by important third-party challenges, we can compare party-vote instability in 1884, 1888, and 1892 with that in 1900, 1904, and 1908.[8] The mean party-vote instability in 1884, 1888, and 1892 was 4.6 percent in the North. In contrast, in the first three presidential elections in the twentieth century, party-vote instability averaged 7.3 percent nationally and 8.0 percent in the North. In high profile presidential elections, at least, the parties could no longer count on receiving the same votes election after election.[9]

Taken together, our various indices of partisan loyalty and stability demonstrate erosion in partisan voting after 1896. Party still guided the electoral behavior of most voters, but an increasing percentage of the active electorate did not vote a straight party ticket on Election Day, nor did they vote for the same party election after election. Further evidence of the weakening of partisan ties can be drawn from the falloff in voter

TABLE 5.2
Mean Presidential and Congressional Party-Vote Instability, 1880–1918

Region	Presidential		Congressional	
	1880–1896	1900–1916	1880–1896	1898–1918
New England	6.0	8.6	4.5	4.4
Mid-Atlantic	3.8	7.8	6.0	7.6
North Central	2.9	9.8	4.5	5.7
Midwest	8.6	13.6	9.9	5.9
South	7.6	6.4	9.7	6.7
Border	3.4	6.0	3.9	4.5
Mountain	25.6	15.8	12.6	10.3
West	7.9	15.8	7.3	7.6
North	7.2	11.2	6.8	6.6
Nation	7.3	10.2	7.5	6.6

NOTE: See "Units of Analyis" in Appendix 1 for a complete list of states in each region.

participation. Since partisan voters rarely switched parties or split their votes between parties, a subsiding of partisan fervor was likely to express itself initially as much in abstention as in partisan disloyalty. For the most part, voters go to the polls to vote for their party. Without the stimulation that partisan commitments provide, and in the absence of alternative incentives, participation drops.[10]

Electoral returns continued to reflect a considerable degree of partisan loyalty, because most participants voted as they had during the 1880s and 1890s. The sharp decline in voter turnout, however, can be seen as an indication that partisanship was on the wane. The trend away from party voting was still inchoate, but by the early twentieth century, parties demonstrably did not control the vote the way they had in the past.[11] They inspired neither the full participation of the electorate nor the same loyalty in those who voted.

Progressive Reform: The Attack on Party Politics

The degeneration of America's mass-based political parties was a complex phenomenon rooted in the social and cultural changes that America underwent in the early years of the twentieth century. Specific political factors, however, contributed to this process by undermining the ability of the parties to mobilize the population. Just as Americans were coming to expect less from their parties, the parties themselves were finding it difficult to give as much as before. Changes in the legal and institutional structure of American electoral politics were largely responsible for this. A wide variety of Progressive reforms restricted partisan control over electoral machinery, regulated the financing and managing of campaigns and other political activities, restructured American government at all levels in order to limit partisan influence, and reshaped the contours of the active electorate. Taken together, these reforms comprised a major assault on partisan participatory politics.[12]

Beginning in the 1880s, the parties had faced a series of scattered challenges. In order to limit partisan control over government, Gilded Age reformers advocated institutional and administrative changes, the restructuring of the Civil Service, the Australian ballot, and stricter anti-corruption laws. Reformers won several victories in the eighties and nineties, but their successes proved ephemeral. The legal changes that they instituted were too few and too limited to harm the powerful parties, which readily adapted and invariably regained control over the political system.

After 1900, however, both the pace and the effectiveness of political reform intensified. The process itself was both gradual and piecemeal, varying throughout the country at different levels of government and depending on the specific forms of institutional changes. It is nevertheless possible to identify an underlying pattern: most of the electoral reforms were designed to curtail partisan control over the political system and regulate mass participation in electoral politics. Historians disagree fundamentally in their interpretation of Progressive reform, but almost all agree that a prominent target was the late-nineteenth-century system of party government.

In contrast to their predecessors, Progressives generally prevailed over their partisan adversaries. Antiparty reforms were increasingly popular among the electorate because it no longer held partisan loyalty sacred. Although partisan interests often affected the specific forms that these reforms took, and in many cases partisan interests mitigated their effects, an amalgam of antiparty forces began to chip away at the resources and the power of political parties. Contemporary scholars recognized the extent to which the parties were restricted; Chester Lloyd Jones observed in 1913:

> The most striking development affecting parties in the last half century has been the increasing degree to which their activities have become subject to regulation by law. The printing of the ballots, the canvassing of votes, the regulation of the time and procedures of caucuses, primaries, and conventions, even the choice of their own committees, has been more and more taken from the parties and put under public supervision and control.[13]

The vast array of Progressive reforms literally rewrote the rules of American electoral politics.

Ballot reform was the first successful movement to limit partisan control over the electoral process. Australian ballot legislation took the country by storm during the late 1880s and the 1890s. Only five years after ballot reform agitation began in 1887, thirty-two states and two territories had replaced the nineteenth-century system of party-printed ballots with official, state-printed, consolidated ballots. By 1896 thirty-nine states had adopted an Australian ballot; by 1916 only Georgia and South Carolina had not passed some sort of ballot reform measure.[14] In the process most states transferred the administration of elections from partisan elected officials to nonpartisan civil servants.

Supporters of the Australian ballot argued that its introduction would eliminate electoral fraud, but its impact was much more far-reaching than simply making an "honest" ballot available to voting Americans. Adoption of an official state-printed ballot necessitated a number of important decisions about the structure of that ballot, including who was listed on the ballot and in what order and whether party designations, double listing of multiparty candidates, and straight ticket check-offs would be allowed. Each decision affected both the power of the parties and the voting behavior of the electorate. As a result, throughout the Progressive Era states repeatedly revised their balloting procedures.[15]

The shift to a government-printed ballot forced states to establish clear standards for determining who could run for office. Typically, electoral contests were restricted to one candidate from any party that had received a specific percentage of the vote (usually 5 percent) in the previous election and to candidates who could produce a nominating petition with a minimum number of signatures (usually 1 to 5 percent of the total vote). Depending on the number of signatures required (a figure that was frequently contested and revised), access to the ballot was generally limited to major party candidates. No longer could political organizations campaign for public offices by printing their own ballots. The vast majority of states also prohibited the double listing of candidates, so that, for example, no candidate could be listed simultaneously as a Republican and a Prohibitionist.[16]

The impact of these changes on the ability of the parties to control who ran for office was both complex and dramatic. In one sense, the new rules strengthened central party organizations, since previously, party-strip balloting had led to intraparty factionalism. District-level party organizations usually printed their own ballots, and these frequently differed slightly from one district to another as local organizations responding to parochial concerns threw their support behind various candidates. Private printing and distribution of ballots thus resulted in an exceptionally fluid and flexible balloting system, which central party machines never fully controlled. With the adoption of an official state-printed ballot, the major parties no longer had to contend with intraparty rivalries. In some states, at least, party leaders recognized the advantages that a reformed ballot would give them over lower-level party organizers and wholeheartedly supported ballot reform.[17] The Australian ballot produced a single "official" party candidate for each office, a simple choice that did not always exist when the parties themselves printed the ballot.[18]

Despite the fact that the Australian ballot strengthened central party control by limiting factionalism, it severely limited the flexibility of the parties in designating candidates. With the advent of a uniform, state-printed ballot, the parties lost one of their most important resources: their ability to structure their tickets according to local needs. Previously, the major parties had used local variation and fusion tickets to expand their appeal and attract additional voters. By virtually eliminating fusion tickets, state control over the balloting process undermined the existence of minor parties and deprived the major parties of a key strategic option.[19] Ballot reform thereby limited the responsiveness of the party system to changing political circumstances. Not only were the resources of each party circumscribed by ever more numerous restrictions, but also the two-party system itself became increasingly inflexible.[20]

Ballot reform also led to a shift in the practice and the meaning of voting itself. With the consolidation of the ballot, voters were given the opportunity to choose between various candidates for specific offices instead of between competing party slates. They were thus able to split their votes between parties much more easily and vote for only those candidates in whom they had an interest. Voting a straight and complete party ticket was no longer unavoidable; it was no longer necessarily even easy to do.[21] The reformed ballot influenced Americans to vote for individual candidates rather than for parties, since party voting was no longer built into the balloting process.

The specific ways in which candidates' names appeared on the ballot also had a significant impact on the party system. Some states adopted an office-block ballot, which grouped candidates by office regardless of political affiliation, while others adopted a party-column format, which arranged candidates by party. Whereas most states required voters to make a mark beside each candidate for whom they wished to vote, some permitted voters to cast a straight party ticket simply by checking a box at the top of the ballot. In 1917 seventeen states used an office-block ballot, and twenty-six utilized the party-column format. Only twelve states provided a check-off for straight party voting.[22] As both contemporaries and later scholars have recognized, the party-column ballot facilitated the continuance of partisan voting, whereas the office-block ballot made it more difficult to vote a straight ticket. The party check-off provision lessened the impact of the new ballot by enabling voters to easily cast a straight party ticket. Depending on the specific shape of the ballot adopted, therefore, ballot reform undercut to a greater or lesser extent the type of party voting that had typified late-nineteenth-century electoral behavior.[23]

The Australian ballot made it significantly more difficult, moreover, for illiterate and non-English-speaking voters to participate in elections. Such voters had no trouble casting a party-printed ticket, which always included party symbols (usually an elephant or a mule), but they could not read a consolidated ballot. In many states, the biggest battles over ballot reform legislation concerned whether party emblems would be allowed on the ballot to guide illiterates and whether to permit personal assistance for these voters.[24] In 1917 fewer than a third of the states allowed party emblems to be printed on ballots, and many refused assistance to those who could not read English.[25]

In effect, the secret ballot functioned as a de facto literacy test, which impacted the participation of the poor, immigrants, and blacks—precisely those voters whose participation rates, as we have seen, dropped most dramatically in the Progressive Era.[26] Meanwhile, some states adopted absentee ballot provisions, which were used most frequently by better educated, higher income voters, thus encouraging their participation.[27]

In a more general way, the shift to a secret ballot undercut both mass partisanship and participation by making voting a less public act. During the late nineteenth century, when people cast flamboyant, party-printed tickets, voting was an open act in which an individual's partisan preference was visible to the entire community. The secret ballot denied public affirmation and was thus part of a process in which politics lost many of its social functions.[28]

Changes in the frequency and timing of elections also altered the electoral experience for many Americans. Since Australian ballot reform increased the cost of elections to the state, many states consolidated elections when they shifted to an official ballot. Terms of office generally were lengthened in the process. Elections therefore became less frequent. This was a significant change from the late nineteenth century, when Americans were almost continually involved in electoral contests. Ironically, as election frequency decreased, many states separated local, state, and national races in order to insulate local and state elections from national trends. The result generally was a decrease in voter turnout in local elections, since high profile offices were no longer on the same ballot. Mass partisanship was undermined as well, because parties were no longer able to use their appeal at one level to attract voters to other levels included on the ticket.[29]

Other Progressive reforms were aimed at the ways parties nominated candidates and financed campaigns. In the nineteenth century, candidates were chosen through a system of district primaries, party caucuses, and conventions. Nominations were indirect, since public participation was mediated through the party delegate selection process. During the first two decades of the twentieth century, state after state adopted sweeping regulations governing both the selection of delegates and the conduct of these partisan affairs. Desiring to limit even further partisan control over the nomination of candidates, some reformers attempted to replace party conventions altogether with state-run, direct primaries.[30]

Although the legislation concerning primary elections varied, more than three-quarters of the states established mandatory direct primaries for all statewide offices by 1917, and many extended this process to local offices as well.[31] Some states, especially in the western and mountain regions, adopted "open" primaries, which enabled voters to cross party lines, thereby denying partisans the exclusive opportunity to choose their own candidates. Even "closed" primaries—those limited to party members—greatly altered electoral politics by taking control of nominations out of the hands of party organizations. In tandem with ballot reform, the establishment of direct primaries completed the transformation from a party-structured to a state-run electoral system.

By 1916, moreover, twenty-six states had established presidential primaries of one sort or another.[32] The parties still chose their standard-bearers at national conventions, but party officials no longer had a free hand in either selecting the delegates to those conventions or determining the guidelines for their political behavior. On the state and local levels, direct primaries replaced conventions altogether, depriving the parties of their ability to draft platforms, construct balanced tickets, and unite party cadres, processes that had been central to nineteenth-century partisan campaigns.[33]

The increased use of primary elections undercut the importance of general elections. In states dominated by one party, as most were during the early twentieth century, victory in the majority party's primary virtually assured election.[34] Where general elections were anticlimactic, public participation declined. In the process, minority parties suffered further atrophy, while the majority party, faced with decreased opposition, saw little need to mobilize mass support. As a result (as many southern reformers in particular recognized), primary elections militated against both mass participation and interparty competition.[35]

Because statewide party organizations were usually able to mobilize enough support to maintain substantial influence over nominations, the direct primary was not so destructive to party organizations, at least at first, as many had expected.[36] In some states the shift to direct primaries contributed, as had the adoption of the Australian ballot, to a centralization of party control as local-level party organizations lost much of their maneuverability.[37] In the long run, however, the loss of firm control over the selection of candidates severely undermined the power of party organizations at the state level as well. A monopoly over nominations made candidates dependent upon their party, whereas direct primaries inevitably resulted in a growing independence from party.[38]

The power of the parties was further sapped by legislation limiting the way they conducted electoral campaigns. After decades of agitation, reformers generally succeeded in outlawing the use of both corporate donations and officeholder assessments to finance campaigns. The 1907 and 1909 federal laws forbidding corporate campaign contributions in national elections were the crowning success of this effort. Federal legislation also limited the total amount of funding for congressional and senatorial campaigns.[39] A wide variety of state and local laws also restricted campaign funding and at the same time mandated how this money could be spent. In particular, the practice of rewarding faithful voters and active supporters with small cash stipends on Election Day, which had contributed to the excitement of the occasion, was widely outlawed.[40] Parties thus found their financial resources diminished and their campaign activities circumscribed. Since the parties had less to offer individual voters, it is not surprising that candidate-centered campaigns became more common.[41]

Additional reforms in the name of popular democracy undercut the position of the parties; other legislation was explicitly designed to insulate political decision making from popular influence. Of the "democratizing" reforms, the initiative, the referendum, and the recall were the most popular. By 1917 twenty-two states, many in the western and mountain regions, had established initiative and referendum procedures permitting the people to bypass legislative bodies and vote directly on legislation. The right to recall public officials was most popular at the local level, although eleven states instituted it as well. Intended to act as a check on party government, these laws helped to undermine partisan control of the legislative process in some states.[42]

The adoption of the Seventeenth Amendment to the Constitution, providing for direct election of U.S. senators, severely weakened state political parties.[43] In the nineteenth century, senators, who were elected by state legislatures, were usually masters of partisan politics. Their position in Washington, moreover, enabled them to link state organizations to national politics. The shift to direct election, especially when senatorial candidates were chosen in primaries rather than by party organizations, dramatically changed the position of senators in many states. Suddenly, they were no longer dependent on state legislatures, nor did they necessarily owe their election to party organizations. Although the ramifications varied from state to state, in much of the country direct election deprived the parties of control over what had been an important strategic position.

At the urban level, where parties had been the strongest in the late nineteenth century, political reforms were devastating. By changing the structure of local government, urban reformers sought to bypass the parties. At the very least, reformers reduced the number of elected officials to a mayor and a single council and replaced ward and district elections with at-large contests. These changes severed the close parochial ties that had existed between city councilmen and their constituents.[44] In some cities reform went further and succeeded in replacing elected mayors by city managers and city councils with commissions.[45] In many cities local elections were transformed into nonpartisan contests in which the parties were not allowed to participate directly. Everywhere, the number of patronage appointments was reduced through an extension of civil service.

Looking at the political system in the broadest terms, the Progressive reforms signaled long-term shifts in the nature of American political decision making, shifts that worked to the disadvantage of political parties.[46] Specifically, the growth of civil service administrations at all levels of government removed important jobs and decisions from the arena of partisan politics. Parties were no longer the only route to political influence. On the federal level, Theodore Roosevelt's extension in 1908 of merit Civil Service to all fourth-class postmasters north of the Ohio River and east of the Mississippi River dried up the principal source of party patronage. In 1912 William Taft abolished most of the remaining federal patronage positions by extending Civil Service to another fifty-two thousand employees.[47]

As administrative government grew during the early twentieth century, political power gradually shifted from local to state to national government and, consequently, away from the level at which political parties had been strongest.[48] The potent, mass-based parties of the nineteenth century, rooted in local politics and dominating legislative activity, were thus divested of their influence both by specific reforms and by gradual evolutionary changes, which together restructured political decision making in early-twentieth-century America. Elections became contests between individual candidates rather than party slates. With both candidate selection and campaign activity now subject to government regulation, political careers were no longer dependent on the parties. A rich variety of patronage appointments and preferments slowly disappeared from the arsenal of partisan resources. Without concrete incentives to offer their adherents, the parties were generally unable to maintain the extensive organizations they had built up in the late nineteenth century and were forced to abandon most labor-intensive electioneering practices. In short, during the early twentieth century both the significance of parties for the mass electorate and the power of parties within government deteriorated, in no small part because of the impact of Progressive reform.

Progressive Reform: The Attack on Mass Participation

Explicit attempts to regulate mass participation in the electoral process accompanied the early-twentieth-century attack on party politics. Progressives sought to use legal reforms to reshape the contours of the voting electorate. Among these were formal changes in suffrage requirements, including the enfranchisement of women voters in many states and the disfranchisement of aliens throughout the nation, and fundamental changes in procedures for establishing voter eligibility (particularly poll taxes, literacy tests, and stringent voter registration systems). The new procedures took the vote away from many men just as women were gaining the franchise for the first time.

The ratification on August 25, 1920, of the Nineteenth Amendment, which granted women nationwide the right to vote, was by far the most far-reaching change in suffrage requirements during this century. Though ratification capped years of struggle, it was only during the teens that women had made significant progress toward winning the vote. In contrast to the late nineteenth century, when only the mountain states enfranchised women, nine additional states granted women the right to vote between 1910 and 1917.[49]

Like the other "democratizing" reforms of the early twentieth century, the enfranchisement of women was a complex political phenomenon. Many of the supporters of women's suffrage hoped that the enfranchisement of women would help to "purify" politics, freeing it from partisan control. They expected that native-born, middle-class women would participate at higher rates than women from immigrant cultures, thus enabling reformers to defeat regular party organizations whose strength was lodged in the working-class and immigrant electorate.[50] To some extent, therefore, the fight for women's suffrage also involved an attempt by reformers to take advantage of vastly different cultural assumptions and use women to restructure the socioeconomic and ethnic balance of the electorate.

Women did not win the vote in most of the country until after its value for male voters had declined appreciably. The irony of women's suffrage coming to fruition at a time when electoral politics was losing much of its customary significance was not lost on some suffragists. Suzanne La Folette noted bitterly, "It is the misfortune for the woman's movement that it has succeeded in securing political rights for women at the very period when political rights are worth less than they have been at any time since the eighteenth century."[51] Women's suffrage nonetheless involved an unparalleled expansion of the right to participate in electoral politics. Whatever cultural prejudices contributed to the passage of the Nineteenth Amendment, women's suffrage represented a major expansion of American democracy. As such, it ran counter to the major trends in electoral reform during the Progressive Era.

Besides women's suffrage, the only formal change in the franchise during the early twentieth century was the repeal of suffrage for noncitizen immigrants, which affected relatively few voters.[52] A vast array of Progressive "procedural" reforms, on the other hand, had a broad impact on both the size and the composition of the American electorate. Poll taxes and literacy tests were powerful devices designed to limit electoral participation of certain segments of the population. Poll taxes required the annual payment of a sum of money, usually one to two dollars, for the "privilege" of voting, constituting a burden on poor families. Some states made the provision even more restrictive by establishing a cumulative poll tax, so that a voter had to pay back poll taxes before regaining the right previously lost. Many states required a voter to pay this tax months before the election and then produce a receipt on Election Day.[53] Literacy tests obliged voters to read and usually to write English. In addition, some states included an "understanding and interpretation" clause, which specified that voters not only had to be able to read a section of the Constitution, but also to understand and frame a "reasonable" interpretation of it. As contemporaries well understood, this provision could be applied capriciously to deny the vote to specific groups of people.[54]

The South pioneered the use of both the poll tax and the literacy test; by 1908 each of the former Confederate states required the payment of a poll tax, and seven out of ten also had enacted literacy requirements.[55] Clearly designed to deprive blacks in the South of their right to participate in the electoral process, these reforms were thoroughly effective.[56] Furthermore, despite attempts in many states to prevent these laws from disfranchising white voters, the white electorate contracted dramatically as poor and illiterate whites were generally excluded from participation as well.[57] The impact of poll taxes and literacy tests on southern voting, both black and white, was immediate and dramatic. On average, turnout declined more than 15 percent in the first election following the adoption of a poll tax and over 13 percent following the adoption of a literacy test and dropped sharply in the next election as well.[58] When the two measures were wielded jointly, popular electoral participation was virtually eliminated.

Though most efficaciously employed in the South, neither the poll tax nor the literacy test was invented there, nor was their use limited to that region. Property requirements dated back to colonial times and survived into the early national period in every state. They had been eliminated in most of the country during the Jacksonian Era, but Delaware continued to enfranchise only taxpayers until 1897, and both Rhode Island and Pennsylvania at least partially restricted the franchise in this way until after World War I.[59] As for literacy requirements, Connecticut was the first state to adopt a literacy test (in 1856), followed by Massachusetts two years later. Whereas property requirements did not become widespread in the North during the Progressive Era, literacy tests did. By 1916 nine northern states limited the franchise to literate citizens, most of them specifying literacy in English. The majority of these states lay on either the West or East Coast, where the tests seem to have been purposefully directed at specific immigrant populations.[60]

Though outwardly not so discriminatory as property and literacy requirements, the enactment of strong voter registration systems also reduced electoral participation, especially among poorer and minority voters. Voter registration began during the early years of the nineteenth century and was the rule in most states by the 1880s and 1890s. Unlike its twentieth-century counterpart, however, nineteenth-century voter registration was generally either nonpersonal (registrars were empowered to draw up lists of eligible voters) or personal and permanent (voters registered in person and were then enfranchised for life). Both systems were administered at the local level, usually by part-time officials nominated by the two parties, and thus operated under partisan influence. In the partisan world of late-nineteenth-century politics, voter registration requirements rarely restricted the franchise significantly.[61]

Reformers were unhappy with partisan control over registration, however, and alleged widespread fraud. They pushed for both periodic and personal voter registration. Beginning in the 1880s, and increasingly over time, they were successful in strengthening registration requirements in one state after another. By 1920 thirty-six states had adopted personal voter registration systems, and the vast majority of these required voters to reregister periodically. Such reform usually also wrested control of the registration process from the parties and turned it over to civil servants.[62]

The tougher regulations adopted during the late nineteenth and early twentieth centuries impeded participation in electoral politics. Personal registration placed the burden on the voter rather than on the state.[63] Individuals had to present themselves personally to a registrar well in advance of an election in order to be eligible to cast a ballot on Election Day. Entry into the electorate thus became a two-step process. Not surprisingly, the added hurdle had the effect of inhibiting the incorporation of new voters into the active electorate.[64] Moreover, the requirement to repeat the registration process periodically made it even more burdensome for voters to maintain their eligibility. Many marginal voters, who might otherwise have been drawn to the polls by the excitement that surrounded elections, probably failed to register and were thus disfranchised in advance of Election Day.[65]

Voter registration requirements discriminated against poor and minority voters. In the North, stringent reregistration requirements were often limited to large cities, where most of the immigrants lived. In both the North and the South, the times and places set for registration were often designed to make it very difficult for the working class to register. In New Jersey, for example, the registration process was limited to four days a year, all workdays, and police surveillance was authorized to verify eligibility.[66] Some states also required that voters provide full information (in English) about a variety of matters, including exact date of birth, street address, and occupation—information that lower-class voters often could not produce.[67] The parties, having lost control over the registration process in much of the country, were often unable to offset these difficulties and thus found it increasingly hard to maintain the eligibility of many of their immigrant and poorer supporters.

Although many reformers and later scholars have claimed that the major impact of Progressive electoral reforms, especially voter registration, was to eliminate fraud from the political process, there is little evidence to substantiate their claims.[68] The passage of ballot reform, stringent registration laws, and other legal safeguards established formal regulations to ensure the honesty of the electoral process, but there is no reason to believe that there had been extensive fraudulent casting and counting of ballots in the 1880s and 1890s, nor that these electoral reforms eliminated a large number of fraudulent votes.[69]

It is clear, however, that Progressive reforms undermined mass participation. The explicit disfranchising legislation enacted and stringently exercised by the southern states was only the most extreme of these legal changes. Throughout the country, the toughening of voter registration laws and balloting procedures deprived many Americans of their right to vote. In addition, these and other legal changes raised the costs of participation to a point where many citizens simply excluded themselves from the electoral process.

Equally important, mass participation was also affected by the wide variety of antiparty reforms. As Progressive reforms sapped party resources, the ability of the parties to act as agents of mass mobilization eroded. Despite the portrayal of Progressive reforms by their supporters as democratizing, mass participation in electoral politics was undercut both indirectly (as party organizations were weakened) and directly (as legal changes made it more difficult for many individuals to vote). By 1918 the legal-institutional structure of American politics facilitated neither strong mass parties nor full political participation.

The Impact of Progressive Reform

Cumulatively, the many Progressive reforms changed the rules of American electoral politics during the early twentieth century. If we are to understand the roots of the decline in mass participation, however, we need to understand the process by which these reforms affected electoral behavior. In particular, we need to explore the relationship between explicit legal and institutional changes and the broader social and political forces that were undermining mass participation.

The impact of electoral reforms on voter behavior, though important, was largely indirect and mediated through the party system. The stringent suffrage restrictions in the South had an immediate and profound effect on voting behavior, but changes in the rules of electoral politics were far less determinate in the rest of the nation. These reforms permitted—indeed facilitated—the emergence of new voting patterns but did not by themselves cause voters to act differently. Sophisticated quantitative studies using multiple regression analysis, both by Paul Kleppner and Stephen Baker and by Richard Carlson, find that outside of the South, Progressive legal changes directly accounted for only a small part of the total decline in voter turnout. [70] The reason is crucial: the effects of reform legislation varied dramatically with the diverse social and especially political circumstances that existed in the states.

An analysis of one specific reform—personal voter registration—to which some scholars attribute the bulk of the falloff in voter turnout[71]— highlights the necessity of placing legal changes within a larger context. For example, voter participation fell off in every county in New York, Ohio, and Pennsylvania after 1896, although some counties had instituted registration requirements and others had not. The additional decline in areas with stringent registration procedures amounted to between one-third and one-fifth of the total statewide decline in each of these states.[72] In a study of the northern states, Paul Kleppner and Stephen Baker find that registration reform could account for one-half of the falloff in 40 percent of the states. In fully 25 percent of the states, however, turnout was higher in areas where personal registration prevailed than in those with less strict requirements.[73] Though registration reform was a significant factor in the nationwide falloff in voting, it was not the only variable involved, nor were the consequences of stringent registration requirements the same throughout the country.

Electoral reforms can best be understood as permissive rather than determinative factors. The adoption of the Australian ballot, for example, made it possible for voters to split their votes between candidates from different parties. Less partisan voting behavior was facilitated to a greater or lesser extent depending upon the shape of the new ballot. The largest increases in ticket splitting, however, occurred twelve to thirty years after the Progressive Era.[74] Ballot reform was a prerequisite for independent voting, but it is not in itself a sufficient explanation for the significant changes in partisan voting patterns.

The impact of Progressive reforms on mass political behavior can only be understood within the context of the larger political and social processes that were restructuring mass politics in the early years of this century. Legal changes raised procedural barriers to participation at a time when voters were already becoming less inclined to cast a ballot. These procedural barriers were most burdensome for poor, immigrant, minority, and young voters, precisely the segments of the electorate most influenced by the erosion of the social and cultural basis of electoral participation.[75] Reforms also stripped political parties of key resources when they were already losing many of their social functions. The early-twentieth-century legal and institutional changes thus exacerbated the ongoing process of partisan degeneration.[76] Reforms interacted with and were mediated by other political and social factors. As a result, both the shape of the electoral reform and its impact varied widely throughout the nation.

The most important variable was the strength of party organizations. Voter registration requirements, for example, affected participation rates more or less severely, depending on the ability of the parties to continue to secure the eligibility of their supporters. In some localities, powerful local parties proved fairly resilient, and many urban party organizations had sufficient resources to continue providing their followers with a wide range of services. In places like New York and Chicago, where parochial ties between parties and voters remained strong, the impact of legal reforms was minimal. Party organizations adapted themselves to the legal changes and maintained control of government as before, through mass mobilization.[77] Local parties in other areas, however, already on the wane, were often overwhelmed by reform. In many places parties were practically legislated out of business. Where they lacked the resources to survive in anything more than a formal sense, the impact of Progressive reform on both the party system and mass electoral participation was devastating.

Far too often, legal changes are treated as givens, as procedural adjustments disembodied from historical context. Progressive reforms were not inevitable but were the result of conscious political activity. Reformers capitalized on a rapidly degenerating system of mass-based partisan politics and sped the process along. Electoral reform was not merely procedural, therefore, but strategic and substantive. Reform not only ensured the dissolution of nineteenth-century participatory politics but also provided the institutional groundwork for a new style of administrative politics that would replace it.

In order to understand both the success of the reform movement and the adaptation of political parties to the new order, we must look more closely at electoral politics in the early years of the twentieth century. In particular, we need to explore the realignment in mass support for the two parties. The evaporation of two-party competition in much of the United States was a vital ingredient in the transformation of American politics. It is largely the specific catalyst of partisan alignments that explains why the parties adapted so readily to an entirely new mode of politics.

CHAPTER SIX

Electoral Politics and Administrative Government

The Shifting Locus of Political Decision Making

The realignment of the American party system in the mid-1890s sapped electoral competition throughout the country. With the Republicans controlling most of the North and the Democrats the South, the early twentieth century experienced few closely fought elections. As competition waned, much of the vitality drained out of the electoral system. Not only did public involvement fall off, but also even the political importance of elections decreased. The primary arena of political decision-making gradually shifted away from electoral politics and representative bodies to administrative and executive agencies and officials. On the national, state and local levels, party government gave way to bureaucratic government, while interest groups gained increasing political influence and power.

This metamorphosis of American government fundamentally altered the exercise of public power. Government was now able and willing to regulate and administer the economy in ways that Gilded Age party government could not attempt. Both the powers of the state and its role in daily life grew dramatically as some of the most severe shortcomings of the late-nineteenth-century political system were resolved. The transformation from a participatory to an administrative political system, however, was not without costs. Whereas the late-nineteenth-century system of party government was handicapped by its absolute dependence on voter support, twentieth-century politics suffered a similar reliance on organized interest groups. The result, ironically, was that as public power grew, it was fragmented and distributed to organized groups. In the process, the ability of American government to address the problems of a modern society increased, but a degree of democratic control over public policy was lost.

Electoral Politics in the Progressive Era

Throughout the nation, electoral competition dissipated after 1896.[1] Whereas nearly every state in the Union had experienced extremely hard-fought contests during the late nineteenth century, early-twentieth-century elections were rarely close. In some states, especially in the South, the plight of the minority party was hopeless; in others the majority party faced stiff competition only occasionally. Electoral competitiveness did not totally vanish, but intense two-party competition was sporadic.[2]

Not only was there substantial regional variation in electoral behavior, but also the rise of candidate-centered campaigns made for great differences in electoral competition for different offices.[3] In addition the 1912 three-way contest between Wilson, Taft, and Theodore Roosevelt resulted in a large short-term deviation from normal voting patterns, which temporarily reinvigorated electoral competition in many northern states. As a result, although electoral competition became less consistent, average electoral competitiveness fell off only slightly during the first two decades of this century. Neither the nation as a whole nor many states experienced a secular decline in electoral competition at all comparable to the decline in voter participation.

Relatively small shifts in partisan voting greatly affected the political system. The close partisan division of the late nineteenth century proved to be a precarious balance that was easily upset both on the national level and in many key northern states. The increase in the average margin of victory in electoral contests was not dramatic, but it was enough to institute stable one-party control over many states and the national government.

Analysis of aggregate election returns reveals the slackening of electoral competition between the two parties (see table 6.1).[4] Electoral competition eroded in every region of the country except the mountain

TABLE 6.1
Mean State-Level Competitiveness Scores in
Presidential Elections, 1880–1916

Region	1880–1896	1900–1916
New England	79.9	79.6
Mid-Atlantic	92.5	85.6
North Central	94.3	85.3
Midwest	82.4	80.6
South	66.9	47.6
Border	92.6	90.0
Mountain	68.1	84.2
West	93.5	79.5
North	85.8	83.4
Nation	81.1	75.7

NOTE: See "Units of Analyis" in Appendix 1 for a complete list of states in each region.

states. In the nation as a whole, mean state-level competitiveness fell from 81.8 to 75.7, while average state-level electoral competition in the North declined from 85.8 to 83.4.[5] In other words, the average state-level margin of victory in early-twentieth-century presidential elections was nearly 25 percent of the total vote.

The steepest decline in electoral competitiveness was in the South, where the mean margin of victory grew to over 50 percent. That disparity translates into a 75-25 division of the vote. Early-twentieth-century electoral contests were less competitive in every southern state than they had been during the eighties and nineties. No southern state averaged over 80 on this index of competitiveness, and only three (Virginia, Arkansas, and North Carolina) averaged over 70.[6] Throughout the South, electoral competition virtually disappeared; gubernatorial and congressional contests were even less closely contested than presidential ones.[7]

Although the nature of electoral contests in the North did not change as dramatically, most northern states experienced a noticeable movement away from close electoral competition. As seen in table 6.2, which presents the competitiveness scores for northern states that participated in national elections from 1880 to 1916, sixteen northern states could be classified as highly competitive during the 1880s and 1890s since they averaged over 90 for the last five nineteenth-century presidential contests.[8] In contrast, early-twentieth-century presidential elections were consistently this close in only five states: Delaware, Indiana, Missouri, Kentucky, and Maryland.[9]

In the populous mid-Atlantic and north central regions, which had been the center of the late-nineteenth-century party system, competition declined significantly. Presidential elections were less closely fought in every single mid-Atlantic and north central state during the first two decades of the twentieth century. The pattern was similar but even more dramatic in the West.[10] In New England as well, competition between

TABLE 6.2

Presidential Competition in the Settled Northern States

State	Mean 1880–1896	1900	1904	1908	1912	1916	Mean 1900–1916
Connecticut	92.6	84.2	80.0	76.5	96.7	96.9	86.9
Maine	81.8	73.0	61.1	70.3	81.1	96.0	76.3
Massachusetts	82.8	80.3	79.3	75.8	96.4	96.1	85.6
New Hampshire	88.2	79.1	77.7	78.3	98.0	99.9	86.6
Rhode Island	79.3	75.3	75.6	73.4	96.5	94.9	83.1
Vermont	54.8	47.1	40.9	46.8	87.3	72.8	59.0
New England	79.9	73.1	69.1	70.2	92.7	92.8	79.6
Delaware	92.0	91.2	90.1	93.8	86.4	97.6	91.8
New Jersey	93.4	85.8	81.4	82.3	79.3	88.3	83.4
New York	94.9	90.7	89.1	87.6	87.4	93.0	89.6
Pennsylvania	89.6	75.4	59.3	76.6	90.0	86.0	77.4
Mid-Atlantic	92.5	85.8	80.0	85.1	85.8	91.2	85.6
Illinois	94.1	91.6	71.7	84.5	86.8	90.8	85.1
Indiana	98.5	96.0	86.2	98.5	80.0	99.0	92.0
Michigan	91.2	80.8	56.3	70.5	99.8	91.7	79.8
Ohio	96.8	93.4	74.6	93.8	85.9	92.3	88.0
Wisconsin	90.7	75.9	64.8	82.2	91.6	93.4	81.6
North Central	94.3	87.5	70.7	85.9	88.8	93.4	85.3
Iowa	89.0	81.4	67.3	85.0	86.7	88.6	81.8
Kansas	73.7	64.5	61.3	90.4	81.2	94.1	78.3
Minnesota	82.6	75.5	44.9	73.8	87.4	99.9	76.3
Missouri	91.5	94.5	96.1	99.9	82.4	96.4	93.8
Nebraska	80.5	96.8	62.1	98.5	78.0	85.7	84.2
Midwest	81.7	82.5	66.3	89.5	83.1	93.0	82.9
Kentucky	90.3	98.3	97.3	98.3	77.0	94.6	93.1
Maryland	91.8	94.7	100.0	99.8	75.1	92.0	92.3
Tennessee	92.3	91.9	89.2	93.2	71.2	86.4	86.4
West Virginia	95.8	90.5	86.8	89.8	79.0	99.1	89.0
Border	92.6	93.9	93.3	95.3	78.2	90.9	90.0
Colorado	71.1	86.4	85.8	98.9	79.1	73.9	84.8
Nevada	77.1	75.5	76.2	98.2	76.2	83.1	81.8
California	98.0	86.8	65.1	77.5	58.8	99.7	77.6
Oregon	90.9	84.0	52.1	77.7	91.0	97.4	80.4
Mountain/ Western	84.3	83.2	69.8	88.1	76.3	88.5	81.2
Totals	89.5	83.6	74.0	84.7	84.5	92.1	83.8

the two parties eroded, although the break with nineteenth-century electoral politics occurred early in these states.[11] Presidential contests were less closely contested in every single New England state from 1900 to 1916 than from 1880 to 1892.[12]

In the Midwest the average margin of victory grew only slightly, but elections were less hard fought after the demise of Populism. Throughout the region, nearly 20 percent of the total vote separated the two major parties. The border states also experienced a slight decline in mean competitiveness in presidential elections, but this region should be seen as an exception to the general pattern. The average margin of victory remained below 10 percent in Kentucky, Maryland, Tennessee, and West Virginia as they all experienced consistently close elections. The other regions of the country all averaged more than a 10 percent gap at the state level between the victor and the loser in early-twentieth-century presidential, gubernatorial, and congressional contests.[13]

Competition did not fall off gradually and cumulatively over a series of elections. Regression analysis shows only the South experiencing a significant secular trend away from electoral competitiveness. In most northern states, electoral competition fell off precipitously in the mid-1890s. Once the competitive balance of the late-nineteenth-century party system had been broken, there were relatively few close elections and competition became increasingly erratic.

In most northern states, some, but not the majority, of elections were bitterly fought. Table 6.2 reveals just how sporadic electoral competition was from 1900 through 1916. Except for Vermont, New Jersey, Iowa, and California, competitiveness in northern states surpassed 90 on the index in at least one election. Seventeen states experienced elections in which less than 4 percent of the total vote separated the winner from the loser. In all but three states, however (Delaware, New York, and Missouri), competition also fell below 80 in at least one of these five presidential elections. In those contests, over 20 percent of the total vote separated the two parties.[14] Electoral competition did not completely disappear after 1896, but fewer contests in fewer states were closely fought, and a stable and close balance between the two parties no longer characterized electoral politics.

Although competition between the Democratic and Republican parties eroded, third parties attracted about the same percentage of the total vote during the first two decades of the twentieth century as they had during the previous twenty years. In both the nation as a whole and the

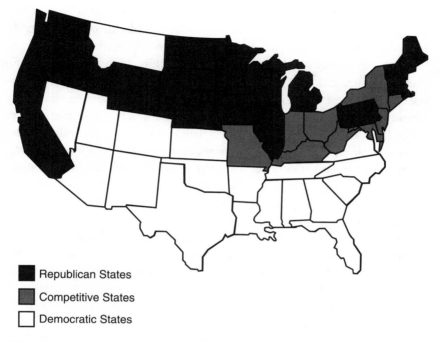

Republican States

Competitive States

Democratic States

Map 6.1

North, minor-party voting averaged in the vicinity of 10 percent of the total vote cast in presidential, gubernatorial, and congressional elections. Moreover, minor parties continued to hold the balance of power in one-fourth to one-third of all state-level presidential, gubernatorial, and congressional contests.[15]

Nonetheless, as the gap in electoral support between the two major parties widened (even if only by a few percentage points), the impact of minor-party voting diminished. Minor-party votes throughout 1900–1918 had little effect on the outcome of elections at any level except during the few years of the Republican party division. In most early-twentieth-century elections, the two parties were simply too widely separated for third parties either to pose a threat to the majority party or to offer hope to the minority one. Third-party political activity no longer ensured a consistently competitive electoral environment.

The decline in electoral competitiveness resulted in one-party domination in an increasing number of states, including several that previously had been highly competitive. Map 6.1 identifies the few states that experienced continually competitive elections and those in which either the Republican or the Democratic party dominated electoral contests.[16] Early-twentieth-century elections were consistently hard fought only in Connecticut, Delaware, New York, Indiana, Ohio, Maryland, Kentucky, West Virginia, and Missouri—a narrow band of states in the middle of the country. Most were either in the border region or, like Delaware and Missouri, could have been classified as border states. Only four other states from the New England, mid-Atlantic, and north central regions remained highly competitive. In contrast, during the 1880s and 1890s, elections were consistently hard fought in all five north central states, the three highly populated mid-Atlantic states (Pennsylvania, New Jersey, and New York), two New England states (New Hampshire and Connecticut), and two western states (California and Oregon) (see map 3.1).

During the early twentieth century, noncompetitive elections resulted in one-party dominance of state government in much of the nation. Research by Walter Dean Burnham on the partisan composition of state legislatures demonstrates the extent of single-party supremacy. Assuming that a "median lead of 40 percent or more for either party (a 70-30 or more extreme two-party imbalance) is indicative of a one-party hegemony at the grass roots level," he identifies those states in which one party was in full control and those in which a substantial political opposition existed.[17] Map 6.2 illustrates Burnham's division of the states into four categories: solidly Republican, leaning Republican, solidly Democratic, and leaning Democratic. The similarity between maps 6.1 and 6.2 is transparent: in most states where one party dominated electoral politics, it was able to translate that ascendancy into clear control over state government. Republicans were dominant throughout the North, facing a viable opposition in only a few of the large states, whereas the Democratic hegemony in the South was unchallenged.

Single-party control over state politics was much more common after the mid-1890s than before. A dozen northern states (Connecticut, Massachusetts, Pennsylvania, Illinois, Michigan, Wisconsin, Iowa, Minnesota, North Dakota, Wyoming, California, and Oregon) that had experienced two-party politics on the state level during the late nineteenth century were dominated by a single party during the early twentieth century. The comparison between periods is dramatic. More than three-fifths of the nation's population and four-fifths of all northerners lived in states with a vibrant two-party system during the late nineteenth century, but only one-third of all Americans and slightly more than two-

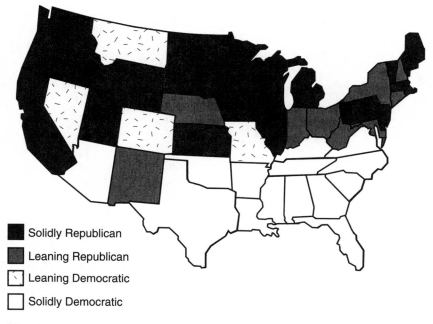

Solidly Republican

Leaning Republican

Leaning Democratic

Solidly Democratic

Map 6.2

fifths of the northern population continued to enjoy the benefits of competitive state politics during the early twentieth century.[18]

The evaporation of the competitive two-party system heightened sectionalism. After 1896 the Republican party was virtually destroyed as an organized political force in the South, and the Democrats ceased to offer a viable opposition in much of the North and West. As the two parties effectively partitioned the nation, the intensity of competition between them lessened because neither represented much of a threat to the other.

With the waning of two-party competition in most states, the competitive balance at the national level was also broken. Control over the late-nineteenth-century federal government, which had rested on small pluralities in a large number of contested states, was usually split between the two parties. After 1896, though, the Republicans gained command over the national government by virtue of their supremacy in the populous North, while the Democrats were institutionalized as the minority party on the basis of the unwavering support of southern voters.[19]

The contrast between the close two-party balance that had distinguished national elections during the Gilded Age and the one-party

TABLE 6.3
Congressional Partisan Divisions, 1881–1921

| Congress | | House | | | Senate | | |
Session	Years	Rep.	Dem.	Other	Rep.	Dem.	Other
47	1881–83	147	135	11	37	37	1
48	1883–85	118	197	10	38	36	2
49	1885–87	183	140	2	43	34	0
50	1887–89	152	169	4	39	37	0
51	1889–91	166	159	0	39	37	0
52	1891–93	88	235	9	47	39	0
53	1893–95	127	218	11	38	44	3
54	1895–97	244	105	7	43	39	6
55	1897–99	204	113	40	47	34	7
56	1899–1901	185	163	9	53	26	8
57	1901–1903	197	151	9	55	31	4
58	1903–1905	208	178	0	57	33	0
59	1905–1907	250	136	0	57	33	0
60	1907–1909	222	164	0	61	31	0
61	1909–11	219	172	0	61	32	0
62	1911–13	161	228	1	51	41	0
63	1913–15	127	291	17	44	51	1
64	1915–17	196	230	9	40	56	0
65	1917–19	210	216	6	42	53	0
66	1919–21	240	190	3	49	47	0

SOURCE: Congressional Quarterly, Guide to U.S. Elections, 928.

dominance of the Progressive Era is striking. McKinley, the first president since Grant to receive over 50 percent of the vote, inaugurated a period in which presidents were routinely elected by majority vote. Every president from McKinley to Truman, with the exception of Wilson, garnered a majority of the votes cast. The only sitting president to be defeated in the early twentieth century was Taft, who had the misfortune to be challenged from within his own party by an ex-president. Whereas late-nineteenth-century presidents stood little chance at reelection, during the first half of the twentieth century incumbent presidents could be beaten only under exceptional circumstances.[20]

After 1896 single-party control over the various branches of the national government became the rule rather than the exception. From 1898 to 1918, one party controlled both houses of Congress and the presidency for every term save one. Table 6.3 presents the partisan composition of Congress from 1881 to 1921. Unlike the 1880s and 1890s, when control over Washington was frequently divided, the Republican party securely ran the federal government from 1896 to 1910. Division within the Republican party allowed the Democrats to usurp this dominant position from 1912 until 1916; but once they reunited, Republicans returned to undisputed command for another decade.

As close pluralities gave way to solid majorities, reelection at all levels became more frequent. The emergence of single-party control over the federal government was accompanied by a decline in the proportion of congressional seats that changed party hands at each election. The rate of party turnover in congressional elections during 1900–1910 was less than half of what it had been during the 1880s as partisan turnover fell off in every region except the border states.[21] With turnover declining, the stability of officeholding on Capitol Hill increased dramatically.

The 52d Congress, elected in 1900, was the first in this nation's history in which more than two-thirds of the House was composed of returning congressmen.[22] Correspondingly, it was also the first in which the average term of congressional service exceeded three years. In contrast to the eighties and nineties, when the biennial turnover rate ranged from 30 to 60 percent, congressional turnover during the Progressive Era never exceeded 40 percent, even in 1912, and generally fluctuated in the mid–20 percent range. The average length of congressional tenure was nearly 50 percent higher during the early twentieth century than during the Gilded Age.[23] Senate tenure increased as well, although turnover rates in the Senate had already begun to decline during the late nineteenth century.[24] In both houses of Congress, as well as in the presidency, the Progressive Era witnessed a sharp break with nineteenth-century patterns of officeholding and the beginning of twentieth-century patterns, which favored reelection of incumbents and stability in government.

Just as the evaporation of a close two-party balance in electoral contests underlay the increased tenure of government officials, stable patterns of officeholding helped to erode electoral competition. For an increasing number of politicians, repeated reelection generated personalized followings. More and more officeholders ran their own campaigns, independent of party control. Incumbents faced less intraparty opposition and thus usually went into general elections unscathed from primary battles. Since incumbents increasingly proved to be formidable candidates, the opposition party was less inclined to devote considerable resources to challenging them, and their own party had little need to marshal support on their behalf. The net result was a general toning down of electoral campaigns. Electoral politics was significantly less vibrant and tumultuous during the early twentieth century because the outcome of elections was rarely in doubt.

The Early-Twentieth-Century Electoral System

As electoral competition waned, political parties had less incentive to mobilize voters, who, in turn, were less inclined to bother to vote. Just when the complexities of voter registration, literacy tests, and poll taxes made participation much more burdensome, the reduction in two-party competition lessened the satisfaction that people derived from casting a ballot. The realignment of partisan politics into a solidly Democratic South and a Republican North made it unnecessary, moreover, for the parties to continue to concentrate on securing active voter support. Occurring when party resources, organizations, and power were eroding, the decline in electoral competition was especially portentous because it meant that the parties had less need or inclination to devote their scarce resources to voter mobilization.

The relationship between the drop in electoral competition and the falloff in voter participation can be explored with regression analysis. Using county-level data, Paul Kleppner estimates that declining electoral competition accounted for between one-quarter and one-third of the early-twentieth-century drop in turnout.[25] We should not place too much weight on these specific figures, because interrelationships among the social and political factors that contribute to the decline in voting confound regression analysis. Even if we cannot determine quantitatively the exact dimensions of the relationship, however, there is no reason to doubt the connection between decreasing electoral competition and voter turnout that Kleppner identifies.

It is possible, nevertheless, to specify more clearly the effect that the erosion of electoral competitiveness had on political participation; the key is the sharply different patterns of change in voter turnout and electoral competition. Whereas the falloff in voter turnout was gradual, cumulative, and extensive, electoral competition eroded in the space of a few elections. After 1896 the nature of electoral contests no longer facilitated extensive voter participation.

Thus, the effect of declining competition on mass electoral behavior was similar to the impact of Progressive Era legal and institutional re-

TABLE 6.4

*Pearson Product-Moment Correlations (r) for the Entire Nation
for Presidential Elections, 1898–1918*

	GTO	CTO	PCOM	GCOM	CCOM	STV	PPVI	CPVI
PTO	.98	.98	.72	.74	.78	-.30	.11*	NS
GTO		.98	.67	.69	.73	-.12*	.15*	NS
CTO			.68	.68	.77	-.18	NS	NS
PCOM				.78	.89	-.20	.19*	NS
GCOM					.87	-.20	.19*	NS
CCOM						-.28	.18*	NS
STV							.23	.20
PPVI								.31

ABBREVIATIONS: NS, Not Significant; PTO, Presidential Turnout; GTO, Gubernatorial Turnout; CTO, Congressional Turnout; PCOM, Presidential Competitiveness; GCOM, Gubernatorial Competitiveness; CCOM, Congressional Competitiveness; STV, Split-Ticket Voting; PPVI, Presidential Party-Vote Instability; CPVI, Congressional Party-Vote Instability
NOTE: All Correlations except starred ones are significant at .001. Starred correlations are significant at .05.

forms. During the early twentieth century, both the absence of consistent electoral competition and the adoption of Progressive reform legislation made voter participation less likely. As the burden involved in voting increased, the incentive to cast a ballot decreased, and the parties were less able and less inclined to mobilize voters. Since the political environment during the early twentieth century no longer favored mass participation, the erosion of the social basis of participatory politics resulted in a substantial demobilization of the American electorate.

The process of political and social change during the early twentieth century was complex, of course, but the end result was a thorough restructuring of electoral politics. Just how thorough becomes clearer when we examine how electoral politics functioned as a system after 1896. The strength of the relationships among the variables that we have been using to represent participation, partisanship, and competitiveness can be examined with correlation analysis.

As table 6.4 shows, voter participation in the entire nation appears to have remained closely related to electoral competitiveness during the first years of the 1900s. Likewise, partisan voting behavior, as inversely represented by split-ticket voting, seems to have been linked somewhat to both participation and competitiveness, although apparently neither of the two was related to partisan stability over time. Comparing this correlation matrix to the comparable one for the late nineteenth century (table 3.7) reveals little evidence of decay in late-nineteenth-century

TABLE 6.5
*Pearson Product-Moment Correlations (r) for the North
for Presidential Elections, 1898–1918*

	GTO	CTO	PCOM	GCOM	CCOM	STV	PPVI	CPVI
PTO	.95	.94	.24	NS	.23	-.19*	-.26	-.16*
GTO		.97	NS	NS	.22	-.14*	-.22*	-.10*
CTO			.15*	NS	.25	-.18	-.31	-.10*
PCOM				.43	.71	-.16*	NS	NS
GCOM					.57	.29	NS	-.10*
CCOM						-.40	NS	-.14*
STV							.35	.21
PPVI								.34

ABBREVIATIONS: NS, Not Significant; PTO, Presidential Turnout; GTO, Gubernatorial Turnout; CTO, Congressional Turnout; PCOM, Presidential Competitiveness; GCOM, Gubernatorial Competitiveness; CCOM, Congressional Competitiveness; STV, Split-Ticket Voting; PPVI, Presidential Party-Vote Instability; CPVI, Congressional Party-Vote Instability
NOTE: All correlations except starred ones are significant at .001. Starred correlations are significant at .05

electoral linkages. In fact, the relationships between electoral competitiveness and mass participation were even stronger during the early twentieth century than during the late nineteenth century.

These correlations, however, were largely a by-product of the vast sectional differences in early-twentieth-century voting behavior between the South, where both mass participation and electoral competitiveness were virtually nonexistent, and the rest of the nation. If the ten southern states are excluded from the analysis, the connection between electoral competitiveness and voter turnout all but vanishes (see table 6.5).[26] Electoral competition in presidential and congressional contests correlated with voter turnout during the early twentieth century, but only slightly. The magnitudes of these correlations were down substantially from those of the late nineteenth century.

Furthermore, competitiveness in gubernatorial elections was no longer significantly related to voter participation. A slight negative relationship between partisan instability and mass participation remains, and the connection to electoral competitiveness disappears. In general, during the early twentieth century, strong interrelationships were no longer evident among mass participation, partisan voting, and electoral competitiveness.

Also, the relationships among various measures of both electoral competitiveness and partisan voting broke down. The magnitude of the correlations between gubernatorial competitiveness and both presidential and congressional competitiveness fell off considerably. As these changes indicate, early-twentieth-century electoral competition varied significantly for different offices. Likewise, the various measures of partisan instability were no longer closely related. Taken together, these changes indicate that early-twentieth-century electoral behavior was more heterogeneous than that of the late nineteenth century. The figures in tables 6.4 and 6.5 thus reflect the shift from a party-centered electoral system to a candidate-dependent one.

Correlation analysis thus illuminates the transformation that American electoral politics underwent during the early twentieth century. We see evidence that electoral behavior was increasingly varied and irregular as turnout, partisanship, and electoral competition ceased to be mutually reinforcing. After the mid-1890s, partisan competition reemerged sporadically, but since neither social nor political conditions facilitated extensive voter participation, close elections usually did not result in massive turnouts. Nor, with the two parties so unevenly matched, did voter mobilization, when it occurred, necessarily reinvigorate electoral competition. Under these conditions, partisan voting behavior served to weaken electoral competition; close contests generally were predicated on deviations from partisan voting. The connection between voter participation and party allegiance weakened as well, since high turnouts became increasingly dependent on the mobilization of less partisan new voters.

The changes in electoral behavior were accompanied, consequently, by a substantial amount of variation from election to election and office to office, signaling the emergence of characteristic twentieth-century patterns of electoral behavior. Heterogeneous electoral results were the product of low levels of public involvement, weak partisan commitments, and erratic electoral competition.

Electoral Demobilization and the Administrative State

The early-twentieth-century transformation of electoral politics thus had broad implications for the American political process. When elections became less participatory, partisan, and competitive, they became less important. Initiative and authority progressively shifted from the local level, where electoral politics had been most vibrant, to the states and ultimately to the national government, where the political process was far removed from popular participation. At all levels political decision making moved from electoral contests and representative bodies to executive officials and independent administrative agencies. In the process the political parties lost their position of dominance, and the exercise of political power was thoroughly restructured.

Since the early twentieth century, extensive scholarly attention has been devoted to explaining the changes in American government during the Progressive Era. Contemporary analysts and politicians, as well as later historians and political scientists, understood that these years witnessed the transition to a larger, more powerful polity that was continuously involved in the daily affairs of its citizens. Both the content and the structure of government changed at all levels as the modern American State was born.[27] Not always fully appreciated, however, was the extent to which this transformation was tied to the demobilization of the mass electorate.[28] The decline in mass electoral participation and the erosion of partisan and competitive electoral politics were both prerequisites for—and exacerbated by—fundamental changes in the way the nation was governed.

During the late nineteenth century, when the American public was fully mobilized by two highly competitive political parties, government power resided largely in the hands of representative bodies—city councils, state legislatures, and Congress—which were dominated by partisan concerns and the relentless need to mobilize electoral support.[29] With the decline of mass participation and partisan competition, much of this electoral pressure faded. In response, the structure of representative bodies gradually began to change, and control over public policy shifted toward the executive branch.

The transformation is clearest on the national level, where Congress was increasingly professionalized during the early twentieth century.[30] As turnover declined and careers lengthened, congressmen and senators gained independence from their parties and began to develop new perspectives on their offices. There was sharp erosion of party loyalty in roll call voting,[31] and seniority, which previously had been a guideline for allocating leadership positions, became the inviolable organizational principle. Under the seniority system, party leadership lost most of its discretionary authority to reward loyalty, punish mavericks, and control policy because access to power now came automatically through accumulated service.[32]

As the significance of seniority grew and the influence of party leadership declined, an elaborate permanent committee system developed in both houses. Increasingly, professional committee staffs did the work involved in drafting legislation, and political battles were fought in committees rather than on the floor. An elaborate division of labor developed as most congressmen and senators gained influence over narrow areas of policy through their committee assignments. The end result was a marked decentralization of decision making; power drifted into the hands of committees and senior congressmen and away from partisan leadership and the House and the Senate as a whole.[33]

The transformation was part of a larger process that undermined Congress's hold on legislative power. Freed from many of the partisan electoral pressures that had limited his predecessors to the role of party mediator, Theodore Roosevelt revolutionized the office of the presidency by taking the lead in proposing legislation. With Roosevelt in the White House, the president, not Congress, set the political agenda. When Taft and Wilson followed Roosevelt in the practice of sending legislative packages to the Hill, the initiative in proposing legislation shifted permanently to the executive branch.[34] The personal qualities of both Roosevelt and Wilson had much to do with this transformation. Giving the appearance of standing above partisan concerns, both presidents developed personalized followings within both the electorate and the government. Thus they dominated the national political stage and fundamentally altered the role of the president within the political process.[35]

Although the charisma of Presidents Roosevelt and Wilson was no doubt a factor in the increasing power of the presidency, far more significant was the commitment of all three Progressive Era presidents to increasing the size and influence of the national administrative apparatus. Each extended the merit system for Civil Service, so that by 1920 patronage on the federal level had largely disappeared. In its place a rapidly growing Civil Service was continually upgraded and professionalized. Executive coordination of a burgeoning administration was strengthened by presidential initiatives, the most important of which was Taft's decision to draw up the first comprehensive federal budget.

The administrative restructuring that undercut party government did not occur without conflict. In a pioneering study of this process, Stephen Skowronek carefully details the extent to which the professionalization and rationalization of the "new American state" was limited by partisan concerns and existing institutional arrangements. Congress, in particular, strenuously resisted presidential efforts to secure control over the new, permanent federal bureaucracy. The result was much confusion, overlapping authority, and institutionalized conflict, which limited both the power of the president and the independence of the federal bureaucracy.

Nevertheless, a powerful federal administration grew up during the early twentieth century. Though not unchecked, the authority and capabilities of the presidency developed as Congress struggled to keep up. Party leadership within government accommodated itself to administrative politics and lower levels of public participation. Participatory electoral politics became increasingly irrelevant to the expanding bureaucratic federal government. The transformation to administrative government continued over the course of the twentieth century, reaching fruition after World War II, but the groundwork for the new system was laid during the early years.[36]

As the new administrative state expanded, so did its ability to regulate the American economy. In many ways a broad mandate to regulate was the driving force behind the growing power and size of the federal government. Economic regulation can take many forms, but during the early twentieth century America generally chose to lodge this power in independent regulatory commissions staffed by nonpartisan experts. The legislation that strengthened the Interstate Commerce Commission and created and empowered the Food and Drug Administration, the Federal Reserve Board, and the Federal Trade Commission was all contained in omnibus, complex bills. In effect, Congress decided not to decide the difficult issues involving regulation directly and instead left the content of regulation almost entirely up to these administrative bodies.[37] In practice, regulatory commissions were not completely independent; they were limited by and responsive to presidential, congressional, and judicial influence.[38] Nonetheless, Progressive Era economic regulation was an extralegislative process that marked a shift in decision making from representative bodies to administrative ones.

The shift toward administrative government began not at the national level, but on the local level of government; it spread upward to state governments and ultimately to Washington.[39] Throughout the nation, local governments reduced the number of elected officials while increasing the size and power of city administrations. In the process the structure and role of both city councils and mayors changed dramatically. City councils generally shrank in size as larger districts and citywide, often nonpartisan, elections replaced ward representation. Inevitably, as their constituencies grew, councilmen were forced to rely on professional city administrators and no longer could respond to strictly parochial concerns. Other urban reforms shifted power away from councils altogether and toward the executive branch of city government. Mayors were often the beneficiaries of this change as they increasingly directed professional city bureaucracies freed from many of the limitations previously imposed by patronage.

In a move to increase efficiency and remove administration from political pressures, many cities experimented with the creation of independent administrative boards and commissions staffed by experts with broad powers to administer and regulate specific areas. At its most extreme, the movement for efficient government led to the complete replacement of elected mayors and city councils with nonpartisan city managers and commissions empowered to run cities like businesses. Although most cities did not go so far as to abandon representative for administrative politics altogether, urban reform during the early twentieth century significantly altered the exercise of public power nationwide on the local level.[40]

Progressive reforms brought similar far-reaching changes to the states, where nineteenth-century partisan legislative government increasingly gave way to twentieth-century administration. The evaporation of two-party competition in most states after 1896 led to an institutionalization of state legislatures comparable to that which occurred in Congress. No longer dependent on massive voter mobilization, twentieth-century state legislators found partisan concerns less pressing. Party government therefore faded in the face of the seniority and committee systems. State legislatures also empowered a myriad of administrative agencies, boards, and commissions, which were given wide latitude to determine their own policies. In state after state, independent bodies were established to regulate railroads and most other public utilities, including gas, electricity, telephones and telegraphs, insurance, banks, and food and drugs.[41] Progressive Era legislatures, in effect, expanded the power of state government to regulate the economy but then surrendered that power to independent administrative boards.[42]

Economic regulation was the most conspicuous achievement of early-twentieth-century administrative government at the state level, but numerous other government concerns, including health, education, crime prevention, taxation, and natural resources, came under the purview of independent boards and commissions.[43] Though the structures of administrative agencies and the extent of their authority varied from state to state, the basic underlying process was the same throughout the nation. State government grew in size and power and established administrative agencies to oversee its burgeoning responsibilities.

At all levels of government, then, there were remarkably similar changes in the ways political power was structured and exercised during the early twentieth century. With the development of extensive executive capabilities, public power no longer lay exclusively in the hands of elected officials. The shift toward administrative government entailed the creation of a wide variety of boards, commissions, and agencies, which enjoyed extensive authority to construct public policy in specific areas. With the proliferation of relatively independent administrative agencies, public power was fractured as it expanded. This process, in turn, was reflected in the internal transformation of legislative bodies themselves, as elaborate committee systems and seniority rules resulted in legislative specialization and dependence on professional staffs. Finally, elected executives—the president, governors, and mayors—gained authority as administrative capabilities increased. In an age of declining political participation, executives became the principal link between administrative government and the mass public.[44]

Extensive scholarly work on Progressive reform has made it clear that the creation of the modern American administrative state was a piecemeal process. Some reformers had a vision of a nonpartisan, businesslike structure and met substantial success in tailoring the final outcome of reforms to fit their goals.[45] The actual process of change, however, was mediated through the give and take of politics.[46] Indeed, there was much uncertainty about the effects of many reforms, since the functioning of new administrative structures had to be worked out over time. As a result unlikely coalitions frequently came together to support various changes, often for contradictory reasons. The historiography of government reform in the early twentieth century is thus filled with accounts of unintended consequences.[47]

Nonetheless, fundamental socioeconomic factors underlay the development of administrative government during the early years of the twentieth century. The enormous social changes that engulfed the nation during the late nineteenth and early twentieth centuries as a result of large-scale industrialization, unprecedented urbanization, massive immigration, and the creation of a complex national economy geometrically increased the demands that American citizens placed upon government at all levels. These pressures were felt first in urban areas, where the need for new utility, sanitation, and transportation services, as well as health and safety protection and regulation, mushroomed with technological improvements and urban growth. In turn, the state and national governments responded as the scale of social dislocation dwarfed local resources and necessitated an integrated political response.

Reform had broad popular support up and down the social scale. The ends sought by various segments of the population differed greatly: the urban poor and the working class desired increased government services; the old nineteenth-century middle class sought to preserve its quality of life, a new professional bourgeoisie sought to restructure American society, and a segment of the corporate elite desired to limit competition and rationalize the national economy. They all called upon government to regulate the economy and administer an increasingly complex and interrelated society.

To a large degree, the increase in the sheer volume of government responsibilities necessitated the creation of administrative government. Legislative bodies were unable to fine tune the decisions now demanded of government and had to delegate the definition of its law to administrative agencies. Such decision making, from how to deliver clean water and safe gas to ensuring the safety of food and drugs and the stability of the nation's banks, required detailed, specialized knowledge.[48] As new social issues emerged, the growing interconnectedness of American society necessitated the coordination of government decision making. If business was to be regulated, as many Americans wanted, the increasing scale of economic activity required state and ultimately national action. The result was the shift of public authority toward the federal government.[49]

Though the upward flow of government decision making and the growth of public administration were necessary, the form of administrative government that emerged was structured by political factors.[50] The great latitude given to administrative bodies and the resulting fragmentation of public power was not inevitable. Legislative bodies could have kept key policy decisions in their own hands while delegating enforcement authority.[51] The dynamics of the late-nineteenth-century political system, however, precluded this option. Stalemated along partisan lines and limited by parochial concerns, legislative bodies from Congress on down were incapable of regulating the economy or managing public administration. The incessant demands of voter mobilization had prevented late-nineteenth-century representatives from enacting legislation that produced clear-cut winners and losers.[52] Economic regulation and intensive public administration seemed possible only if decision making could be insulated from the vicissitudes of electoral politics. As a result, administrative agencies were empowered with broad mandates as autonomous bodies. Administration was to be "independent" from legislative control and partisan direction. It was therefore the limitations of the late-nineteenth-century participatory political system, as much as the demands of the modern economy, that led to the creation of a unique American form of administrative political system during the early twentieth century.

At the heart of this transformation of American politics was a dramatic confluence of social and political factors. The fundamental changes in American social life that necessitated the development of the government's administrative capabilities also worked to erode the political culture of mass participation. As voting declined, the removal of electoral pressures permitted the development of independent administrative agencies and the institutionalization of legislative bodies. In the process the participatory political system of the last century was supplanted by an administrative one.

Shifting the primary arena of political decision making to administrative bodies greatly expanded the capacity of twentieth-century American government. The political achievements of the Progressive Era stand in sharp contrast to the stalemates of the Gilded Age. At the local level, urban reform began the difficult task of managing the complex social problems associated with massive urbanization. The creation of independent regulatory boards by state and federal governments began to bring the national economy under political control. Everywhere, administrative government was beginning to address the fundamental concerns of a rapidly industrializing and urbanizing society. The new American State was able to regulate and administer, as well as distribute concrete goods and services on an unprecedented level.[53] The structure was in place for a century-long expansion of the role of government in American life.

With the increased capabilities, however, came a fundamental change in the way Americans related to government. Whereas the political parties served as the principal link between Americans and government during the nineteenth century, they had little function in the new administrative state. By definition the new bureaucracy was to be nonpartisan. In place of party guidance, administrative agencies sought to balance conflicting interests with technical expertise.

An essential element in this process was a close working relationship with organized interest groups, which multiplied during the early twentieth century.[54] Organized special interests, especially occupation-based groups, sought to provide the facts necessary to facilitate administrative decisions, particularly those involving economic regulation, as well as the experts to interpret those facts. The interaction between administrative government and private interest organizations therefore became continuous and routine.

Special interests lobbied their concerns at all levels of the government, from legislative and city council committee rooms to independent regulatory board meetings.[55] Whereas parties had once controlled the agenda of political discussion through their dominance of legislative bodies, interest groups now structured political decision making through their symbiotic ties to legislative committees and administrative agencies. Political representation by mass-based parties thus became relatively less important, and small, specialized, functional interest groups dominated the arena of administrative politics.[56]

The contrast between twentieth-century administrative politics primarily responsive to interest groups and the nineteenth-century system of partisan electoral politics should command our attention. In the rough-and-tumble nineteenth-century political universe, Americans directly participated in the political process by voting for their party. Balloting was a democratizing force as almost all voters turned out on Election Day. The ballot made late-nineteenth-century government responsible to the entire electorate—so much so that the process of governing was severely circumscribed.

During the early twentieth century, the limitations imposed by partisan, participatory electoral politics on American government were surmounted by the creation of the modern administrative state. But this achievement was compromised by the fragmentation of state power and the increasing influence of organized private interests. Thus government power devolved to administrative bodies, legislative committees, and regulatory commissions, and construction and implementation of government policy in the broader public interest proved difficult.

The development of the administrative state substantially insulated government from public involvement. Mass participation in electoral politics fell off precipitously and unevenly, creating an electorate that no longer accurately represented the American public. Not only did Americans stop voting, but also elections lost much of their meaning, for the arena of political decision making had shifted to one in which organized interests and their financial resources counted, rather than ballots. Although the transformation of American politics at the turn of the century created a government capable of responding to the demands of a modern society, the nature of this transformation raised serious questions about the quality of twentieth-century American democracy.

Measuring Voter Turnout

Although scholars who utilize quantitative sources work with hard data, in this case election returns, the interpretation of those data is anything but straightforward. As with any source, the scholar must evaluate the accuracy of historical records and the degree to which they reflect or distort past behavior. Numerous classification and evaluatory decisions have to be made before meaningful analysis can begin. In the end, the value of quantitative analysis often rests as much on those preliminary decisions, which determine the quality of the database and how it is structured, as on the analysis itself.

Mass participation in electoral politics is most often gauged through estimating voter turnout. I estimate the latter by dividing the total number of votes cast in an election for an office by the potential eligible voter population. Unfortunately, the process is problematic, since the terms used to calculate turnout—the number of votes cast and the size of the eligible electorate—are subject to interpretation and error.

The Issue of Fraud and the Accuracy of Election Returns

The number of votes recorded for a particular office in a particular election does not necessarily accurately reflect the total number of voters.

Besides occasional human error, fraud may affect vote totals. Some people may be coerced to vote or abstain, and some may vote more than once; furthermore, some votes may be inaccurately recorded, counted more than once, or not counted at all.

The question of corruption is vital for this study. Late-nineteenth-century reformers argued that fraudulent practices were so widespread that they contaminated election results and misrepresented the will of the people.[1] Many scholars have accepted and elaborated upon these charges, presenting long lists of alleged abuses, including the miscounting of votes, the illegal naturalization of foreigners, the stuffing of ballot boxes, voting repeaters, voting the dead, and bribery and intimidation. Philip Converse concludes that "the standard form of vote fraud before 1900 involved the addition of illegitimate votes to a pile of legitimate ones by one or another mechanism." The result was "an utter travesty on democratic process."[2] Scholars have regarded America's cities as hotbeds of nefarious electoral practices, but rural areas have received their share of censure as well.[3]

Under close examination, however, there is little reason to believe that extensive fraud contaminates the historical value of nineteenth-century election returns.[4] Many of the complaints of corruption focused on the inadequacies of election machinery, including the use of party-printed ballots, loose voter registration requirements, and partisan election supervision. These conditions certainly were permissive, but they are not in themselves confirmation of pervasive fraud.[5] On the contrary, there is little hard evidence of voter intimidation or the casting and counting of fraudulent ballots in the North during the 1880s and 1890s.[6]

Notorious cases of ballot box stuffing and the like certainly occurred. They were challenged in the courts and reported in the press, but their very notoriety points to their exceptional nature.[7] Ample legal remedies existed to contest the outcome of suspicious elections. The results of southern congressional elections, for example, were frequently appealed in Congress. However, despite the closeness of most late-nineteenth-century elections, only a handful of northern elections were challenged.[8]

Most nineteenth-century Americans lived in a face-to-face world where they knew their neighbors and could observe their behavior closely. Elections were public events. The crowds that gathered to observe the voting severely limited the opportunity for fraud, particularly since political parties, which were well organized and bitterly competitive, usually kept a close watch on each other during the casting and counting of ballots. It is hard to imagine extensive fraud thriving in such a social and political climate.[9]

The only substantive evidence of the systematic casting of fraudulent ballots comes from voter registration lists that contained an excessive number of names and from postelection surveys that could not track down registered voters. The rapid geographic mobility of the American population, however, can account for most of these discrepancies in registration lists. Some ballot boxes certainly were stuffed, some voters voted repeatedly, and some votes were deliberately miscounted. Yet, what is remarkable is how little proof there is of actual vote fraud. My feeling is that this is not too surprising because there was little need for extensive fraud. A few votes could swing most elections; since participation was so massive, the percentage of fraudulent votes was probably quite small.[10]

Most accounts of political corruption focused not on fraudulent acts that distorted election results but on electioneering tactics such as "excessive campaign expenditures, vote buying, the purchase of drinks at the corner saloon, political barbecues, and free rides to the poll."[11] These campaign practices offended observers who thought that voters should cast their votes strictly on the basis of the issues involved in a campaign. We need to recognize, however, that many voters apparently considered these payments and services a legitimate form of patronage. Voters who allowed their votes to be "bought" in this way were casting their ballots for the party of their choice. They were simply using different criteria to make that choice. The parties utilized these inducements as they would any other campaign strategy—in order to motivate voters to participate.[12] The use of such tactics does not reduce the historical validity of the election results.

In the absence of substantial evidence to the contrary, we can accept the fact that the number of votes cast in late-nineteenth-century elections generally reflected the number of voters who went to the polls. We can be relatively confident therefore in using unadjusted election returns to calculate voter turnout.

Estimating the Size of the Electorate

Determining the number of voters is only half of the process involved in estimating turnout. Reliable estimates of the size of the eligible voter population must also be developed, and this is more problematic.[13] Like other scholars, I derive my estimates from decennial federal census tables, using linear interpolations between census periods. Since federal census takers did not count the electorate directly, the size of the electorate has to be determined from a variety of census tables on the basis of state-level voter eligibility requirements.[14]

In most states, eligibility was limited to male citizens over the age of twenty-one; this figure is readily obtainable. Since all states enfranchised voters at the age of twenty-one, age is not a problem in calculating the size of the electorate. Nor is race, since the Fifteenth Amendment had already been adopted. In the few states that enfranchised women before the passage of the Nineteenth Amendment, the eligible voter population is quite easily adjusted to include all adult citizens.[15]

Citizenship introduces some problems in estimating the size of the electorate. Citizenship did not become a universal prerequisite for voting in this country until 1928. During the late nineteenth and early twentieth centuries, some states gave the vote to noncitizen immigrants who had declared their intention to become citizens.[16] In these states the number of aliens who, according to census tables, had taken out naturalization papers must be included in calculations of the eligible voter population.[17]

Unfortunately, it is impossible to know how strictly suffrage laws relating to citizenship were enforced in different states. Sometimes immigrants were permitted to vote regardless of their status; at other times and in other places, laws permitting their participation were violated. The problem in estimating the size of the potential electorate in alien-suffrage states is compounded by the fact that census tables frequently listed a large number of aliens of "unknown" status. Since immigrants without naturalization papers and those of "unknown" status are excluded from calculation of the potential eligible voter population, my figures inevitably include a small error for states where alien suffrage was a question.[18]

I do not consider state restrictions on the franchise beyond those of age, race, gender, and citizenship in estimating the size of the potential electorate. State laws disfranchising prisoners, convicted felons, and the mentally ill affected a numerically insignificant number of people. Other restrictions, ranging from residency and voter registration requirements to literacy tests and poll taxes, were much more far-reaching. These restrictions were generally applied irregularly, and thus it is difficult to ascertain how many Americans were disfranchised by them. Scholars do not take such restrictions into account when determining the size of the potential electorate because to do so would hide the deleterious effect that they had on voter participation. Not adjusting voter eligibility levels for these qualitative restrictions enables us to explore that impact directly.[19]

The most serious problem in determining the size of the electorate is posed not by variations in state suffrage restrictions but by systematic inaccuracies in census data upon which all estimates are based. Nineteenth-century censuses undercounted the nation's population. Census takers were usually untrained and poorly supervised. Many houses were missed, especially corner houses on the border between census takers. The major cause of census underenumeration, however, was the population's mobility: the count took too long to be accurate when Americans moved so frequently.[20]

If nineteenth-century censuses undercounted the population, then census-based estimates of the number of eligible voters are too low. Underestimating the size of the electorate in this way will cause us to overestimate voter turnout percentages. This problem is severe enough, some scholars have argued, to cause nineteenth-century turnout to be vastly overstated. Claiming that the census enumeration error approached 10 percent, Ray Shortridge demonstrates that recalculating turnout on the basis of adjusted census figures would produce an 8.5 percent lower estimate of voter participation, not an inconsiderable amount. Shortridge concluded that high nineteenth-century turnout levels are mainly an artifact of census enumeration errors.[21] The problem posed by census underenumeration is not as troubling as it first appears, though. In the first place, the counting error apparently was relatively consistent across the entire period. There is no reason to suspect, for example, that early-twentieth-century censuses were substantially more accurate than those of the late nineteenth century. Thus, undercounting may artificially increase our estimates of the absolute level of voter turnout, but it has no significant effect on long-term voter participation patterns.[22]

Furthermore, the source of most counting errors—geographical mobility—must be factored in if we are to understand the impact of census-based estimates of the size of the electorate on voter turnout figures.[23] Both rural and urban nineteenth-century Americans moved at phenomenal rates. On the basis of the work of Stephen Thernstrom, Peter R. Knights, and other historical demographers, it seems safe to conclude that each year during the late nineteenth century, more than one-quarter of the population in American cities, towns, and rural areas moved.[24] In any four-month period, therefore, 8 to 10 percent of the eligible voter population were in transit or were new migrants. Consequently, more than four times as many Americans moved each year as were missed by census counters.[25]

Migration had a significant impact on both voter eligibility and participation. Most states had minimum residency requirements in both a locality and in the state, ranging from six months to two years.[26] Since it is not known how strictly these laws were enforced, it is impossible to determine how many voters were affected by such restrictions. Nonetheless, even if the number of people legally disfranchised by residency requirements was small, the realities of geographic migration in the late nineteenth century took the vote out of the hands of many.[27] Voting was impossible for Americans in transit, since few states had absentee voter provisions, and extremely difficult for new arrivals, who had to acquire a rudimentary knowledge of local politics (including where, when, and how to vote) before they could vote.[28] For most migrants the physical necessities of relocating were so enormous that voter participation probably had to wait until they were settled.[29]

In this light, census underenumeration loses much of its significance since many of those missed were either legally or practically unable to vote. Excluding these recent migrants from our estimates of the electorate, because they were left uncounted by the census, does not obscure the voter participation rates of the stable portion of the electorate. Indeed, in my view, census underenumeration has the effect of partially adjusting voter turnout figures to account for geographic mobility. Many more migrants were included in the census (and thus in my estimates of the size of the eligible electorate) than stable residents were excluded. In evaluating voter participation levels, the inclusion of these recent migrants, many of whom could not vote, more than makes up for the exclusion of a small percentage (3–4 percent) of stable residents.

In the end, the issue of census underenumeration, like that of voter fraud, is real but far from fatal. The consistency of census errors over time and the close connection between these errors and geographic mobility makes it unnecessary to try to correct estimates of the size of the electorate for census undercounting. Not only does the use of census figures allow for comparisons with other voting studies, but there is no doubt in my mind that deriving estimates of the electorate directly from census data also provides the best available means to calculate voter participation rates over time.

Units of Analysis

Having decided to use unadjusted election returns and census data to calculate voter turnout, I also had to make important decisions regarding the units of analysis for this study. Historians who work with quantitative sources face a trade-off in designing research projects, between the closely detailed picture that can be developed in a micro-level study and the breadth afforded by a larger project. The key is to design a project that can produce the appropriate level of explanation. Since I ask questions about mass political behavior that are national and systemic in scope, I analyze returns for the entire nation from 1880 to 1918. I also use returns for presidential, gubernatorial, and congressional elections.[30]

Conducting a national study necessitates the use of returns aggregated to the state level. Although computer-readable county-level returns and census information are now available for the nation, the size of this data base and the knowledge of local politics necessary to work with changing jurisdictional boundaries and local partisan idiosyncrasies are enormous.[31] Returns below the county level are even more burdensome. The breadth gained in a national study offsets the sacrifice in detail lost in state-level analysis. In any case, the "ecological fallacy" caused by inferring individual behavior from aggregate data is not a problem since I address aggregate-level questions.

Though state-level data provided the basis of analysis, these data are aggregated further to examine regional and national political behavior.[32] In partitioning the nation, I chose to use the eight standard groupings that the U.S. Bureau of the Census employs:

New England
Connecticut
Maine
Massachusetts
New Hampshire
Rhode Island
Vermont

Mid-Atlantic
Delaware

New Jersey
New York
Pennsylvania

North Central
Illinois
Indiana
Michigan
Ohio
Wisconsin

Midwest	*Border*
Iowa	Kentucky
Kansas	Maryland
Minnesota	Oklahoma
Missouri	Tennessee
Nebraska	West Virginia
North Dakota	
South Dakota	*Mountain*
	Arizona
South	Colorado
Alabama	Idaho
Arkansas	Montana
Florida	Nevada
Georgia	New Mexico
Louisiana	Utah
Mississippi	Wyoming
North Carolina	
South Carolina	*West*
Texas	California
Virginia	Oregon
	Washington

To facilitate analysis, I specifically examine political behavior in the North, which includes all regions except the South.

The regions designated by the Bureau of the Census are not always ideal for our purposes. For example, Missouri voters often behaved more like those in the border states than midwesterners, and Delaware differed dramatically in politics from the other mid-Atlantic states. However, the advantages of utilizing standard regions, which permits ready comparison to other work, clearly outweigh the inconvenience in the categorization of a few states.[33]

Quantitative Measures

Measures of the Composition of the Active Electorate

Roll-Off

Roll-off is a measure of the percentage of those who vote but do not cast a full ticket.[1] (Other scholars use roll-off as a measure of the percentage of the electorate who do not vote a full ticket.)[2] Roll-off was calculated for all presidential-year elections on the basis of vote returns for presidential, gubernatorial, and congressional races. When there was not a gubernatorial race on the November ballot, the votes cast for presidential and congressional candidates were utilized to measure roll-off. If a gubernatorial election was held and fewer votes were cast for governor than for congressional candidates, votes for the former were used.

When the total votes cast for congressional candidates were less than the total votes cast for governor *(VTG)*, roll-off was calculated by dividing the total votes cast for congressional candidates *(VTC)* by the total votes cast for presidential candidates *(VTP)* and subtracting that fraction from 100 percent. If fewer votes were cast for gubernatorial than for congressional candidates, roll-off was calculated as 100 percent minus the total votes cast for governor divided by the total votes cast for president.

If $VTC < VTG$ then roll-off $= 100 - (VTC/VTP)$.

If $VTG < VTC$ then roll-off $= 100 - (VTG/VTP)$.

The higher the roll-off, the greater is the percentage of marginal voters in the electorate. A negative roll-off is possible but would cast doubt on the usefulness of this index.

Roll-off is severely affected by different balloting procedures. Prior to the adoption of ballot reform, party-strips almost invariably listed candidates for all offices. Where it was harder to vote an incomplete ballot than a complete one, as it was during much of the nineteenth century, roll-off is not a useful indicator of voter marginality.[3]

Drop-Off

Drop-off is an index of the percentage of actual voters who are marginal.[4] (Other scholars measure drop-off as a percentage of the electorate who are marginal.)[5] Drop-off was calculated on the basis of presidential, gubernatorial, and congressional returns. When off-year congressional turnout (CTO_{y+2}) was less than gubernatorial turnout (GTO_{y+2}), drop-off was determined by dividing off-year congressional turnout by presidential turnout (PTO_y) in the previous presidential election and subtracting that fraction from 100 percent. If fewer votes were cast for governor than for congressional candidates in an off-year election, then drop-off equals 100 percent minus the gubernatorial turnout divided by presidential turnout in the previous election.

If $CTO_{y+2} < GTO_{y+2}$ then drop-off $= 100 - (CTO_{y+2}/PTO_y)$

If $GTO_{y+2} < CTO_{y+2}$ then drop-off $= 100 - (GTO_{y+2}/PTO_y)$

The higher the drop-off, the greater is the percentage of marginal voters. A negative drop-off is possible but would cast doubt on the usefulness of this index.

It should be noted that this method of calculating drop-off (utilizing the lowest turnout figures for off-year elections and the highest for presidential elections) has the effect of including roll-off in the drop-off index. The combination is desirable since roll-off and drop-off are both measures of the same thing. Defined this way, drop-off is an inclusive measure of voter marginality.

Measures of Partisan Loyalty and Stability

The partisan loyalty of individual voters cannot be inferred directly from aggregate indices. Since individual partisan shifts in opposite directions balance out in aggregate data, measures of partisanship based on election returns do not directly reveal the absolute level of individual partisan consistency. Indeed, there is no necessary relationship between the aggregate measure and the actual degree of partisanship. When party voting shifts in one direction, aggregate measures provide a fair estimation of the actual amount of partisan movement. But when shifts occur in both directions, aggregate measures underestimate instability. It is entirely possible that over time an aggregate index of partisan instability will rise even though the actual amount of movement declines.[6] What aggregate measures indicate, then, is only the net partisan instability in the electorate at large. They provide a minimal estimate of aggregate partisan loyalty. We can partially compensate for this limitation of aggregate indices with the use of several different measures that can be compared to check for consistency.

All measures of party loyalty are calculated from party vote percentages. Thus, they are affected by decisions made in determining the percentage of the total vote that each party received in each election. When a candidate runs as the nominee of only one party, there is no problem in calculating party vote percentages. However, many candidates, especially in the 1890s, were nominated by more than one party (e.g., Prohibitionists and Republicans) or by splinter groups within a party (e.g., Silver-Republicans, Gold-Democrats). Decisions have to be made about how to classify the votes cast for these candidates. For the sake of comparison with other work, the party codings provided by the Inter-University Consortium for Political and Social Research were used. In general, the ICPSR codes all votes cast for fusion and splinter tickets as third-party votes and does not credit them to a major party. (The main exception to this rule is that for the years 1896 and 1898, the Democratic party is credited with all the votes cast for Democratic, Populist, and Democratic-Populist fusion candidates.) One effect of not assigning the votes from fusion tickets and splinter parties to the major parties is that these indices slightly exaggerate partisan instability.

Split-Ticket Voting

Ticket splitting was estimated by subtracting the lowest percentage of the total vote cast for a Democrat from the highest percentage cast for a

Democrat in the same election. State-level election returns for presidential, gubernatorial, and congressional races are utilized in constructing this index.[7] It is important to recognize that the use of state-level data for only national and state races affects the findings. If election results for more offices were examined, more partisan instability would be found. In any index like this one, split-ticket voting is in part a function of the number of contests examined.[8]

Split-ticket voting, like roll-off, is also affected by different balloting procedures. Prior to ballot reform, party-strips almost always listed candidates exclusively from one party. Only in the case of fusion with a third party did a party-strip include candidates from different parties. Since party-strip balloting strongly favored straight party voting, the value of split-ticket voting as an index of partisan loyalty in the nineteenth century is limited. The Australian ballot, in contrast, facilitates split-ticket voting by listing all candidates for all offices. In analyzing split-ticket voting over time, then, it is essential to treat the balloting system as an important intervening variable.

Correlation and Regression Analysis of Partisan Loyalty

Pearson product-moment correlations were calculated on the basis of state-level election returns. Correlation analysis reveals the amount of stability or instability in the relative ordering of the states in terms of the support accorded each party. This statistical technique will show partisan instability only when shifts in support for one party or the other varied in different states. This analysis, therefore, is relatively insensitive to across-the-board variation in partisan voting since such shifts may leave the relative ordering of the states almost undisturbed.[9]

Several scholars suggest that ecological regression analysis may be more useful than correlation analysis to measure aggregate partisan loyalty over time. By using least-squares regression analysis to estimate the cell entries in contingency tables, it is possible to measure the percentage of each party's voters that remained loyal in subsequent elections and trace the pattern of defection of those voters who switched parties.[10] Unfortunately, there are insurmountable problems associated with the use of the technique in this way with state-level data. Gudmund Iversen explains that "essential for this estimating procedure is the assumption of only individual level effect."[11] The reliability of this method is thus based on the assumption that the behavior of partisans varies randomly in relation to the voting strength of the various parties within a state.[12] We cannot make this assumption for the late nineteenth century. The presence or absence of third-party challenges in different states certainly affected partisan voting behavior. More generally, the assumption of strictly individual-level effects is contrary to any model of voter mobilization in which party strength is related to partisan voting.

Since this assumption is not appropriate for our purposes, it was not surprising that ecological regression analysis of partisan stability did not yield meaningful results. In voter transition tables, cell entries repeatedly fell outside of the admissible range from zero to one.[13] Therefore, I chose not to use this technique to measure partisan stability over time.

Party-Vote Instability

Party-vote instability is the average of the difference between the percentages of the total vote polled by the major parties in consecutive elections.[14] To calculate party-vote instability, the absolute difference between the percentage of the total vote cast for the Democratic presidential candidate in one election $(P\%D_y)$ and the percentage of the total vote cast for the Democratic presidential candidate in the subsequent election $(P\%D_{y+4})$ was added to the absolute difference between the percentage of the total vote cast for the Republican presidential candidates in the same elections $(P\%R_y$ and $P\%R_{y+4})$. That sum was divided by two to produce the average presidential partisan-vote instability $(PPVI)$. To create a party-vote instability index for congressional elections $(CPVI)$, the process was repeated using the percentage of the total vote cast in consecutive elections for Democratic $(C\%D_y$ and $C\%D_{y+2})$ and Republican $(C\%R_y$ and $C\%R_{y+2})$ congressional candidates. The absolute difference in partisan vote percentages was used because we are interested in the total amount of partisan instability and not the direction of that instability.

$$PPVI = [\text{abs}(P\%D_y - P\%D_{y+4})] + [\text{abs}(P\%R_y - P\%R_{y+4})]/\ 2$$
$$CPVI = [\text{abs}(C\%D_y - C\%D_{y+2})] + [\text{abs}(C\%R_y - C\%R_{y+2})]/\ 2$$

It should be noted that this congressional partisan-vote instability index measures party swing over a two-year period between congressional elections, whereas the presidential party-vote index measures party swing over four years. Congressional party-vote instability is calculated on the basis of state-level averages of the percentage of the total vote received by each party.

This index weighs shifts between the major parties twice as heavily as movement between a major and minor party because shifts between the major parties enter into both terms of the calculation (increasing the percentage of one party and decreasing the percentage of the other), whereas shifts involving minor parties affect only one term. A 1 percent vote shift between the major parties produces 1 point on this index of party-vote instability; a 1 percent increase or decrease in minor-party voting registers as a 1/2 point on this index. This bias is advantageous for measuring partisan loyalty in this period, since it reflects the fact that voters found movement between the major parties more difficult than movement into and out of minor parties.

Many different indices are used to measure partisan stability. The advantage of this one is that it measures shifts in the electoral support accorded to both parties. It is thus less vulnerable to over- or underemphasizing changes in the voting behavior of partisans of one party or the other. This neutrality is particularly important because at different times and in different places during this period, third parties drew their support disproportionately from partisans of each of the two major parties.

Measures of Political Competition

To evaluate political competition, political scientists and historians construct many different indices that measure the number or percentage of offices won by each party, the rate of alternation in office, the percentage of votes cast for each party, the margin of victory, and the extent of minor-party voting, as well as combinations of these factors.[15] These various indices can be divided into two categories: measures of vote division and of officeholding. Because of the winner-take-all electoral system in the United States, under certain circumstances the two different types of indices can produce divergent estimates of competitiveness.[16] Officeholding, however, is a function of vote division. In a predominantly two-party electoral system, the partisan division of the vote is a good predictor of electoral success over time.[17] For the purpose of studying the political behavior of the American electorate, competitiveness can best be analyzed using the partisan division of the vote to measure the margin of victory between the winner and the runner-up.[18]

Measures of electoral competitiveness, which are based on the partisan division of the vote, are affected by decisions made in determining the percentage of the total vote that each party receives in each election. The problem here is the same one faced in measuring party loyalty and is discussed above.

Electoral Competitiveness

My index of electoral competitiveness is a measure of the percentage of the total vote that separates the two major parties subtracted from 100. This index was computed by taking the absolute value of the difference between the percentages of the total vote cast for the Democratic *(%DEM)* and Republican *(%REP)* candidates. This approach was followed for presidential *(PCOMP)*, gubernatorial *(GCOMP)*, and congressional *(CCOMP)* races.[19]

$$PCOMP = 100 - [\text{abs}(P\%DEM - P\%REP)]$$

$$GCOMP = 100 - [\text{abs}(G\%DEM - G\%REP)]$$

$$CCOMP = 100 - [\text{abs}(C\%DEM - C\%REP)]$$

On this index, 100 indicates full competition; 0 indicates the absence of competition. The index score declines as the gap between the two parties widens. This index has all the properties of a ratio scale, which facilitates comparisons and enables one to make inferences about public perception of electoral competition.

Decisions about how to treat minor-party voting are extremely important when measuring electoral competition. By calculating this index on the basis of the percentage of the total vote that separated the two major parties, the implicit assumption is made that votes cast for minor parties were available to be won by the major parties. For example, the competitiveness score for a three-way vote division of 40%-38%-22% is the same as for a two-way 51%-49% division (98). Other scholars measure competition between the major parties on the basis of the percentage of the two-party vote.[20]

Nonetheless, the usefulness of this index, like any summary measure of electoral competition, is still hampered by extensive fluctuation in minor-party voting, particularly when minor parties draw their votes unevenly from one or the other major party. In elections where a third party disrupts a competitive two-party system by attracting a significant number of votes from one of the major parties, the competitiveness scores on this index will be low, although the possibility of fusion between the minor party and a major party could have produced an intensely competitive political climate.[21]

Notes

NOTE TO THE PREFACE

1. The historical literature on the transformation of American society during the Progressive Era is vast. My view of these changes is most influenced by Robert H. Wiebe's *The Search for Order, 1877–1920* (New York: Hill and Wang, 1967) and Samuel P. Hays's essays, *American Political History as Social Analysis: Essays* (Knoxville: University of Tennessee Press, 1980).

NOTES TO THE INTRODUCTION

1. J. Morgan Kousser has called upon political historians to use rational-choice theory that posits strictly individual-level decision making; Kousser, "Toward 'Total Political History': A Rational-Choice Program," *Journal of Interdisciplinary History* 20 (Spring 1990): 521–60. For a detailed analysis of individual-choice models of voting behavior, see William R. Shaffer, *Computer Simulations of Voting Behavior* (New York: Oxford University Press, 1972). The limitations of using an individual-choice model to explain aggregate electoral behavior are explored by V. O. Key, Jr., and Frank Munger in "Social Determinism and Electoral Decisions: The Case of Indiana," in *Voters, Parties, and Elections: Quantitative Essays in the History of American Popular Voting Behavior,* ed. Joel H. Silbey and Samuel T. McSeveney (Lexington, Mass.: Xerox College Press, 1972), 29–45. See also Jack Dennis, "Theories of Turnout: An Empirical Comparison of Alienationist and Rationalist Perspectives," in *Political Participation and American Democracy,* ed. William Crotty (New York: Greenwood Press, 1991), 33–6.

2. Charles Tilly provides a valuable conceptual vocabulary to analyze voting as collective action; Charles Tilly, *From Mobilization to Revolution* (Reading, Mass.: Addison-Wesley, 1978). See also Michael J. Avey, *The Demobilization of American Voters: A Comprehensive Theory of Voter Turnout* (New York: Greenwood Press, 1989).

3. Walter Dean Burnham, "The Changing Shape of the American Political Universe," *American Political Science Review* 59 (March 1965): 7–28. Although a rich and contentious literature on the decline in voter participation developed in political science in response to Burnham's work, few historians have been engaged in this debate. Paul Kleppner's *Who Voted? The Dynamics of Electoral Turnout, 1870–1980* (New York: Praeger, 1982) examines quantitative changes in voter participation nationwide; John F. Reynolds's *Testing Democracy: Electoral Behavior and Progressive Reform in New Jersey, 1880–1920* (Chapel Hill: University of North Carolina Press, 1988) focuses on one state. Michael E. McGerr's *The Decline of Popular Politics: The American North, 1865–1928* (New York: Oxford University Press, 1986) provides a full-scale treatment of the decline in mass participation that eschews analysis of voting behavior.

4. Walter Dean Burnham, *The Current Crisis in American Politics* (New York: Oxford University Press, 1982); Paul Kleppner, ed., *The Evolution of American Electoral Systems* (Westport, Conn.: Greenwood Press, 1981); Philip E. Converse, "Change in the American Electorate," in *The Human Meaning of Change*, ed. Angus Campbell and Philip E. Converse (New York: Russell Sage Foundation, 1972), 263–337; Philip E. Converse, "Comment on Burnham's 'Theory and Voting Research,'" *American Political Science Review* 68 (September 1974): 1024–7; Jerrold Rusk, "Effect of the Australian Ballot Reform on Split-Ticket Voting: 1876–1908," *American Political Science Review* 64 (December 1970): 1220–38; and Frances Fox Piven and Richard A. Cloward, *Why Americans Don't Vote* (New York: Pantheon Books, 1988).

5. Richard L. McCormick, *From Realignment to Reform: Political Change in New York State, 1893–1910* (Ithaca, N.Y.: Cornell University Press, 1981); and Reynolds, *Testing Democracy*.

6. See chapters 4 and 5.

7. Samuel P. Hays labels this approach "the social analysis of political history"; see his collected essays, *American Political History as Social Analysis: Essays* (Knoxville: University of Tennessee Press, 1980).

8. Richard L. McCormick, "The Social Analysis of American Political History—After Twenty Years," in *The Party Period and Public Policy* (New York: Oxford University Press, 1986), 89–140; J. Morgan Kousser, "Restoring Politics to Political History," *Journal of Interdisciplinary History* 12 (Spring 1982): 569–95; and "Are Political Acts Unnatural?" *Journal of Interdisciplinary History* 15 (Winter 1985): 467–80.

9. In their detailed study of political participation in America, Sidney Verba and Norman H. Nie define political participation as "an instrumental act by which citizens influence government; Verba and Nie, *Participation in America: Political Democracy and Social Equality* (New York: Harper and Row, 1972), 5. For a discussion of this definition, see Robert R. Alford and Roger Friedland, "Politi-

cal Participation and Public Policy," *Annual Review of Sociology*, vol. 1, ed. Alex Inkeles (Palo Alto: Annual Review, 1975), 430.

10. Paula Baker concludes that "men and women operated, for the most part, in distinct political subcultures, each with its own bases of power, modes of participation, and goals"; P. Baker, "The Domestication of Politics: Women and American Political Society," *American Historical Review* 89 (June 1984): 622. See also Anne Firor, "On Seeing and Not Seeing: A Case of Historical Invisibility," *Journal of American History* 71 (June 1984): 7–21.

11. See chapter 1.

12. It is true, however, that my focus on electoral politics privileges male political activity over the realm of female politics in nineteenth-century America. In part this reflects contemporary understanding of political activity among both men and women, many of whom were working to gain the franchise. In part it also reflects a historical evaluation of the power differential between the realms of male electoral politics and female associational politics. Nevertheless, this focus unfortunately replicates historical inequality in historical analysis. It is important to recognize this, for as Joan Wallach Scott explains, "If one grants that meanings are constructed through exclusions, one must acknowledge and take responsibility for the exclusions involved in one's own project"; J. Scott, *Gender and the Politics of History* (New York: Columbia University Press, 1988), 7.

13. Rosalyn Terborg-Penn, "Discontented Black Feminists: Prelude and Postscript to the Passage of the Nineteenth Amendment," in *"We Specialize in the Wholly Impossible": A Reader in Black Women's History*, ed. Darline Clark Hine et al. (New York: Carlson Publishing, 1995), 487–503.

14. Some political scientists, most notably Bernard Berelson, Paul Lazarsfeld, and William McPhee, suggest that all measures of electoral participation are basically interchangeable because they measure the same thing; Berelson, Lazarsfeld, and McPhee, *Voting: A Study of Opinion Formation in a Presidential Campaign* (Chicago: University of Chicago Press, 1954). In contrast, Lester Milbraith concludes that there is a hierarchy of participatory activity ranging from exposure to political stimuli to voting, petitioning, campaigning, and officeholding. In his view all participatory acts can be placed on a continuum from easy to more difficult; Milbraith, *Political Participation: How and Why Do People Get Involved in Politics?* (Chicago: Rand McNally, 1965), 6, 19, 22.

15. See Appendix 1.

16. There is an extensive political science and historical literature on party systems and realignments. V. O. Key, Jr., and Walter Dean Burnham are usually credited with first developing these fertile constructs; Key, "A Theory of Critical Elections," *Journal of Politics* 17 (February 1955): 3–18; and "Secular Realignments and the Party System," *Journal of Politics* 21 (May 1959): 198–210; and Burnham, *Critical Elections and the Mainsprings of American Politics* (New York: W. W. Norton, 1970); and "Party Systems and the Political Process," in *The American Party Systems: Stages of Political Development*, 2d ed., ed. William Nisbet Chambers and Walter Dean Burnham (New York: Oxford University Press, 1975), 277–307. The most detailed quantitative analysis of realignments and party systems is a work by Jerome M. Clubb, William H. Flanigan, and Nancy

H. Zingale, *Partisan Realignment: Voters, Parties, and Government in American History* (Beverly Hills, Calif.: Sage, 1980). For a critical analysis of this work and the development of realignment historiography, see Richard L. McCormick, "The Realignment Synthesis in American History," reprinted in his collection of essays, *The Party Period and Public Policy*, 64–88. The harshest critic of the party systems approach has been Allan J. Lichtman; see Lichtman, "Critical Election Theory and the Reality of American Presidential Politics," *American Historical Review* 81 (April 1976): 317–48; and "The End of Realignment Theory? Toward a New Research Program for American Political History," *Historical Methods* 15 (Fall 1982): 170–88.

17. See for example Kleppner, *The Cross of Culture: A Social Analysis of Midwestern Politics, 1850–1900* (New York: Free Press, 1970); *The Third Electoral System, 1853–1892: Parties, Voters, and Political Cultures* (Chapel Hill: University of North Carolina Press, 1979); and *Continuity and Change in Electoral Politics, 1893–1928* (New York: Greenwood, 1987); Richard Jensen, *The Winning of the Midwest: Social and Political Conflict, 1888–1896* (Chicago: University of Chicago Press, 1971); John M. Allswang, *A House for All People: Ethnic Politics in Chicago, 1890–1936* (Lexington: University of Kentucky Press, 1971); and Ronald P. Formisano, *The Birth of Mass Political Parties: Michigan, 1827–1861* (Princeton, N.J.: Princeton University Press, 1971).

18. There is a tension in Walter Dean Burnham's work between his identification of generational party systems and his recognition of the significance of the changes that American politics underwent at the turn of the century; see Burnham, *Critical Elections*. Joel H. Silbey has developed a revised concept of political eras with a full-scale look at nineteenth-century politics; Silbey, *The American Political Nation, 1838–1893* (Stanford, Calif.: Stanford University Press, 1991).

NOTES TO CHAPTER 1

1. See Appendix 1 for a discussion of the issues involved in measuring voter turnout.

2. These figures are true regional and national means, not the average of state-level figures. Averaging state-level turnout rates has the unfortunate effect of obscuring the full extent of political participation during this period because, for the most part, turnout was highest in the most populous states and lowest in the least populous states. Average state-level turnout for the 1880s and 1890s was 74.4 percent nationwide and 80.0 percent in the North.

3. Indiana's mean presidential turnout for these five elections was a remarkable 95 percent. Turnout also averaged over 90 percent in New Jersey, Ohio, Wisconsin, and Iowa and over 88 percent in New York, Michigan, Illinois, and West Virginia.

4. Illinois, Indiana, Kentucky, Maryland, Michigan, Missouri, Ohio, Oregon, Texas, and Wisconsin.

5. These figures are state-level averages.

6. In the nineteenth century, Pennsylvania and Delaware both limited the

franchise to taxpayers. In these states nontaxpayers could vote only if they paid a poll tax ranging from twenty-five cents to ten dollars. Although it is not known how strictly these restrictions were enforced, they doubtlessly suppressed turnout in both states. Dudley O. McGovney, *The American Suffrage Medley: The Need for a National Uniform Suffrage* (Chicago: University of Chicago Press, 1949), 114–6; and Kirk H. Porter, *A History of Suffrage in the United States* (Chicago: University of Chicago Press, 1969), 111.

7. In 1880, 67.1 percent of America's eligible voters lived in these four regions, and in 1890, 66.8 percent lived there.

8. Whereas electoral laws in most of the nation facilitated mass participation, the New England states made it relatively more difficult both for voters to participate and for the parties to mobilize supporters. Most New England states strengthened their voter registration requirements during the 1880s, thus making voting a two-step process. Philip E. Converse, "Change in the American Electorate," in *The Human Meaning of Change*, ed. Angus Campbell and Philip E. Converse (New York: Russell Sage Foundation, 1972), 285; and Richard John Carlson, "The Effects of Voter Registration Systems on Presidential Turnout in Non-Southern States: 1912–1924" (Ph.D. dissertation, University of Illinois at Urbana-Champaign, 1976). See chapter 5 (this volume) for a discussion of the impact of electoral regulations on political behavior.

9. Massachusetts restricted participation by requiring eligible voters to pass a literacy test. Richard Dana, "The Practical Workings of the Australian System of Voting in Massachusetts," *Annals of the American Academy of Political and Social Science* 2 (May 1892): 741–5.

10. McGovney, *American Suffrage Medley*, 50, 117–8.

11. In 1880 the only states in the region were Colorado, Nevada, California, and Oregon. Not until 1892 did Wyoming, Montana, Idaho, and Washington vote for a president, and Utah did not participate until 1896. Neither Arizona nor New Mexico participated in a national election during the nineteenth century. Barely 3.3 percent of the nation's eligible voters lived in these two regions in 1880, and this rose to only 5.5 percent in 1890.

12. Paul Kleppner, "Voters and Parties in the Western States, 1876–1900," *Western Historical Quarterly* 14 (January 1983): 49–69; and Jerrold G. Rusk and John J. Stucker, "Measuring Patterns of Electoral Participation in the United States," *Micropolitics* 3 (Winter 1984): 475.

13. Alabama, Arkansas, Florida, North Carolina, South Carolina, Texas, and Virginia.

14. Peak presidential turnouts in the southern states were Florida (1880), 86.3 percent; North Carolina (1884), 86.1 percent; South Carolina (1880), 83.1 percent; Texas (1896), 86.6 percent; and Virginia (1888), 83.1 percent.

15. See J. Morgan Kousser, *The Shaping of Southern Politics: Suffrage Restriction and the Establishment of the One-Party South, 1880–1910* (New Haven, Conn.: Yale University Press, 1974); Jerrold G. Rusk and John J. Stucker, "The Effect of the Southern System of Election Laws on Voting Participation: A Reply to V. O. Key, Jr.," in *The History of American Electoral Behavior*, ed. Joel H. Silbey, Allan G. Bogue, and William H. Flanigan (Princeton, N.J.; Princeton University Press,

1978), 198–250; and Frederic D. Ogden, *The Poll Tax in the South* (University: University of Alabama Press, 1958).

16. Arkansas, Florida, Georgia, Mississippi, and South Carolina. See Kousser, *Shaping of Southern Politics*, 41, 239; and Ogden, *Poll Tax*, 111–22.

17. C. Vann Woodward, *Origins of the New South 1877–1913* (Baton Rouge: Louisiana University Press, 1951).

18. Kousser, *The Shaping of Southern Politics*, 27–9, 243.

19. The classic work delineating core and peripheral voters is Angus Campbell, "Surge and Decline: A Study of Electoral Change," *Public Opinion Quarterly* 24 (Fall 1960): 397–418. See also James E. Campbell, "The Revised Theory of Surge and Decline," *American Journal of Political Science* 31 (November 1987): 965–79; and Albert D. Cover, "Surge and Decline in Congressional Elections," *Western Political Quarterly* 38 (December 1985): 606–19. Analytical concepts such as core and peripheral voters that are derived from middle- to late-twentieth-century voter surveys can be of heuristic value to us. Nonetheless, for elections before the advent of surveys, the composition of the electorate and the extent of its involvement in electoral politics must be inferred from electoral behavior. The inference made here is that the more fully Americans participated in elections, the more involved they were. Other political historians have come to the same conclusion; see for example William E. Gienapp, "Politics Seem to Enter into Everything: Political Culture in the North, 1840–1860," in *Essays in Antebellum American Politics, 1840–1860*, ed. Stephen E. Maizlish and John J. Kushma (College Station: University of Texas Press, 1982), 20.

20. Appendix 2 explains how roll-off was measured.

21. Appendix 2 explains how drop-off was measured.

22. These are regional and national figures, not the averages of state-level means.

23. Spencer D. Albright, *The American Ballot* (Washington, D.C.: American Council on Public Affairs, 1942), 26–30; and Joseph B. Bishop, "The Secret Ballot in Thirty-Five States," *Forum* 2 (January 1892): 592. In 1892 the average state-level roll-off in Australian-ballot states was 2.5 percent. In reform-ballot states, roll-off increased significantly in 1896 to 4.7 percent. This is not surprising, however, since the 1896 election drew an exceptionally large turnout, including many marginal voters who did not normally participate.

24. Maine, New Hampshire, Delaware, Illinois, Indiana, Iowa, Kansas, Minnesota, North Dakota, South Dakota, North Carolina, and West Virginia.

25. In 1894, 67.5 percent of the nation's voters cast ballots in congressional elections, including 72.9 percent of all voters in the North. Record turnouts were registered in the mid-Atlantic (72 percent), north central (79.2 percent), border (67.8 percent), and western regions (70.2 percent).

26. During the nineteenth century, only a few mountain states enfranchised women in federal elections: Wyoming (1890), Colorado (1893), Utah (1896), and Idaho (1897).

27. The expansion of suffrage had begun in the colonial period. By 1776 all of the colonies had abolished religious restrictions on voting and most had relaxed their economic requirements. In the North only Rhode Island, Delaware,

and Pennsylvania continued to limit the franchise to taxpayers; Chilton Williamson, *American Suffrage from Property to Democracy, 1760–1860* (Princeton, N.J.: Princeton University Press, 1960); Jerrold G. Rusk and John J. Stucker, "Legal-Institutional Factors in American Voting" (unpublished paper, revised June 1975); McGovney, *American Suffrage Medley;* Porter, *History of Suffrage,* 77–111; and Kousser, *Shaping of Southern Politics.* See chapter 5 for a discussion of the laws designed to restrict access to the ballot.

28. Walter Dean Burnham, "The Changing Shape of the American Political Universe," *American Political Science Review* 59 (March 1965): 16.

29. Gary W. Cox and J. Morgan Kousser, "Turnout and Rural Corruption: New York as a Test Case," *American Journal of Political Science* 25 (November 1981): 652. See also Albert C. Parker, "Empire Stalemate: Voting Behavior in New York State, 1860–1892" (Ph.D. dissertation, Washington University, 1975), 39–40. Voter participation in the five most rural counties in New Jersey averaged 93.6 percent in 1888 and 89.6 percent in 1892, respectively 5.5 percent and 1.7 percent higher than turnout in the five largest cities in the state; John F. Reynolds, "Testing Democracy: Electoral Participation and Progressive Reform in New Jersey, 1880–1919" (Ph.D. dissertation, Rutgers University, 1980), 39–42.

30. On the moderately positive correlation with turnout in Indiana, see Melvyn Hammarberg, *The Indiana Voter: The Historical Dynamics of Party Allegiance during the 1870s* (Chicago: University of Chicago Press, 1977), 162–6. See also Paul Kleppner, *The Third Electoral System, 1853–1892: Parties, Voters, and Political Cultures* (Chapel Hill: University of North Carolina Press, 1979), 47.

31. Lester W. Milbraith, *Political Participation: How and Why Do People Get Involved in Politics?* (Chicago: Rand McNally, 1965), 42; and Angus Campbell, Philip E. Converse, Warren E. Miller, and Donald E. Stokes, *The American Voter* (New York: John Wiley and Sons, 1960), 211–3.

32. John M. Allswang, *A House for All People: Ethnic Politics in Chicago, 1890–1936* (Lexington: University of Kentucky Press, 1971), 15–37.

33. Converse, "Change in the American Electorate," 285. For comparative turnouts among Boston's various wards, see Dana, "Practical Workings of the Australian System of Voting," 743.

34. Kleppner estimates that in most of the country foreign-born voters went to the polls at a 12–14 percent lower rate than native-stock voters, but the descendants of foreign-born voters voted at a 2–3 percent higher rate; Paul Kleppner, *Who Voted? The Dynamics of Electoral Turnout, 1870–1980* (New York: Praeger, 1982), 36–8. Reynolds also uses ecological regression analysis to estimate the turnout rates of native-born, foreign-born, and black voters in New Jersey. He finds similar evidence of substantial participation of all segments of the electorate; John F. Reynolds, *Testing Democracy: Electoral Behavior and Progressive Reform in New Jersey, 1880–1920* (Chapel Hill: University of North Carolina Press, 1988), 179.

35. See for example Charles Stephenson, "A Gathering of Strangers? Mobility, Social Structure and Political Participation in the Formation of Nineteenth-Century American Working Class Culture," in *American Working Class Culture:*

Explorations in American Labor and Social History, ed. Milton Cantor (Westport, Conn.: Greenwood Press, 1979), 31–60. In contrast, Martin Shefter argues that the working class was intensely involved both in electoral politics and in workplace politics; Martin Shefter, "Trade Unions and Political Machines: The Organization and Disorganization of the American Working Class in the Late Nineteenth Century," in *Working Class Formation: Nineteenth Century Patterns in Western Europe and the United States*, ed. Ira Katznelson and Aristide Zolberg (Princeton, N.J.: Princeton University Press, 1986), 197–276.

36. Kleppner, *Who Voted?* 34–5.

37. This strong relationship between class and participation has been one of the major findings of survey research on twentieth-century voting; Campbell, Converse, Miller, and Stokes, *American Voter*, 184–210; Milbraith, *Political Participation*, 110–28; Sidney Verba and Norman H. Nie, *Participation in America: Political Democracy and Social Equality* (New York: Harper and Row, 1972), 125–37; and Michael J. Avey, *The Demobilization of American Voters: A Comprehensive Theory of Voter Turnout* (New York: Greenwood Press, 1989), 5.

38. The national electorate grew from 11,436,836 to 17,490,112, an increase of 51 percent. The number of votes cast for presidential candidates rose from 9,210,420 in 1880 to 13,936,068, also an increase of 51 percent. The eligible voter pool in the North grew 55.2 percent, from 8,996,593 to 13,963,333, and the total votes cast grew 56.3 percent, from 7,664,160 to 11,976,520.

39. Of course not all of these were young voters. Many were naturalized immigrants. However, since foreign-born citizens most likely voted at a somewhat lower rate than other citizens, voters coming of age in the eighties and nineties must have participated extensively; Kleppner, *Who Voted?* 36–8.

40. Campbell, Converse, Miller, and Stokes, *American Voter*, 49, 261–5; Milbraith, *Political Participation*, 134–5; Raymond E. Wolfinger and Steven J. Rosenstone, *Who Votes?* (New Haven, Conn.: Yale University Press, 1980), 23–30; Verba and Nie, *Participation in America*, 138–48; and Avey, *Demobilization of American Voters*, 33.

41. Geographic mobility introduced some socioeconomic bias into electoral participation since poor people moved more often and social status was highly related to geographic persistence; Kenneth J. Winkle, "A Social Analysis of Voter Turnout in Ohio, 1850–1860," *Journal of Interdisciplinary History* (Winter 1983): 428.

42. See chapter 2.

43. Mary P. Ryan, *Women in Public: Between Banners and Ballots, 1825–1880* (Baltimore: Johns Hopkins University Press, 1990); Theda Skocpol, *Protecting Soldiers and Mothers: The Political Origins of Social Policy in the United States* (Cambridge, Mass.: Harvard University Press, 1992); Paula Baker, "The Domestication of Politics: Women and American Political Society," *American Historical Review* 89 (June 1984): 167–94; and *The Moral Framework of Public Life: Gender, Politics and the State in Rural New York, 1870–1930* (New York: Oxford University Press, 1991); Theda Skocpol and Gretchen Ritter, "Gender and the Origins of Modern Social Policies in Britain and the United States," *Studies in Political Development* 5 (Spring 1991): 75–80; Rosalyn Terborg-Penn, "Discontented Black

Feminists: Prelude and Postscript to the Passage of the Nineteenth Amendment," in *"We Specialize in the Wholly Impossible": A Reader in Black Women's History*, ed. Darline Clark Hine (New York: Carlson Publishing, 1995), 487–503; and Rebecca Brooks Edwards, "Gender in American Politics: 1880–1900" (Ph.D. dissertation, University of Virginia, 1995).

44. Reynolds, *Testing Democracy*, 29–30; Gienapp, "Politics Seem to Enter into Everything," 16–7; Michael McGerr, "Political Style and Women's Power, 1830–1930," *Journal of American History* 77 (December 1990): 864–85; and Edwards, "Gender in American Politics."

45. According to James Bryce, women had the right to vote on at least some issues concerning schools in fourteen states during the 1880s: Colorado, Indiana, Kansas, Kentucky, Massachusetts, Michigan, Minnesota, Nebraska, New Hampshire, New York, New Jersey, Oregon, Vermont, Wisconsin, and the territories of Idaho and Wyoming; Bryce, *The American Commonwealth*, 2 vols., 2d ed., rev. (London: MacMillan, 1892), 2:441–2, 1:465–6, 1:575, 2:441. See also Elizabeth Cady Stanton, Susan B. Anthony, and Ida Husted Harper, *History of Woman Suffrage*, vol. 4 (New York: Fowler and Wells, 1881–1922); Alan P. Grimes, *The Puritan Ethic and Women's Suffrage* (New York: Oxford University Press, 1967), 3–77; and John J. Stucker, "The Impact of Women's Suffrage on Patterns of Voter Participation in the U.S.: Quasi-Experimental and Real-Time Analysis, 1890–1920" (Ph.D. dissertation, University of Michigan, 1973).

46. Ryan, *Women in Public*, 174.

47. P. Baker, *Moral Framework of Public Life*, 56–61.

48. Morton Keller, *Affairs of State: Public Life in Late Nineteenth Century America* (Cambridge, Mass.: Harvard University Press, 1977), 241. See also Walter Dean Burnham, "Party Systems and the Political Process," in *The American Party Systems: Stages of Political Development*, 2d ed., ed. William Nisbet Chambers and Walter Dean Burnham (New York: Oxford University Press, 1975), 279; Gienapp, "Politics Seemed to Enter into Everything," 36; and Joel H. Silbey, *The American Political Nation, 1838–1893* (Stanford, Calif.: Stanford University Press, 1991), 13, 47, and 70.

49. Richard McCormick, *The History of Voting in New Jersey: A Study in the Development of Election Machinery, 1664–1911* (New Brunswick, N.J.: Rutgers University Press, 1953), 163.

50. John D. Stewart, "Philadelphia Politics in the Gilded Age" (Ph.D. dissertation, St. Johns University, 1973), 138; and Wharton School of Finance and Economy, *The City Government of Philadelphia: A Study in Municipal Administration as Prepared by Members of the Senior Class in the Wharton School of Finance and Economy* (Philadelphia: University of Pennsylvania Press, 1893) 28. Many of the more closely contested states held state and congressional elections in September and October before November national elections; Robert J. Dinkin, *Campaigning in America: A History of Election Practices* (Westport, Conn.: Greenwood, 1989), 70.

51. Bryce, *American Commonwealth*, 1:573–80, 2:73, 2:87–90.

52. Seymour Mandlebaum, *Boss Tweed's New York* (New York: John Wiley and Sons, 1965), 50–1. Two or more bodies legislated for most large cities.

Philadelphia, for example, elected both a common council and a select council; Wharton School of Finance and Economy, *City Government of Philadelphia*, 28. See also Bryce, *American Commonwealth*, 1:596–605, 1:632–3.

53. Albert Shaw, "Local Government in Illinois" (Baltimore: Johns Hopkins University Studies, 1883), quoted in Bryce, *American Commonwealth*, 1:573. Iowa townships elected three trustees, one clerk, a road supervisor, justices of the peace, *and* constables (579). On legislative function, see 586. See also Estelle F. Feinstein, *Stamford in the Gilded Age: The Political Life of a Connecticut Town, 1868–1893* (Stamford, Conn.: Stamford Historical Society, 1973), 28.

54. Bryce, *American Commonwealth*, 1:580.

55. The preponderance of elected offices, in part the result of Jacksonian Era reforms, was something of which contemporary politicians were well aware. See for example B. Gratz Brown, *How the People Govern: An Address by Ex-Gov. at Booneville, Missouri, July 5th, 1880* (St. Louis: Slawson and Perrot, 1880), 8; and M. Ostrogorski, *Democracy and the Organization of Political Parties*, 2 vols., trans. Frederick Clarke (New York: McMillan Co., 1902), 2:539.

56. Keller, *Affairs of State*, 240; see also 534.

57. Robert W. Cherny, *Populism, Progressivism and the Transformation of Nebraska Politics* (Lincoln: University of Nebraska Press, 1981), 2. See also chapter 3.

58. For example, in Philadelphia Republican district leaders were elected and then met to choose ward leadership and a representative to the Republican city committee. John T. Salter, "The End of Vare," *Political Science Quarterly* 2 (June 1935): 214–35. In New Jersey as well, city and county conventions formed city and county party committees for each election. These committees, however, were appointed by convention chairmen, rather than being elected by the convention; John R. Williams, "Testing the Iron Law of Oligarchy: The Formal Structure of the New Jersey Democratic Party in the 1880s," *Shippensburg State College Review* (May 1971): 16–7.

59. Jean H. Baker, "The Ceremonies of Politics," in *A Master's Due: Essays in Honor of David Herbert Donald*, ed. William J. Cooper et. al. (Baton Rouge: Louisiana State University Press, 1985), 169–70; and *Affairs of Party; The Political Culture of Northern Democrats in the Mid-Nineteenth Century* (Ithaca, N.Y.: Cornell University Press, 1983), 291–2.

60. On political clubs and marching bands, see Ostrogorski, *Democracy and the Organization of Political Parties*, 2:333; Dinkin, *Campaigning in America*, 62; Michael E. McGerr, *The Decline of Popular Politics: The American North, 1865–1928* (New York: Oxford University Press, 1986), 23–9; Philip R. Vandermeer, *The Hoosier Politician: Officeholding and Political Culture in Indiana, 1896–1920* (Urbana: University of Illinois Press, 1985), 32–3; and James Edward Wright, *The Politics of Populism: Dissent in Colorado* (New Haven, Conn.: Yale University Press, 1974), 82.

61. Ostrogorski, *Democracy and the Organization of Political Parties*, 2:290–1. See also Bryce, *American Commonwealth*, 2:197.

62. McGerr, *Decline of Popular Politics*, 26. For example, McGerr finds that "during the campaign of 1880, New Haven, a city of 62,000 people living in thirteen wards, produces 42 clubs and 68 companies for the two major parties. Per-

haps 5000 out of 16,000 eligible voters signed a club constitution or marched in the city's campaign army"; McGerr, *Decline of Popular Politics*, 26. In 1888 the Republican party alone formed more than 1,100 clubs in just Indiana; Richard Jensen, *The Winning of the Midwest: Social and Political Conflict, 1888–1896* (Chicago: University of Chicago Press, 1971), 24. Nationwide, Ostrogorski estimated that 1.5 or 2 million electors belonged to campaign clubs; Ostrogorski, *Democracy and the Organization of Political Parties*, 2:292.

63. Ostrogorski, *Democracy and the Organization of Political Parties*, 2:332; J. Baker, "Ceremonies of Politics," 170–1; and *Affairs of Party*, 297–8; Reynolds, *Testing Democracy*, 34.

64. Ostrogorski, *Democracy and the Organization of Political Parties*, 2:333.

65. For descriptions of nineteenth-century election parades, see Bryce, *American Commonwealth*, 2:202–3; J. Baker, *Affairs of Party*, 292–7; and "Ceremonies of Politics," 161–3; Richard Jensen, "Armies, Admen, and Crusaders: Types of Presidential Campaigns," *History Teacher* 2 (January 1969): 34–6; and McGerr, *Decline of Popular Politics*, 28.

66. For a firsthand description of stump speaking, see David Turpie, *Sketches of My Own Time* (Indianapolis: Bobbs-Merrill, 1903), 289–95. See also Ostrogorski, *Democracy and the Organization of Political Parties*, 2:309–10; Albert V. House, "The Democratic State Central Committee of Indiana in 1880," *Indiana Magazine of History* 58 (June 1982): 195–200; Parker, "Empire Stalemate," 42–4; and Dinkin, *Campaigning in America*, 66.

67. Important national and state politicians drew large crowds in big cities and small towns alike. Robert Kelley writes:

> In a nation that had no national sports or common folk activity save evangelism, politics attracted the passions that later generations would center around mass spectator athletic events. Men like Daniel Webster could attract 100,000 people to their open air speeches and their orations ran on for hours. On those occasions insignificant lives took on expanded dimensions by being identified with great men and great causes.

Kelley, *The Cultural Pattern in American Politics: The First Century* (New York: Alfred A. Knopf, 1979), 153.

68. Gil Troy, *See How They Ran: The Changing Role of the Presidential Candidate* (New York: Free Press, 1991), 104–5; Murat Halstead, *Life and Distinguished Services of William McKinley: Our Martyr President* (H. L. Barber, 1901), 226.

69. Pre-election sermons were common regardless of denomination; Bryce, *American Commonwealth*, 2:200–1; and J. Baker, *Affairs of Party*, 273.

70. See chapter 2.

71. For reproductions of political buttons, badges, and ribbons, see Edmund B. Sullivan, *American Political Badges and Medalets, 1789–1892* (Lawrence, Mass.: Quarterman Publications, 1981), 447–636; and Roger A. Fischer, *Tippecanoe and Trinkets Too: The Material Culture of American Presidential Campaigns, 1828–1984* (Urbana: University of Illinois Press, 1988), 108–43.

72. Ostrogorski, *Democracy and the Organization of Political Parties*, 2:333–4.

73. Ryan, *Women in Public*, 130–71; McGerr, "Political Style and Women's Power," 867; J. Baker, "Ceremonies of Politics," 162–3; Gienapp, "Politics Seemed to Enter into Everything," 16–7; Reynolds, *Testing Democracy*, 29–30; Don Doyle, "Social Theory and New Communities in Nineteenth Century America," *Western Historical Quarterly* 8 (April 1977): 160–1; and Bryce, *American Commonwealth*, 2:200–1, 603. In contrast, Paula Baker argues that women in rural New York were hardly involved in campaign activity; P. Baker, *The Moral Framework of Public Life*, 39.

74. Fischer, *Tippecanoe and Trinkets Too*, 121. See also Edith P. Mayo, "Campaign Appeals to Women," *Journal of Popular Culture* 3 (Winter 1980): 722–42.

75. Ostrogorski disapprovingly described the button "craze" among young children; Ostrogorski, *Democracy and the Organization of Political Parties*, 2:337.

76. Quoted in Reynolds, *Testing Democracy*, 28.

77. McGerr, *Decline of Popular Politics*, 24–5; and Dinkin, *Campaigning in America*, 64.

78. Vandermeer, *Hoosier Politician*, 26–7.

79. Reynolds, *Testing Democracy*, 35; J. Baker, "Ceremonies of Politics," 174–5; and McGerr, *Decline of Popular Politics*, 28.

80. J. Baker, *Affairs of Party*, 276, 306.

81. J. Baker, "Ceremonies of Politics," 177; and *Affairs of Party*, 310–1.

82. P. Baker, *Moral Framework of Public Life*, 39; Reynolds, *Testing Democracy*, 34–5.

83. Lewis Atherton, *Main Street on the Middle Border* (Bloomington: Indiana University Press, 1954), 213.

84. For a similar view, see Robert D. Marcus, *Grand Old Party: Political Structure in the Gilded Age, 1880–1896* (New York: Oxford University Press, 1971). Marcus suggests that with so many offices up for election in so many different contests, politics became the "national pastime: campaigns were major events offering entertainment, information and emotional satisfaction" (4).

85. Lawrence W. Levine, *Highbrow/Lowbrow: The Emergence of Cultural Hierarchy in America* (Cambridge: Harvard University Press, 1988).

86. See John F. Kasson, *Amusing the Million: Coney Island at the Turn of the Century* (New York: Hill and Wang, 1978), 3–5.

87. P. Baker, "Domestication of Politics," 628–9; see also *Moral Framework of Public Life*, 24–37. Jensen highlights the martial side of nineteenth-century politics: "Even the language of politics was cast in military terms. From the *opening gun* of the *campaign* the *standard bearer*, along with the other *war-horses fielded* by the party, *rallied* the *rank and file* around the party *standard*, the *bloody shirt* and other *slogans*. Precinct *captains aligned* their *phalanxes shoulder-to-shoulder* to mobilize voters for the *Old Guard*"; Jensen, *Winning of the Midwest*, 11.

88. P. Baker, *Moral Framework of Public Life*, 24–37. The quotations are on 28 and 29.

89. McGerr, *Decline of Popular Politics*, 30–3. See also Alan Dawley and Paul Faler, "Working-Class Culture and Politics in the Industrial Revolution: Sources of Loyalism and Rebellion, *Journal of Social History* 9 (Summer 1976): 474–7.

90. Robert H. Wiebe, *The Search for Order, 1877–1920* (New York: Hill and

Wang, 1967), 4. He refined and modified the concept of "island communities" in *The Segmented Society: An Introduction to the Meaning of America* (New York: Oxford University Press, 1975). See also Thomas Bender, *Community and Social Change in America* (New Brunswick, N.J.: Rutgers University Press, 1978).

91. Samuel Kernell, "The Early Nationalization of Political News in America," *Studies in American Political Development* (1986): 275–6.

92. Wiebe, *Segmented Society*, 21. For a description of the effect of mobility on small towns, see Atherton, *Main Street*, 17–9.

93. The same is true for religious identities.

94. Stephen Thernstrom and Peter R. Knights speculate about the significance of political ties in holding together this mobile social order; Thernstrom and Knights, "Men in Motion; Some Data and Speculations about Urban Population Mobility in Nineteenth-Century America," *Journal of Interdisciplinary History* 1 (Summer 1970): 34–5. Don Harrison Doyle writes: "The legendary vigor of frontier politics may have owed as much to this need to integrate a transient society as it did to the egalitarian democracy that Turner saw coming out of the American forest. . . . The role of political parties as mechanisms for integrating newcomers . . . provided important antidotes to the mobility and fragmentation of new communities"; Doyle, "Social Theory and New Communities," 160–1.

95. Studies of voting behavior generally find that voters who are cross-pressured are less involved in politics. Campbell, Converse, Miller, and Stokes, *American Voter*, 42–8; and Milbraith, *Political Participation*, 55.

96. J. Baker, "Ceremonies of Politics," 166–8. See also *Affairs of Party*; and Silbey, *American Political Nation*, 69–71, 86–90.

97. In this I differ strongly with some of the scholars who have focused on nineteenth-century political culture. Paula Baker, for example, presents late-nineteenth-century electoral politics almost strictly as "an imaginative politics where manhood received its reward"; P. Baker, *Moral Framework of Public Life*, xvi. Likewise, Jean Baker locates the meaning of elections in their ceremonial (i.e., "nonrational") significance in building a sense of nationhood; J. Baker, *Affairs of Party*, 316; see also 261–316.

NOTES TO CHAPTER 2

1. See William Nisbet Chambers and Philip C. Davis, "Party Competition and Mass Participation: The Case of the Democratizing Party System, 1824–1862," in *The History of American Electoral Behavior*, ed. Joel H. Silbey, Allan G. Bogue, and William H. Flanigan (Princeton, N.J.: Princeton University Press, 1978), 174–97; William Nisbet Chambers, "Party Development and the American Mainstream," in *The American Party Systems: Stages of Political Development*, ed. William Nisbet Chambers and Walter Dean Burnham, 2d ed. (New York: Oxford University Press, 1975), 3–33; William G. Shade, "Political Pluralism and Party Development: The Creation of a Modern Party System, 1815–1852," in *The Evolution of American Electoral Systems*, ed. Paul Kleppner (Westport, Conn.: Greenwood Press, 1981), 33–76, 77–112; and Ronald P.

Formisano, *The Birth of Mass Political Parties: Michigan, 1827–1861* (Princeton, N.J.: Princeton University Press, 1971).

2. Other scholars of late-nineteenth-century political behavior have also assigned a central role to the party. See Walter Dean Burnham, "The System of 1896: An Analysis," in *The Evolution of American Electoral Systems*, ed. Paul Kleppner (Westport, Conn.: Greenwood Press, 1981), 190; Joel H. Silbey, *The American Political Nation, 1838–1893* (Stanford, Calif.: Stanford University Press, 1991), 9; and Paul Kleppner, *Who Voted? The Dynamics of Electoral Turnout, 1870–1980* (New York: Praeger, 1982), 47.

3. As quoted in Paul Kleppner, "Partisanship and Ethnoreligious Conflict: The Third Electoral System, 1853–1892," in *The Evolution of American Electoral Systems*, ed. Paul Kleppner (Westport, Conn.: Greenwood Press, 1981), 113.

4. See Philip E. Converse and Roy Pierce, "Measuring Partisanship," *Political Methodology* 11 (1985): 143–4.

5. Split-party voting would be a more accurate label for this behavior since it often involved the voting of fusion tickets or other tickets that listed candidates from more than one party, especially before the passage of ballot reform legislation standardized voting procedures. This index of split-ticket voting, therefore, is an aggregate measure of voters who did not vote a single-party ticket. Appendix 2 explains how ticket splitting was measured.

6. The 6 percent figure is somewhat arbitrary, but it is reasonable to use a percentage that does not eliminate too many elections but still captures the difference between races with and without meaningful minor-party candidates. See Jerrold Rusk, "Effect of the Australian Ballot Reform on Split-Ticket Voting: 1876–1908," *American Political Science Review* 64 (December 1970): 1222.

7. As low as these figures are, they are still somewhat higher than Rusk's figures for split-ticket voting in races between major party candidates. For the North these figures are only slightly higher than Rusk's (.1 percent to .5 percent), but for the nation as a whole they exceed his by a considerable amount (.7 percent to 1.5 percent). Since both studies use state-level voting returns provided by the ICPSR to compute our measures, it is not readily apparent why our results should diverge in this way. At the very least, however, it is clear that we are not underestimating aggregate split-ticket voting; Rusk, "Effect of the Australian Ballot Reform on Split-Ticket Voting: 1876–1908" (Ph.D. dissertation, University of Michigan, 1968), 197.

8. Mean split-ticket voting in two-party elections calculated on the basis of presidential and congressional races alone was only 1.9 percent (*n* = 23) for the South and 1.2 percent (*n* = 85) for the North. The national split-ticket voting mean calculated in this manner was a mere 1.3 percent (*n* = 111).

9. Reynolds and McCormick's findings are therefore consistent with the picture that I am painting of a partisan, but contentious, electorate; John Reynolds and Richard McCormick, "'Outlawing Treachery': Split Tickets and the Ballot Laws in New York and New Jersey, 1880–1910," *Journal of American History* 72 (March 1986): 848–58. See also John F. Reynolds, *Testing Democracy: Electoral Behavior and Progressive Reform in New Jersey, 1880–1920* (Chapel Hill: University of North Carolina Press, 1988), 43–6.

10. See Appendix 2.

11. Eldon C. Evans, *A History of the Australian Ballot System in the United States* (Chicago: University of Chicago Press, 1917); Spencer D. Albright, *The American Ballot* (Washington, D.C.: American Council on Public Affairs, 1942), 26–30; and Joseph B. Bishop, "The Secret Ballot in Thirty-Five States," *Forum 2* (January 1892): 592.

12. Walter Dean Burnham, "Communications to the Editor," *American Political Science Review* 65 (December 1971): 1150–2; John Reynolds and Richard McCormick, "'Outlawing Treachery'"; Rusk, "Effect of the Australian Ballot Reform," *American Political Science Review*. See chapter 5 for further discussion of the effects of ballot reform.

13. For a discussion of correlation analysis and why I do not use ecological regression analysis, see Appendix 2.

14. Kleppner, "Partisanship and Ethnoreligious Conflict," 115.

15. Appendix 2 explains how party-vote instability is measured.

16. These are state-level averages. Mean regional party-vote instability percentages for the four presidential elections from 1884 to 1896 were the following: New England, 6.0 percent; mid-Atlantic, 3.8 percent; north central, 2.9 percent; midwest, 8.6 percent; south, 7.6 percent; border, 3.4 percent; mountain, 25.6 percent; and west, 7.3 percent.

17. Here again, the 6 percent figure is somewhat arbitrary. It was used to discriminate between two-party and multiparty states. In order to test the use of this cutoff figure, exactly the same calculations were performed using other cutoffs for minor-party voting (10 percent average, and ten percent in any given election) with similar results. The vast majority of states in which minor-party candidates averaged over 6 percent of the votes cast were multiparty states. Any cutoff under 6 percent eliminates too many states that were generally two-party states.

18. Connecticut, Maine, Massachusetts, New Hampshire, Rhode Island, Vermont, Delaware, New Jersey, New York, Pennsylvania, Illinois, Indiana, Ohio, Wisconsin, Iowa, Missouri, Kentucky, Maryland, Tennessee, West Virginia, and California.

19. This conclusion is supported by case studies of voting in several states that did not experience significant third-party activity. These studies all utilize county-level election returns. See Reynolds, "Testing Democracy: Electoral Participation and Progressive Reform in New Jersey, 1880–1919" (Ph.D. dissertation, Rutgers University, 1980), 52–5; Lee Benson, Joel H. Silbey, and Phyllis F. Field, "Toward a Theory of Stability and Change in American Voting Patterns: New York State, 1792–1970," in *The History of American Electoral Behavior*, ed. Joel H. Silbey, Allan G. Bogue, and William H. Flanigan (Princeton, N.J.: Princeton University Press, 1978), 92–3; Charles Hyneman, Richard Hofstadter, and Patrick F. O'Connor, *Voting in Indiana: A Century of Persistence and Change* (Bloomington: Indiana University Press, 1979), 91; V. O. Key, Jr., and Frank Munger, "Social Determinism and Electoral Decisions: The Case of Indiana," in *Voters, Parties, and Elections: Quantitative Essays in the History of American Popular Voting Behavior*, ed. Joel H. Silbey and Samuel T. McSeveney (Lexington, Ky.: Xerox College Press, 1972), 31–3.

20. Chapter 3 examines third-party voting in greater depth.

21. Allan Peskin makes the same point in "Who Were the Stalwarts? Who Were Their Rivals? Republican Factions in the Gilded Age," *Political Science Quarterly* 99 (Winter 1984–5): 703.

22. See for example Richard P. McCormick, *The History of Voting in New Jersey: A Study in the Development of Election Machinery, 1664–1911* (New Brunswick, N.J.: Rutgers University Press, 1953), 165–70; Ballard C. Campbell, *Representative Democracy: Public Policy and Midwestern Legislatures in the Late Nineteenth Century* (Cambridge, Mass.: Harvard University Press, 1980), 176; Morton Keller, *Affairs of State: Public Life in Late Nineteenth Century America* (Cambridge, Mass.: Harvard University Press, 1977), 242–3; James Albert Woodburn, *American Politics: Party Politics and Party Problems in the United States* (New York: G. P. Putnam's Sons, 1903), 275–8; and Peter H. Argersinger, "Regulating Democracy: Election Laws and Dakota Politics, 1889–1902," *Midwest Review* 5 (Spring 1983): 1–19; and "The Value of the Vote: Political Representation in the Gilded Age," *Journal of American History* 76 (June 1989): 59–90.

23. Walter C. Hamm, "The Art of Gerrymandering," *Forum* 9 (July 1890): 538–51; and Argersinger, "Value of the Vote."

24. Partisan considerations also contributed to the extension of federal Civil Service as outgoing presidents sought to secure their party's appointees. Most of these positions were technical and clerical, however, and left the chief sources of party patronage undisturbed. See Stephen Skrowronek, *Building a New American State: The Expansion of National Administrative Capacities, 1877–1920* (N.Y.: Cambridge University Press, 1982), 68–74; Paul P. Van Riper, *History of the United States Civil Service* (White Plains, New York: Dow, Peterson, 1958), 118, 130; Martin Shefter, "Party, Bureaucracy, and Political Change in the United States," in *Political Parties: Development and Decay*, ed. Louis Maisel and Joseph Cooper (Beverly Hills, Calif.: Sage Publications, 1978), 228–9; and James A. Morone, *The Democratic Wish: Popular Participation and the Limits of American Government* (New York: Basic Books, 1990), 102–6.

25. M. Ostrogorski, *Democracy and the Organization of Political Parties*, 2 vols., trans. Frederick Clarke (New York: McMillan Co., 1902), 2:304–5. Reynolds quotes the *Newark Daily Advertiser,* which "reported in 1880 that 80 percent of the city's new citizens had been sponsored by party representatives, who also paid their naturalization fees"; Reynolds, *Testing Democracy,* 26, 28. See also Frederick C. Luebke, *Immigrants and Politics: Germans of Nebraska, 1880–1900* (Lincoln: University of Nebraska Press, 1969), 136.

26. Surveying the administration of elections, Rusk finds that "the states had virtually abandoned the electoral machinery to the parties;" Rusk, "Effect of the Australian Ballot Reform" (Ph.D. dissertation), 39.

27. James Albert Woodburn, a contemporary political scientist explains,

"In the actual conduct of the election the party organizations are the chief factors. The inspector of the election board will be a township trustee, or some other public officer appointed or elected by party influence and party process, and the judges and clerks are appointed by party committeemen or at the behest of party interests. . . . The agents of the two large parties are there to keep one another in check."

Woodburn, *American Politics*, 214.

28. Albright, *American Ballot*, 99–100.

29. James Bryce, *The American Commonwealth*, 2 vols., 2d ed., rev. (London: MacMillan, 1892), 2:136–8; Rusk, "Effect of the Australian Ballot Reform" (Ph.D. dissertation), 20; Evans, *History of the Australian Ballot System*, 6–16; Reynolds, "The 'Silent Dollar,': Vote Buying in New Jersey," *New Jersey History* 98 (Fall–Winter 1980): 193; and *Testing Democracy*, 36. Philip E. Converse calls this a "visible" voting system; Converse, "Change in the American Electorate," in *The Human Meaning of Change*, ed. Angus Campbell and Philip E. Converse (New York: Russell Sage Foundation, 1972), 277.

30. For example, see Bryce, *American Commonwealth*, 2:145; and Reynolds and McCormick, "'Outlawing Treachery,'" 843–8.

31. Lionel E. Fredman, *The Australian Ballot: The Story of an American Reform* (East Lansing: Michigan State University Press, 1968), esp. 83–4; Albright, *American Ballot*; Evans, *History of the Australian Ballot System*; Jerrold G. Rusk and John J. Stucker, "Legal-Institutional Factors in American Voting" (unpublished paper, revised June 1975); and Bishop, "Secret Ballot," 589–98.

32. See chapter 5.

33. Although all but a few ballot reform laws provided for official, consolidated ballots distributed at the polling place, states differed on what these ballots should look like. Some states followed the lead of Massachusetts and adopted an "office-block" ballot, which listed candidates by office regardless of their political party. Others followed Indiana and adopted a "party-column" ballot, which organized candidates' names by party. Both ballot forms enabled voters to split their votes between parties. However, the party-column ballot facilitated straight-ticket voting. Moreover, some states instituted a party check-off, which permitted voters to cast a straight-party ticket by checking one box. See Philip Loring Allen, "Ballot Laws and Their Workings," *Political Science Quarterly* 21 (1906): 38–58; Rusk, "Effect of the Australian Ballot Reform," *American Political Science Review*, 1222; Evans, *History of the Australian Ballot System*, 36–40; and Robert C. Brooks, *Political Parties and Electoral Problems* (New York: Harper and Brothers, 1923), 389–404. Evans and Brooks provide facsimiles of both ballot forms.

34. Reynolds, *Testing Democracy*, 49–70. For a detailed discussion of ballot reform, see chapter 5.

35. Once ballot reform passed, most states permitted independent candidates to petition for a place on the ballot. Nominating petitions, however, invariably required a large number of signatures, usually 5 percent of the total vote cast in the previous election, and this effectively limited the ballot to party nominees. During the 1890s reformers started working for nonpartisan elections.

36. Bryce, *American Commonwealth*, 2:80–5; Ostrogorski, *Democracy and the Organization of Political Parties*, 2:226–37; Reynolds, *Testing Democracy*, 19–20; and John R. Williams, "Testing The Iron Law of Oligarchy: The Formal

Structure of the New Jersey Democratic Party in the 1880s," *Shippensburg State College Review* (May 1971): 15–23.

37. Charles Merriam and Louise Overacker conclude that primaries as well as party conventions remained "almost wholly under party control"; Merriam and Overacker, *Primary Elections* (Chicago: University of Chicago Press, 1928), 22, 20–59. See also V. O. Key, Jr., *American State Politics: An Introduction* (New York: Alfred A. Knopf, 1956), 85–169. For local primaries, see Williams, "Testing the Iron Law of Oligarchy," 16–7.

38. See Bryce, *American Commonwealth*, 2: 97–8.

39. The time span between nominations and elections in New Jersey, according to John Williams, was approximately two months for governor, six weeks for congressmen, three weeks for state senators and county officials, and one week for ward officials; J. Williams, "Testing the Iron Law of Oligarchy," 18. At the city level, J. Roger Hollingsworth likewise finds that "it was not at all unusual for elections to be held three or four days following the parties' nomination of candidates." Several states, in response, passed laws requiring that nominations be made at least fourteen days prior to election day. J. Roger Hollingsworth, "The Impact of Electoral Behavior on Public Policy: The Urban Dimension, 1900," in *The History of American Electoral Behavior*, ed. Joel H. Silbey, Allan G. Bogue, and William H. Flanigan (Princeton, N.J.: Princeton University Press, 1978), 367. See also Reynolds, *Testing Democracy*, 19–20; B. Campbell, *Representative Democracy*, 10.

40. For a similar view, see Michael McGerr, *The Decline of Popular Politics: The American North, 1865–1928* (New York: Oxford University Press, 1986), 35–7. In contrast, Patrick F. Palermo argues that each candidate had to "develop his own campaign organization," which he held together through personal appeals to his "friends"; Palermo, "The Rules of the Game: Local Republican Political Culture in the Gilded Age," *Historian* (August 1985): 490.

41. Reynolds, *Testing Democracy*, 22; and B. Campbell, *Representative Democracy*, 13–5.

42. "The sums they pay are accordin' to their salaries and length of their terms in office, if elected," claimed George Washington Plunkitt, one of the nation's best-known wardheelers; William L. Riordon, *Plunkitt of Tammany Hall* (New York: E. P. Dutton, 1963), 73. Jeremiah Jenks, a late-nineteenth-century political scientist, estimated that candidates for local office in Illinois were assessed 5 percent of the annual salary of the office for which they were running; Jenks, "Money in Practical Politics," *Century* 44 (October 1892): 942.

43. This was well understood at the time. As Jenks wrote: "When candidates have been nominated and elected through the efforts of a committee, they, of course, are likely to feel under personal obligations to their party." Jeremiah Jenks, "Political Party Machinery in the United States," *Chautauquan* (April–September 1896): 27.

44. Gil Troy, *See How They Ran: The Changing Role of the Presidential Candidate* (New York: Free Press, 1991), 82–112.

45. Samuel Kernell, "The Early Nationalization of Political News in America," *Studies in American Political Development* 1 (1986): 275–6; and Paula Baker,

"The Culture of Politics in the Late Nineteenth Century: Community and Political Behavior in Rural New York," *Journal of Social History* 18 (Winter 1984): 170. Conducting "an examination of a few of the chief newspapers during the months of September and October 1884," Bryce found that "'campaign matter' of all kinds formed between one-half and one-third of the total letterpress of the paper (excluding advertisements), and this, be it remembered every day during those two months"; Bryce, *American Commonwealth*, 2:199.

46. Jensen, "Armies, Admen, and Crusaders: Types of Presidential Crusaders," *History Teacher* 2 (January 1969): 37. See also Frank Luther Mott, *American Journalism: A History of Newspapers in the United States through 250 years, 1690–1940* (New York: Macmillan, 1941), 253–91.

47. Paul David Nord, *Newspapers and New Politics: Midwestern Municipal Reform, 1890–1900* (Ann Arbor: University of Michigan Research Press, 1981), 26; Alfred McClung Lee, *The Daily Newspaper in New York* (New York: Macmillan, 1937), 174–7. Historians interested in the origins of modern journalism pay scant attention to the small partisan "rags" that most people read in the nineteenth century. For example, see Nord, *Newspapers and New Politics*; and Michael Schudson, *Discovering the News: A Social History of American Newspapers* (New York: Basic Books, 1978).

48. McGerr, *Decline of Popular Politics*, 17.

49. Ostrogorski, *Democracy and the Organization of Political Parties*, 2:320; Woodburn, *American Politics*, 209.

50. Bryce, *American Commonwealth*, 2:199.

51. Jensen, "Armies, Admen, and Crusaders," 37. See also Seymour Mandlebaum, *Boss Tweed's New York* (New York: John Wiley and Sons, 1965), 23. Sally Foreman Griffith's description of the *Emporia Gazette* during the 1890s provides a good example; Griffith, *Hometown News: William Allen White and the Emporia Gazette* (New York: Oxford University Press, 1989), 32–63.

52. Mott, *American Journalism*, 411–519; McGerr, *The Decline of Popular Politics*, 107–30; and Philip R. Vandermeer, *The Hoosier Politician: Officeholding and Political Culture in Indiana, 1896–1920* (Urbana: University of Illinois Press, 1985), 25.

53. As quoted in Troy, *See How They Ran*, 84.

54. McGerr, *Decline of Popular Politics*, 120. McGerr gathered these statistics by counting each paper listed in N. W. Ayer & Son's *American Newspaper Annual* (Philadelphia: N. W. Ayer and Son, 1891), 257.

55. Schudson, *Discovering the News*, 90. Schudson compares the ways Pulitzer's Democratic *New York World* and the Republican *New York Times* characterized the same political campaign (108–9).

56. Wilson continued: "It would seem to be scarcely an exaggeration to say they are homogenous only in name. Neither of the two principal parties is of one mind with itself. Each tolerates all sorts of difference of creed and variety of aims within its own ranks. . . . They are like armies without officers." Woodrow Wilson, *Congressional Government: A Study in American Politics* (Cleveland: World Publishing, 1956), 210.

57. Richard Jensen's extended use of the military metaphor to describe

nineteenth-century politics is thus problematic; "Armies, Admen, and Crusaders"; and Jensen, *The Winning of the Midwest: Social and Political Conflict,
1888–1896* (Chicago: University of Chicago Press, 1971), 11–2. See also Michael
Les Benedict, "Factionalism and Representation: Some Insights from the Nineteenth-Century United States," *Social Science History* 9 (Fall 1985): 361–89.

58. Hays, "The Politics of Reform in Municipal Government in the Progres-
sive Era," *Pacific Northwest Quarterly* 55 (October 1964): 157–69; and "Political
Parties and the Community-Society Continuum," in *The American Party System:
Stages of Political Development*, ed. William Nisbet Chambers and Walter Dean
Burnham (New York: Oxford University Press, 1975), 152–81.

59. Ostrogorski, *Democracy and the Organization of Political Parties*, 2:281.

60. Marcus, *Grand Old Party: Political Structure in the Gilded Age, 1880–1896*
(New York: Oxford University Press, 1971), 58; McGerr, *Decline of Popular Poli-
tics*, 34–5; and Robert J. Dinkin, *Campaigning in America: A History of Election
Practices* (Westport, Conn.: Greenwood, 1989), 71–2.

61. Marcus, *Grand Old Party*, 22; Peskin, "Who Were the Stalwarts?"

62. H. Wayne Morgan, *From Hays to McKinley: National Political Parties,
1877–1896* (Syracuse, N.Y.: Syracuse University Press, 1969), 84. See also
Leonard D. White, *The Republican Era: A Study in Administrative History,
1869–1901* (New York: Macmillan, 1958), 11.

63. Philip S. Klein and Ari Hoogenboom, *A History of Pennsylvania* (New
York: McGraw-Hill, 1973), 321.

64. Eric McKitrick, "The Study of Corruption," *Political Science Quarterly* 72
(December 1957): 502–14.

65. Mandlebaum, *Boss Tweed's New York*, 120–8, 162; Martin Shefter, "The
Electoral Foundation of the Political Machine: New York City, 1884–1897," in
The History of American Electoral Behavior, ed. Joel H. Silbey, Allan G. Bogue, and
William H. Flanigan (Princeton, N.J.: Princeton University Press, 1978),
263–98; Ira Katznelson, *City Trenches: Urban Politics and the Patterning of Class in
the United States* (Chicago: University of Chicago Press, 1981), 56–7; David C.
Hammack, *Power and Society: Greater New York at the Turn of the Century* (New
York: Russell Sage Foundation, 1982); Reynolds, *Testing Democracy*, 17–28; and
Kleppner, "From Party to Factions: The Dissolution of Boston's Majority Party,
1876–1908," in *Boston, 1700–1980: The Evolution of Urban Politics*, ed. Ronald P.
Formisano and Constance K. Burns (Westport, Conn.: Greenwood Press, 1984),
111–32.

66. Palermo, "Rules of the Game," 483; James D. Norris and Arthur H. Shaffer, eds., *Politics and Patronage in the Gilded Age: The Correspondence of James A.
Garfield and Charles E. Henry* (Madison: State Historical Society of Wisconsin,
1970), xvi.

67. Kleppner, *Who Voted?* 48–50; Chester Lloyd Jones, "The County in Politics," *Annals of the American Academy of Political and Social Science* 47 (May 1913):
92–3.

68. Ostrogorski, *Democracy and the Organization of Political Parties*, 2:207–26;
Reynolds, *Testing Democracy*, 25–8; Kleppner, "From Party to Factions," 117–9;

White, *Republican Era*, 11; and John T. Salter, *Boss Rule: Portraits in City Politics* (New York: Arno Press, 1974).

69. Ostrogorski, *Democracy and the Organization of Political Parties*, 2:285.

70. Plunkitt remembered the time when he began as a block leader with the support of about sixty voters: "You ought to have seen how I was courted and petted by the leaders of rival organizations. I had marketable goods and there was bids for them from all sides, and I was a risin' man in politics." Riordon, *Plunkitt of Tammany Hall*, 10; Reynolds, *Testing Democracy*, 26. See also Ostrogorski, *Democracy and the Organization of Political Parties*, 2:368; and Kleppner, "From Party to Factions," 118–22.

71. Williams, "Testing the Iron Law of Oligarchy," 19.

72. Kleppner, *The Cross of Culture: A Social Analysis of Midwestern Politics, 1850–1900* (New York: Free Press, 1970); *The Third Electoral System, 1853–1892: Parties, Voters, and Political Cultures* (Chapel Hill: University of North Carolina Press, 1979); and *Continuity and Change in Electoral Politics, 1893–1928* (New York: Greenwood, 1987); Jensen, *Winning of the Midwest*; Robert Kelley, *The Cultural Pattern in American Politics: The First Century* (New York: Alfred A. Knopf, 1979); McGerr, *Decline of Popular Politics*, 3–42; Jean H. Baker, *Affairs of Party: The Political Culture of Northern Democrats in the Mid-Nineteenth Century* (Ithaca, N.Y.: Cornell University Press, 1983); Paula Baker, *The Moral Framework of Public Life: Gender, Politics, and the State in Rural New York, 1870–1930* (New York: Oxford University Press, 1991), 24–55.

73. Jenks, "Political Party Machinery," 26–7; and "Money in Practical Politics," 941. See also Ostrogorski, *Democracy and the Organization of Political Parties*, 2:306–7, 340–1; and Gerson Harry Smoger, "Organizing Political Campaigns: A Survey of Noneteenth and Twentieth Century Trends" (Ph.D. dissertation, University of Pennsylvania, 1982), 19–23.

74. Riordon, *Plunkitt of Tammany Hall*, 90–8; and Jane Addams, "Why the Ward Boss Rules," *Outlook* 58 (2 April 1898): 879.

75. Riordon, *Plunkitt of Tammany Hall*, 25; See also Ostrogorski, *Democracy and the Organization of Political Parties*, 2:377.

76. Thomas J. Schlereth, *Victorian America: Transformations in Everyday Life, 1876–1915* (New York: HarperCollins, 1991), 226–9; and Roy Rosenzweig, *Eight Hours for What We Will: Workers and Leisure in an Industrial City, 1870–1920* (New York: Cambridge University Press, 1983), 35–65.

77. Many ward leaders were saloon keepers themselves; see James Michael Curley, *I'd Do It All Again: A Record of All My Uproarious Years* (Englewood Cliffs, N.J.: Prentice Hall, 1957), 27. See also Smoger, "Organizing Political Campaigns," 206–7.

78. Ostrogorski, *Democracy and the Organization of Political Parties*, 2:286–92; Shefter, "Electoral Foundation of the Political Machine," 294–5; and "Emergence of the Political Machine: An Alternative View," in *Theoretical Perspectives on Urban Politics*, ed. Willis D. Hawley and Michael Lipsky (Englewood Cliffs, N.J.: Prentice-Hall, 1976), 34–5; John D. Buenker, *Urban Liberalism and Progressive Reform* (New York: W. W. Norton, 1973), 5; Samuel P. Orth, *The Boss and the*

Machine: A Chronicle of the Politicians and Party Organization (New Haven, Conn.: Yale University Press, 1919), 88–91; and J. Baker, *Affairs of Party*, 286–7.

79. Reynolds, *Testing Democracy*, 26; Riordon, *Plunkitt of Tammany Hall*, 25–6; Addams, "Why the Ward Boss Rules," 881; J. Baker, *Affairs of Party*, 286–7; and John H. Cutler, *"Honey Fitz": Three Steps to the White House* (Indianapolis: Bobbs-Merrill, 1962), 51–2.

80. Riordon, *Plunkitt of Tammany Hall*, 28. John F. Fitzgerald ("Honey Fitz"), Democratic party leader in Boston's Sixth Ward, likewise kept a card index of all the men in his district who needed work and prevailed upon city contractors and public utility executives for positions; Cutler, *"Honey Fitz,"* 52–3.

81. Addams, "Why the Ward Boss Rules," 879.

82. Wharton School of Finance and Economy, *The City Government of Philadelphia: A Study in Municipal Administration as Prepared by Members of the Senior Class in the Wharton School of Finance and Economy* (Philadelphia: University of Pennsylvania Press, 1893), 103. See also John D. Stewart, "Philadelphia Politics in the Gilded Age" (Ph.D. dissertation, St. Johns University, 1973), 135–8.

83. Keller, *Affairs of State*, 239. Steven P. Erie has suggested that Tammany Hall controlled forty thousand jobs in the 1880s out of a labor force of nearly one million, or 1 in 25 workers; Erie, *Rainbow's End: Irish-Americans and the Dilemmas of Urban Machine Politics* (Berkeley: University of California Press, 1988), 59.

84. Harold F. Gosnell, *Boss Platt and His New York Machine* (Chicago: University of Chicago Press, 1924), 220; Keller, *Affairs of State*, 239.

85. Richard Jensen, *Grass Roots Politics: Parties, Issues, and Voters, 1854–1983* (Westport, Conn.: Greenwood Press, 1983).

86. Van Riper, *History of the United States Civil Service*, 118, 130; Keller, *Affairs of State*, 239; Skowronek, *Building a New American State*, 69; and Martin Shefter, "Party, Bureaucracy, and Political Change," 228–9.

87. First-, second- and third-class postmasterships were nominated by the president with the consent of the Senate. Fourth-class postmasterships were named directly by the postmaster general, who was himself a presidential appointee; Malcolm M. Willey and Stuart A. Rice, *Communication Agencies and Social Life* (New York: McGraw-Hill, 1933), 106.

88. Skowronek, *Building a New American State*, 72; Benedict, "Factionalism and Representation," 373–4.

89. Jensen, *Winning of the Midwest*, 162.

90. Skowronek, *Building the New American State*, 72. Over sixty-three hundred of these positions were held by women during the 1890s; Marshall Cushing, *The Story of Our Post-Office: The Greatest Government Department in All Its Phases* (Boston: A. M. Thayer, 1893), 442–3.

91. White, *Republican Era*, 258–9; Norris and Shaffer, *Politics and Patronage*, xxii–xxiii.

92. As quoted in Morgan, *From Hays to McKinley*, 251–2.

93. Riordon, *Plunkitt of Tammany Hall*, 74.

94. Ari Hoogenboom, *Outlawing the Spoils* (Urbana: University of Illinois Press, 1963), 225–6. See also Philadelphia Department of Public Works, "The

Political Assessment of Office-Holders: A Report on the System as Practiced by the Republican Organization in the City of Philadelphia, 1883–1913" (1913); Lloyd Abernathy, "Insurgency in Philadelphia, 1905," *Pennsylvania Magazine of History and Biography* 86 (January 1963): 3–20; and Ostrogorski, *Democracy and the Organization of Political Parties*, 2:143–7, 425.

95. For examples, see Ostrogorski, *Democracy and the Organization of the Political Parties*, 2:378–9; John M. Allswang, *Bosses, Machines and Urban Voters: An American Symbiosis* (Port Washington, N.Y.: Kennikat Press, 1977); Salter, *Boss Rule*; Sonya Forthal, *Cogwheels of Democracy: A Study of the Precinct Captain* (New York: William-Frederick Press, 1946); Moses Rischin, *The Promised Land: New York's Jews, 1870–1914* (New York: Harper and Row, 1970), 223; Elmer Cornwall, "Bosses, Machines, and Ethnic Groups," *Annals of the American Academy of Political and Social Science* 353 (May 1964): 27–39; and Buenker, *Urban Liberalism*, 4–6.

96. Local partymen thus acted as a buffer between voters and the government. Salter, *Boss Rule*, 21–5.

97. Writing in February 1882, Representative Roswell G. Horr of Michigan laboriously described the particularist requests made by his constituents:

> I think it is safe to say that each member of the House receives fifty letters each week; many receive more. . . . Growing out of these letters will be found during each week a large number of errands. . . . One-quarter of them will be from soldiers asking aid in their pension cases. . . . Another man writes to you to look up some matter in reference to a land patent. Another says his homestead claim should be looked after. . . . Another has a son or brother in the Regular Army whom he would like to have discharged. Another has a recreant son whom he would like to get into the Regular Army or Navy. Another wants you to drop into the Treasury and see about some claims of his. . . . Another has his boat tied up and he wants her released. Another would like you to go to the Post-Office Department and see if extra clerk hire cannot be allowed for his office. Another wants a new post-route established. . . . Another would like to have you call at the Navy Department and see if his boy cannot get into school at Annapolis or on some training ship.

Quoted in White, *Republican Era*, 72. Congressional inquiries to the Pension Bureau alone exceeded 40,000 in 1980, 90,000 in 1888 *and* 150,000 in 1891—over 500 each working day (75).

98. See Ostrogorski, *Democracy and the Organization of Political Parties*, 2:380; Jenks, "Money in Practical Politics"; Reynolds, "'Silent Dollar'"; and Jensen, *Winning of the Midwest*, 34–9.

99. Margaret Thompson, *The "Spider Web": Congress and Lobbying in the Age of Grant* (Ithaca, N.Y.: Cornell University Press, 1985); Bryce, *American Commonwealth*, 1:161, 520–4, 645–7; Gosnell, *Boss Platt*, 180; Robert D. Bowden, *Boies Penrose: Symbol of an Era* (New York: Greenberg, 1937); and William S. Vare, *My Forty Years in Politics* (Philadelphia: Roland Swain, 1933).

100. Robert K. Merton, "Manifest and Latent Functions: Toward the Codification of Functional Analysis in Sociology," in *Social Theory and Social Structure* (Glencoe, Ill.: Free Press, 1957), 19–84.

101. This constituent focus thus helps explain how late-nineteenth-century parties were able to mobilize all segments of the electorate, including poor, immigrant, *and* rural voters. See chapter 1.

102. Addams, "Why the Ward Boss Rules," 881.

103. Riordon, *Plunkitt of Tammany Hall*, 27–8.

104. Kleppner, "Partisanship and Ethnoreligious Conflict"; Burnham, "The United States: The Politics of Heterogeneity," in *Electoral Behavior: A Comparative Handbook*, ed. Richard Rose (New York: Free Press, 1974), 654.

105. J. Morgan Kousser, *The Shaping of Southern Politics: Suffrage Restriction and the Establishment of the One-Party South, 1880–1910* (New Haven, Conn.: Yale University Press, 1974), 11–46; Kleppner, "Partisanship and Ethnoreligious Conflict"; and *Third Electoral System*, 98–120; and Robert C. Kenzer, *Kinship and Neighborhood in a Southern Community: Orange County, North Carolina, 1849–1881* (Knoxville: University of Tennessee Press, 1987), 134–47.

106. Kleppner, *Third Electoral System*, 55–9, 173–6; and *Cross of Culture*, 65, 91; B. Campbell, *Representative Democracy*, 17–21; Jensen, *Winning of the Midwest*, 7.

107. James Edward Wright, *The Politics of Populism: Dissent in Colorado* (New Haven, Conn.: Yale University Press, 1974), 57; and Moses Rischin, *Promised Land*, 221.

108. Republicans used this tactic extensively in the nineties in the battle against Populists, whom they labeled "rebels;" Peter Argersinger, *Populism and Politics: William Alfred Peffer and the People's Party* (Lexington: University of Kentucky Press, 1974), 3, 14–5, 43–5, 89, 147, 304–5; and Lawrence Goodwyn, *The Populist Moment: A Short History of the Agrarian Revolt in America* (New York: Oxford, 1978), 131–2.

109. For illustrations of the sectional nature of the late-nineteenth-century party system, see Congressional Quarterly, *Guide to U.S. Elections* (Washington, D.C.: Congressional Quarterly, 1975), 237–41; and Kleppner, *Third Electoral System*, 45.

110. Jensen, *Winning of the Midwest*; and "The Religious and Occupational Roots of Party Identification: Illinois and Indiana in the 1870s," *Civil War History* 16 (December 1970): 325–43; Kleppner, *Cross of Culture*; and *Third Electoral System*; Robert W. Cherny, *Populism, Progressivism, and the Transformation of Nebraska Politics* (Lincoln: University of Nebraska Press, 1981); Roger E. Wyman, "Wisconsin Ethnic Groups and the Election of 1890," *Wisconsin Magazine of History* 51 (Summer 1968); and Allswang, *Bosses, Machines, and Urban Voters*.

111. Allan G. Bogue, Jerome M. Clubb, and William H. Flanigan, "The New Political History," *American Behavior Scientist* 21 (November/December 1988): 201–21; William G. Shade, "'New Political History': Some Statistical Questions Raised," *Social Science History* 5 (Spring 1981): 171–96; Walter Dean Burnham, "Quantitative History: Beyond the Correlation Coefficient: A Review Essay," *Historical Methods Newsletter* 4 (March 1971): 62–6; James E. Wright, "The Ethnocultural Model of Voting," *American Behavioral Scientist* 16 (May/June 1973):

35–56; Richard L. McCormick, "Ethnocultural Interpretations of American Voting Behavior," *Political Science Quarterly* 89 (June 1974): 351–77; J. Morgan Kousser, "The 'New Political History': A Methodological Critique," *Reviews in American History* 4 (March 1976): 1–14; Melvyn Hammarberg, *The Indiana Voter: The Historical Dynamics of Party Allegiance during the 1870s* (Chicago: University of Chicago Press, 1977), 108–12; Peter H. Argersinger, "Religious Politics and the Party System," review of *The Third Electoral System, 1853–1892: Parties, Voters, and Political Cultures,* by Paul Kleppner, *Reviews in American History* 7 (December 1979): 547–52; and Allan J. Lichtman, "Political Realignment and 'Ethnocultural' Voting in Late Nineteenth Century America," *Journal of Social History* 16 (Spring 1983): 55–82.

112. Jensen, "Religious and Occupational Roots," 333; and *Winning of the Midwest,* 89–121, 178–88; B. Campbell, "Did Democracy Work? Prohibition in Late Nineteenth-Century Iowa: A Test Case," *Journal of Interdisciplinary History* 8 (Summer 1977): 87–116; and Norman H. Clark, *Deliver Us from Evil: An Interpretation of American Prohibition* (New York: W. W. Norton, 1976).

113. Wyman, "Wisconsin Ethnic Groups"; Jensen, *Winning the Midwest,* 122–53; Samuel T. McSeveney, *Politics of Depression: Political Behavior in the Northeast, 1893–1896* (New York: Oxford University Press, 1972), 25; B. Campbell, *Representative Democracy,* 28, 62–3, 114–7; Kleppner, *Cross of Culture,* 158–79; and Robert J. Ulrich, *The Bennett Law of 1889: Education and Politics in Wisconsin* (New York: Arno Press, 1980); and Luebke, *Immigrants and Politics,* 146.

114. John F. Kasson, *Amusing the Million: Coney Island at the Turn of the Century* (New York: Hill and Wang, 1978), 11–7; Mandlebaum, *Boss Tweed's New York,* 73–4; McSeveney, *Politics of Depression,* 45–8, 57–62; Roy Rosenzweig, "Middle-Class Parks and Working-Class Play: The Struggle over Recreational Space in Worcester, Massachusetts, 1870–1910," *Radical History Review* 21 (Fall 1979): 31–48; and *Eight Hours for What We Will,* 127–52; and Terrence J. McDonald, "Putting Politics Back into the History of the American City," *American Quarterly* 34 (Summer 1982): 200–9.

115. Jensen, *Winning of the Midwest,* 59, 146; and "Religious and Occupational Roots," 328–31; Kleppner, *Cross of Culture,* 158–61; Wyman, "Wisconsin Ethnic Groups"; Luebke, *Immigrants and Politics,* 145–8; J. Baker, *Affairs of Party,* 273; Wright, *Politics of Populism,* 82.

116. Jensen, *Winning of the Midwest,* 15–6; Kleppner, *Third Electoral System,* 6–7; McSeveney, *Politics of Depression,* 18–9; Formisano, *Birth of Mass Political Parties,* 135; Luebke, *Immigrants and Politics,* 49–52; and McCormick, "Ethnocultural Interpretations."

117. Kleppner, *Cross of Culture,* 47–8, 112; and *Third Electoral System,* 153–8, 198–237; Jensen, *Winning the Midwest,* 146; and Luebke, *Immigrants and Politics,* 6, 39, 66, 71–116, 148–9.

118. Reynolds, *Testing Democracy,* 40–2.

119. Melvyn Hammarberg, "Indiana Farmers and the Group Basis of Late-Nineteenth-Century Political Parties," *Journal of American History* 61 (June 1974): 91–115; and *Indiana Voter;* Luebke, *Immigrants and Politics,* 63–4; and

Robert J. Kolesar, "Limits of Partisanship in Gilded Age Worcester: The Citizens Coalition," *Historical Journal of Massachusetts* 16 (January 1988): 94–106

120. Rosenzweig, *Eight Hours for What We Will*, 93–103, 127–52; Jensen, "Religious and Occupational Roots"; and *Winning of the Midwest*, 309–15; Hammarberg, *Indiana Voter*, 118–41, 177–8; B. Campbell, *Representative Democracy*, 21, 24; Roger Dewey Petersen, "The Reaction to a Heterogeneous Society: A Behavioral and Quantitative Analysis of Northern Voting Behavior, 1845–1870, Pennsylvania a Test Case" (Ph.D. disssertation, University of Pittsburgh, 1970), 182–211; and Luebke, *Immigrants and Politics*, 530–70, 117–21.

121. Samuel P. Hays, "History as Human Behavior," *Iowa Journal of History* 58 (July 1960): 196.

122. Kleppner, *Cross of Culture*, 35. See also Formisano, *Birth of Mass Political Parties*, 47, 55.

123. Kleppner, *Cross of Culture*, 22–34; Cherny, *Populism, Progressivism, and the Transformation of Nebraska Politics*, 18–20; and Albert C. Parker, "Empire Stalemate: Voting Behavior in New York State, 1860–1892" (Ph.D. dissertation, Washington University, 1975), 193–302.

124. Kleppner, *Who Voted?* 46; and "Partisanship and Ethnoreligious Conflict," 139; Silbey, *American Political Nation*, 174; and Pamela Johnston Conover, "The Influence of Group Identifications on Political Perceptions and Evaluations," *Journal of Politics* 46 (August 1984): 760–85.

125. B. Campbell, *Representative Democracy*, 25–6.

126. Jensen, "Armies, Admen, and Crusaders"; *Winning of the Midwest*, 1–21; and "Religious and Occupational Roots"; Marcus, *Grand Old Party*, ii; McCormick, "Ethnocultural Interpretations," 351–74; J. Baker, *Affairs of Party*; Geoffrey Blodgett, "A New Look at the American Gilded Age," *Historical Reflections* 6 (Winter 1974): 237.

127. We should not overemphasize the success that the parties had in nationalizing politics. At times Kleppner, Jensen, and other ethnocultural historians seem to describe politics in this period as a national battle between a pietist party and a liturgical party; Kleppner, *Third Electoral System*, 383; and "Partisanship and Ethnoreligious Conflict"; and Jensen, *Winning of the Midwest*, 3. For criticism of this approach, see McCormick, "Ethnocultural Interpretations"; and Bogue, Clubb, and Flanigan, "New Political History," 201–21.

128. Parties thus performed what Theodore J. Lowi has labeled "constituent functions. . . . Constituent means that which constitutes. . . . necessary in the formation of the whole, forming, composing, making an essential part"; "Party, Policy, and Constitution in America," in *The American Party Systems: Stages of Political Development*, ed. William Nisbet Chambers and Walter Dean Burnham, 2d ed. (New York: Oxford University Press, 1975), 238–76. See also Walter Dean Burnham, "Party Systems and the Political Process," in *The American Party Systems: Stages of Political Development*, ed. William Nisbet Chambers and Walter Dean Burnham, 2d ed. (New York: Oxford University Press, 1975).

129. Samuel Hays, "Society and Politics: Politics and Society," *Journal of Interdisciplinary History* 15 (Winter 1985): 254.

130. As quoted in Wright, *Politics of Populism*, 151.

131. The closest things to voter surveys of the late-nineteenth-century electorate were city and county directories. Jensen found nonpartisan directories that listed residents in several counties in Indiana and Illinois in the 1870s. Only two percent of the adult residents in these counties failed to name a party preference; Jensen, *Winning of the Midwest*, 6–7.

132. As quoted in Argersinger, *Populism and Politics*, 30–1.

133. Political scientists associated with the Survey Research Center at the University of Michigan developed this understanding of partisanship as an affective orientation; Angus Campbell, Philip E. Converse, Warren E. Miller, and Donald E. Stokes, *The American Voter* (New York: John Wiley and Sons, 1960); Philip E. Converse, *Elections and the Political Order* (New York: John Wiley and Sons, 1966); Philip E. Converse, "Of Time and Partisan Stability," *Comparative Political Studies* 2 (July 1969): 139–67; and *The Dynamics of Party Support: Cohort Analyzing Party Identification* (Beverly Hills, Calif.: Sage Publications, 1976); and Paul Allen Beck and M. Kent Jennings, "Pathways to Participation," *American Political Science Review* 76 (March 1982): 74–108.

134. Morris P. Fiorina, *Retrospective Voting in American National Elections* (New Haven, Conn.: Yale University Press, 1981), 102, x. See also Morris P. Fiorina, "An Outline for a Model of Party Choice," *American Journal of Political Science* 21 (August 1977): 601–25; and "Economic Retrospective Voting in American National Elections: A Micro-Analysis," *American Journal of Political Science* 22 (May 1978): 426–43.

135. Kleppner, *Continuity and Change*, 13.

NOTES TO CHAPTER 3

1. See Appendix 2 for a discussion of the measurement of electoral competitiveness and the properties of this index.

2. That represents a 55–45 vote in two-party elections. See Paul T. David, *Party Strength in the United States, 1872–1970* (Charlottesville: University Press of Virginia, 1972), 36–8.

3. Connecticut, 92.6; Delaware, 92.0; New Jersey, 93.4; New York, 94.9; Illinois, 94.1; Indiana, 98.5; Michigan, 91.2; Ohio, 96.8; Wisconsin, 90.7; Missouri, 91.5; Virginia, 90.5; North Carolina, 93.5; Kentucky, 90.3; Maryland, 91.8; Tennessee, 92.3; West Virginia, 95.8; California, 97.0; and Oregon, 90.0. In addition, three states rated over 88: Pennsylvania, 89.6; Iowa, 89.0; and Washington, 88.7.

4. Mark Stern, "Measuring Inter-Party Competition: A Proposal and a Test of a Method," *Journal of Politics* 39 (August 1972): 889–904.

5. Late-nineteenth-century politicians recognized the importance of these states in electing a president. See Robert D. Marcus, *Grand Old Party: Political Structure in the Gilded Age, 1880–1896* (New York: Oxford University Press, 1971), 94–6, 138–45, 190; H. Wayne Morgan, *From Hays to McKinley: National Political Parties, 1877–1896* (Syracuse, N.Y.: Syracuse University Press, 1969), 119–20, 231–4, 310–1; and Samuel T. McSeveney, *The Politics of Depression:*

Political Behavior in the Northeast, 1893–1896 (New York: Oxford University Press, 1972), 5–8.

6. In the north central states, for example, Richard Jensen finds extensive county-level competition; Jensen, *The Winning of the Midwest: Social and Political Conflict, 1888–1896* (Chicago: University of Chicago Press, 1971), 10–1. On the stable balance between the two parties in New York state, see Richard McCormick, *From Realignment to Reform: Political Change in New York State, 1893–1910* (Ithaca, N.Y.: Cornell University Press, 1981), 24–5.

7. Maryland had a score of 93.5 in one contest.

8. Connecticut, Delaware, Iowa, Minnesota, Nebraska, Tennessee, West Virginia, and California also had scores over 98.

9. Connecticut, New Hampshire, New Jersey, New York, Pennsylvania, Illinois, Indiana, Ohio, West Virginia, and California. Five other states—Massachusetts, Michigan, Wisconsin, Tennessee, and Oregon—averaged over 88. On congressional competitiveness, see James C. Garand and Donald A. Gross, "Changes in the Vote Margins for Congressional Candidates: A Specification of Historical Trends," *Journal of Politics* 46 (February 1984): 17–30. See also Melvyn Hammarberg, *The Indiana Voter: The Historical Dynamics of Party Allegiance during the 1870s* (Chicago: University of Chicago Press, 1977), 32.

10. Congressional Quarterly, *Guide to U.S. Elections* (Washington, D.C.: Congressional Quarterly, 1975), 798–842.

11. Deciding whether to credit votes for particular candidates to one of the major parties or to classify them as third-party votes was not always straightforward. See Appendix 2 for a discussion of this issue. In general, votes cast for all candidates running on any party label other than Democrat or Republican were classified as minor-party votes. (This includes Silver-Republicans and Gold-Democrats.) In 1896, however, votes cast for candidates on a Democratic-Populist fusion ticket were credited to the Democratic party.

12. Paul Kleppner, *The Cross of Culture: A Social Analysis of Midwestern Politics, 1850–1900* (New York: Free Press, 1970), 15; and *The Third Electoral System, 1853–1892: Parties, Voters, and Political Cultures* (Chapel Hill: University of North Carolina Press, 1979), 238–97; McSeveney, *Politics of Depression*, 20–4; and Ballard Campbell, *Representative Democracy: Public Policy and Midwestern Legislatures in the Late Nineteenth Century* (Cambridge, Mass.: Harvard University Press, 1980), 28.

13. J. Morgan Kousser, *The Shaping of Southern Politics: Suffrage Restriction and the Establishment of the One-Party South, 1880–1910* (New Haven, Conn.: Yale University Press, 1974), 11–44.

14. Peter H. Argersinger, "'Place on the Ballot': Fusion Politics and Antifusion Laws," *American Historical Review* 85 (April 1980): 287–306; and "Regulating Democracy: Election Laws and Dakota Politics, 1889–1902," *Midwest Review* 5 (Spring 1983): 1–19; John F. Reynolds, *Testing Democracy: Electoral Behavior and Progressive Reform in New Jersey, 1880–1920* (Chapel Hill: University of North Carolina Press, 1988), 45–6; Kousser, *Shaping of Southern Politics*; and James E. Wright, *The Politics of Populism: Dissent in Colorado* (New Haven, Conn.: Yale University Press, 1974), 149.

15. For discussion of the impact of ballot reform on third-party challenges and fusion strategies, see chapter 5.

16. Kleppner, *Third Electoral System*, 238–97.

17. This table understates the effect of third-party voting because the Democrats are credited with all the Democratic/Populist vote in 1896.

18. In the mid-Atlantic and north central regions, third-party candidates averaged over 5 percent of the presidential vote in only one state, Michigan. Minor parties had greater success in congressional and gubernatorial races, but even for these offices, they drew over 5 percent of the average vote only in Delaware, Michigan, and Wisconsin.

19. In all four of the border states, third parties averaged less than 4 percent of the presidential vote. Only in Tennessee did minor parties average over 5 percent of the vote in both congressional and gubernatorial elections.

20. Voter turnout in New England also fell considerably in 1896 because the late-nineteenth-century electoral system was already crumbling in these states. See chapter 4.

21. See table 3.2. Until the Populist revolt, the Nebraska Republicans had faced little statewide competition from the Democratic party; that state was one of the least competitive in the North. See Robert W. Cherny, *Populism, Progressivism, and the Transformation of Nebraska Politics* (Lincoln: University of Nebraska Press, 1981), 13–30, 53–73.

22. In presidential elections, competitiveness scores averaged 93.5 in North Carolina, 90.5 in Virginia from 1880 to 1896, and 88.6 in Florida from 1880 to 1888. Peak levels reached 99.9 in Virginia, 97 in North Carolina, and 94 in Florida. On electoral competition in these states, see Kousser, *Shaping of Southern Politics*, 91–103, 171–95.

23. Electoral competitiveness peaked at 90 in Louisiana and 85 in Arkansas. On electoral competition in Louisiana and Arkansas, see Kousser, *Shaping of Southern Politics*, 123–9, 152–65.

24. In the other seven states, opposition parties garnered over 40 percent of the vote in state elections in the eighties and nineties. See Kousser, *Shaping of Southern Politics*, 245–6.

25. Kousser concludes that opponents to the Democratic party challenged its dominance in the South and came close to succeeding in many states; Kousser, *Shaping of Southern Politics*, 27–9, 34–5. Voter turnout rose with the increase in political competition.

26. Congressional Quarterly, *Guide to U.S. Elections*, 461–86.

27. Margaret Thompson, *The "Spider Web": Congress and Lobbying in the Age of Grant* (Ithaca, N.Y.: Cornell University Press, 1985), 74–9; Nelson W. Polsby, "The Institutionalization of the House of Representatives," *American Political Science Review* 62 (March 1968): 144–68; H. Douglas Price, "The Congressional Career, Then and Now," in *Congressional Behavior*, ed. Nelson W. Polsby (New York: Random House, 1971), 14–27; and "Careers and Committees in the American Congress: The Problem of Structural Change," in *The History of Parliamentary Behavior*, ed. William O. Aydelotte (Princeton, N.J.: Princeton University Press, 1977), 31–40; David W. Brady, *Congressional Voting in a Partisan Era*

(Lawrence: University Press of Kansas, 1973), 150–1; and Morris P. Fiorina, David W. Rohde, and Peter Wissel, "Historical Change in House Turnover," in *Congress in Change: Evolution and Reform*, ed. Norman J. Ornstein (New York: Praeger, 1975), 24–57.

28. James Bryce, *The American Commonwealth*, 2 vols., 2d ed., rev. (London: MacMillan, 1892), 1:192.

29. B. Campbell, *Representative Democracy*, 31–2; Cherny, *Populism, Progressivism, and the Transformation of Nebraska Politics*, 30.

30. For example, in Indiana in 1888, the Republican party polled a majority of 5,378 votes in congressional races, but a Democratic districting plan concentrated those votes in three districts. The Democrats thereby won the remaining ten seats; Walter C. Hamm, "The Art of Gerrymandering," *Forum* 9 (July 1890): 544. See also Argersinger, "The Value of the Vote: Political Representation in the Gilded Age," *Journal of American History* 76 (June 1989): 66–72, 81.

31. Marcus, *Grand Old Party*, 135.

32. Kleppner, *Third Electoral System*, 32–40.

33. Congressional Quarterly, *Guide to U.S. Elections*, 818–21, 828–32.

34. McSeveney, *Politics of Depression*, 8–9; Kleppner, *Cross of Culture*, 15–9; and *Third Electoral System*, 32–43, 198–237.

35. Agrarian activism was at least partially responsible for the Democratic landslide in 1890 and its equally dramatic failure four years later.

36. It is not surprising that these correlations were of a smaller order. As indices of aggregate partisan instability, these variables are not very precise ways to measure mass partisanship.

37. The reductions in the magnitudes of the correlation coefficients ranged up to .15. The correlations between turnout and partisan stability were the most affected by the inclusion of the 1896 election. These correlations declined by as much as 40 percent.

38. Since both participation and electoral competition were consistently high, correlation analysis is not very effective in measuring the relationship between the two factors.

39. Although ticket splitting did not have a significant relationship to voter turnout in the North, party-vote instability, a measure of partisanship over time, did.

40. In 1880 and 1884 the correlations between party-vote instability, on the one hand, and turnout and competitiveness, on the other, were not strong enough to be statistically significant. In 1896 the correlation between party-vote instability and competitiveness was significant, but the correlation between party-vote instability and turnout was not.

41. The scholarship on political participation consistently highlights the impact of electoral competitiveness on voter turnout; Lester W. Milbraith, *Political Participation: How and Why Do People Get Involved in Politics?* (Chicago: Rand McNally, 1965), 96; Kevin V. Mulcahy and Richard S. Katz, *America Votes: What You Should Know about Elections Today* (Englewood Cliffs, N.J.: Prentice-Hall, 1976), 51–74; and William H. Flanigan, *Political Behavior of the American Electorate*, 2d ed. (Boston: Allyn and Bacon, 1972), 12, 34–5.

42. Competitiveness plays a central role in individual-choice theories of voter participation. See Jack Dennis, "Theories of Turnout: An Empirical Comparison of Alienationist and Rationalist Perspectives," in *Political Participation and American Democracy*, ed. William Crotty (New York: Greenwood Press, 1991), 33–6.

43. Martin Shefter persuasively argues that it is necessary to pay attention to forces on the "'supply side' as well as the 'demand' side of the electoral marketplace." Only under certain conditions do parties use their resources to mobilize mass support; Shefter, "Political Parties, Political Mobilization, and Political Demobilization," in *The Political Economy*, ed. Thomas Ferguson and Joel Rogers (Armonk, N.Y.: M. E. Sharpe, 1984), 140, 140–8.

44. Walter Dean Burnham, "The System of 1896: An Analysis," in *The Evolution of American Electoral Systems*, ed. Paul Kleppner (Westport, Conn.: Greenwood Press, 1981), 190.

45. Samuel Hays, *American Political History as Social Analysis: Essays* (Knoxville: University of Tennessee Press, 1980); Kousser, *Shaping of Southern Politics*; and "Restoring Politics to Political History," *Journal of Interdisciplinary History* 12 (Spring 1982): 569–95; McCormick, "The Party Period and Public Policy: An Exploratory Hypothesis," *Journal of American History* 66 (September 1979): 279–98; *From Realignment to Reform*; and "Political Parties in the United States: Reinterpreting Their Natural History," *History Teacher* 19 (November 1985): 15–31; and Martin Shefter, "Party, Bureaucracy, and Political Change in the United States," in *Political Parties: Development and Decay*, ed. Louis Maisel and Joseph Cooper (Beverly Hills, Calif.: Sage Publications, 1978): 211–4.

46. Joel Silbey, *The American Political Nation, 1838–1893* (Stanford, Calif.: Stanford University Press, 1991), 187; McCormick, "Party Period and Public Policy"; Skowronek, *Building a New American State: The Expansion of National Administrative Capacities, 1877–1920* (New York: Cambridge University Press, 1982), 125; Seymour Mandlebaum, *Boss Tweed's New York* (New York: John Wiley and Sons, 1965), 122; and Robert Wiebe, *The Search for Order, 1877–1920* (New York: Hill and Wang, 1967), 30–5.

47. Bryce, *American Commonwealth*, 2:3.

48. Michael Abram and Joseph Cooper, "The Rise of Seniority in the House of Representatives," *Polity* 1 (Fall 1968): 52–85; Polsby, "Institutionalization of the House of Representatives," 75–84; Nelson W. Polsby, Miriam Gallaher, and Barry Spencer Rundquist, "The Growth of the Seniority System in the House of Representatives," *American Political Science Review* 63 (September 1969): 787–807; Price, "Careers and Committees," 46–57; and David Brady and David Epstein, "Intra-Party Preferences, Heterogeneity, and the Origins of the Modern Congress: Progressive Reformers in the House and Senate, 1890–1920," presented to the Political Economy Seminar, Washington University, St. Louis, Missouri, November, 1989.

49. Woodrow Wilson, *Congressional Government: A Study in American Politics* (Cleveland: World Publishing, 1956), 212–3.

50. William G. Shade, Stanley D. Hooper, David Jacobson, and Stephen E. Moiles, "Partisanship in the United States Senate," *Journal of Interdisciplinary History* 4 (Autumn 1973): 198, 191–200; David J. Rothman, *Politics and Power:*

The United States Senate, 1869–1901 (Cambridge, Mass.: Harvard University Press, 1966); Jerome M. Clubb and Santa A. Traugott, "Partisan Cleavage and Cohesion in the House of Representatives, 1861–1974," *Journal of Interdisciplinary History* 7 (Winter 1977): 375–401; David W. Brady and Philip Althoff, "Party Voting in the U.S. House of Representatives, 1890–1910: Elements of a Responsible Party System," *Journal of Politics* 36 (August 1974): 753–75; and David W. Brady, Joseph Cooper, and Patricia A. Hurley, "The Decline of Party in the U.S. House of Representatives, 1887–1968," *Legal Studies Quarterly* 4 (August 1979): 384–5; Margaret Susan Thompson and Joel H. Silbey, "Research on 19th Century Legislatures," *Legislative Studies Quarterly* 9 (May 1984): 327–8, 332; and Silbey, *American Political Nation*, 188.

51. B. Campbell, *Representative Democracy*, 84–8, 194–204; Peter H. Argersinger, "Populist in Power: Public Policy and Legislative Behavior," *Journal of Interdisciplinary History* 28 (Summer 1987): 81–105.

52. Silbey, *American Political Nation*, 191.

53. Morgan, *From Hays to McKinley*, 121–37, 231–54, 320–32; Leonard D. White, *The Republican Era: A Study in Administrative History, 1869–1901* (New York: Macmillan, 1958), 6–8; Marcus, *Grand Old Party*, 28–9; and Skowronek, *Building a New American State*, 48–56.

54. M. Thompson, *"Spider Web."*

55. McCormick, "Party Period and Public Policy," 284; see also 280–95; and *From Realignment to Reform*, 2–22. See also Theodore J. Lowi, "American Business, Public Policy, Case Studies, and Political Theory," *World Politics* 16 (July 1964): 689–90; Samuel P. Hays, *The Response to Industrialism: 1885–1914* (Chicago: University of Chicago Press, 1957), 17–9; Harry N. Scheiber, "Government and the Economy: Studies of the 'Commonwealth' Policy in Nineteenth-Century America," *Journal of Interdisciplinary History* 3 (Summer 1972): 135–51; and "Federalism and the American Economic Order," *Law and Society Review* 10 (Fall 1975): 57–118; and Robert A. Lively, "The American System: A Review Article," *Business History Review* 29 (March 1955): 81–96. James Willard Hurst, *Law and the Conditions of Freedom in the Nineteenth-Century United States* (Madison: University of Wisconsin Press, 1956); Carter Goodrich, *Government Promotion of American Canals and Railroads, 1800–1890* (New York: Columbia University Press, 1960); and Gerald Nash, *State Government and Economic Development: A History of Administrative Policies in California, 1849–1933* (Berkeley: University of California Press, 1964); and Theda Skocpol, *Protecting Soldiers and Mothers: The Political Origins of Social Policy in the United States* (Cambridge, Mass.: Harvard University Press, 1992).

56. Morgan, *From Hays to McKinley*, 167; and McCormick, "Party Period and Public Policy," 284.

57. White, *Republican Era*, 70–92; M. Thompson, *"Spider Web"*; Skocpol, *Protecting Mothers and Soldiers*.

58. Skowronek, *Building a New American State*, 22–9; both contemporary reformers and later historians have castigated Gilded Age party government for precisely this reason; Richard Hofstadter, *The American Political Tradition and the Men Who Made It* (New York: Random House, 1948), 164–86; Matthew Joseph-

son, *The Politicos, 1865–1896* (New York: Harcourt, Brace, and World, 1963); and Wiebe, *Search for Order,* 5–6.

59. Scheiber, "Federalism and the American Economic Order," 63–4; and Silbey, *American Political Nation,* 179.

60. Scheiber, "Federalism and the American Economic Order," 110–1; and Nash, *State Government and Economic Development.*

61. B. Campbell, *Representative Democracy,* 151–2.

62. Wright, *The Politics of Populism,* 85–92. Other state legislatures were equally concerned with parochial matters. For example, in Pennsylvania from 1867 to 1875, 50 to 86 general bills were passed each year as compared with 1,099 to 1,478 private bills; John D. Stewart, "Philadelphia Politics in the Gilded Age" (Ph.D. dissertation, St. Johns University, 1973), 97.

63. McCormick, "Party Period and Public Policy," 288.

64. McCormick, *From Realignment to Reform,* 69, 145; James A. Kehl, *Boss Rule in the Gilded Age: Matt Quay of Pennsylvania* (Pittsburgh: University of Pittsburgh Press, 1981); and Harold F. Gosnell, *Boss Platt and His New York Machine* (Chicago: University of Chicago Press, 1937).

65. McCormick, "Party Period and Public Policy," 288.

66. Mandlebaum, *Boss Tweed's New York,* 122.

67. McCormick, "Party Period and Public Policy," 290.

68. Geoffrey Blodgett, "A New Look at the American Gilded Age," *Historical Reflections* 6 (Winter 1974): 139; and David M. Potter, *People of Plenty: Economic Abundance and the American Character* (Chicago: University of Chicago Press, 1954), 123–5.

69. Morton Keller, *Affairs of State: Public Life in Late Nineteenth Century America* (Cambridge, Mass.: Harvard University Press, 1977), 410–1.

70. Skowronek, *Building a New American State,* 121–62; Keller, *Affairs of State,* 171–81, 409–38; McCormick, *From Realignment to Reform,* 22–7; Naomi Lamoreaux, "Regulatory Agencies," in *Encyclopedia of American Political History,* ed. Jack P. Greene (New York: Charles Scribner and Sons, 1984), 1113–4; Mandlebaum, *Boss Tweed's New York,* 141–53; and Nash, *State Government and Economic Development,* 159–75.

71. Keller, *Affairs of State,* 422; McCormick, *From Realignment to Reform,* 22; and "Party Period and Public Policy," 284.

72. My account follows Skowronek, *Building a New American State,* 138–50.

73. Keller, *Affairs of State,* 178–81; and Thomas K. McCraw, "Regulation in America: A Review Article," *Business History Review* 49 (Summer 1975): 161.

74. See Wright, *Politics of Populism,* 69, 96, 99; and Nash, *State Government and Economic Development,* 159–64.

75. Wright, *Politics of Populism,* 96–7. See also Nash, *State Government and Economic Development,* 164–75; and Mandlebaum, *Boss Tweed's New York,* 149–50.

76. Keller, *Affairs of State,* 425; and Scheiber, "Federalism and the American Economic Order," 110.

77. As quoted in Skowronek, *Building a New American State,* 138–9. See also McCraw, "Regulation in America," 166–8.

78. Skowronek, *Building a New American State,* 149.

79. Ibid., 121, 130; Albro Martin, "The Troubled Subject of Railroad Regulation in the Gilded Age—A Reappraisal," *Journal of American History* 61 (September 1974): 325–71.

80. Blodgett, "New Look at the American Gilded Age," 139; and Potter, *People of Plenty*, 123–5.

81. Richard Oestreicher, "Urban Working-Class Political Behavior and Theories of American Electoral Politics, 1870–1940," *Journal of American History* 74 (March 1988): 1272; and Martin Shefter, "Trade Unions and Political Machines: The Organization and Disorganization of the American Working Class in the Late Nineteenth Century," in *Working Class Formation: Nineteenth Century Patterns in Western Europe and the United States*, ed. Ira Katznelson and Aristide Zolberg (Princeton, N.J.: Princeton University Press, 1986), 267–71.

82. Herbert Gutman, *Work, Culture, and Society in Industrializing America: Essays in American Working-Class and Social History* (New York: Random House, 1977), 234–92; and "The Workers' Search for Power: Labor in the Gilded Age," in *The Gilded Age*, ed. H. Wayne Morgan, rev. and enlarged ed. (Syracuse, N.Y.: Syracuse University Press, 1970), 31–54; and Shefter, "Trade Unions and Political Machines," 211, 238–42.

83. Leon Fink, *Workingmen's Democracy: The Knights of Labor and American Politics* (Urbana: University of Illinois Press, 1983); Alan Dawley and Paul Faler, "Working-Class Culture and Politics in the Industrial Revolution: Sources of Loyalism and Rebellion," *Journal of Social History* 9 (Summer 1976): 466–80; and Shefter, "Trade Unions and Political Machines," 222–30.

84. Oestreicher, "Urban Working-Class Political Behavior," 1272; and Fink, *Workingmen's Democracy*, 226.

85. This led the opponents of party politics to try to remove large areas of policy formation from the realm of partisan politics. See chapter 6.

86. Jensen, *Winning of the Midwest*, 122–61, 178–208, 291–308; Kleppner, *Cross of Culture*, 161–8, 347–51, 366–8; and *Third Electoral System*, 303–56; McSeveney, *Politics of Depression*, 25; and Ballard C. Campbell, "Did Democracy Work? Prohibition in Late Nineteenth-Century Iowa: A Test Case," *Journal of Interdisciplinary History* 8 (Summer 1977), 89, 94, 108–16.

87. Keller, *Affairs of State*, 298.

88. Marcus, *Grand Old Party*, 74.

89. Skowronek, *Building a New American State*, 8, 45–84. See also Wallace Farnham, "'The Weakened Springs of Government': A Study in Nineteenth-Century American History," *American Historical Review* 68 (April 1963): 677, 664–9; Nash, *State Government and Economic Development*, 164, 175, 178, 187; Blodgett, "New Look at the American Gilded Age," 240–1; McCormick, "Party Period and Public Policy," 284; and "Political Parties in the United States," 22; Shefter, "Party, Bureaucracy, and Political Change."

90. McCormick, "Political Parties in the United States," 28.

91. McCormick, *From Realignment to Reform*; Martin J. Schiesl, *The Politics of Efficiency: Municipal Administration and Reform in America, 1880–1920* (Berkeley: University of California Press, 1977); Mandlebaum, *Boss Tweed's New York*, 141–68; Blodgett, "New Look at the American Gilded Age," 241–4; and *The*

Gentle Reformers: Massachusetts Democrats in the Cleveland Era (Cambridge: Harvard University Press, 1966); Lee Benson, *Merchants, Farmers and Railroads: Railroad Regulation and New York Politics, 1850–1887* (Cambridge, Mass.: Harvard University Press, 1955); and Skowronek, *Building a New American State*, 1–163.

92. John D. Hicks, *The Populist Revolt: A History of the Farmer's Alliance and the People's Party* (Lincoln: University of Nebraska Press, 1931); Norman Pollack, *The Populist Response to Industrial America* (Cambridge, Mass.: Harvard University Press, 1962); Robert C. McMath, Jr., *Populist Vanguard: A History of the Southern Farmers' Alliance* (Chapel Hill: University of North Carolina Press, 1975); Goodwyn, *Democratic Promise: The Populist Moment in America* (New York: Oxford University Press, 1976); Wright, *Politics of Populism*; and Steven Hahn, *The Roots of Southern Populism: Yeoman Farmers and the Transformation of the Georgia Upcountry, 1850–1890* (New York: Oxford University Press, 1983).

93. See chapter 5. Samuel Hays, "The Politics of Reform in Municipal Government in the Progressive Era," *Pacific Northwest Quarterly* 55 (October 1964): 157–69; and Michael McGerr, *The Decline of Popular Politics: The American North, 1865–1928* (New York: Oxford University Press, 1986); Clinton R. Woodruff, "The Municipal League of Philadelphia," *American Journal of Sociology* 11 (September 1905): 336–58; E. V. Smalley, "The Philadelphia Committee of 100," *Century Magazine*, July 1883, 395–9; Joseph Lincoln Steffens, "Philadelphia: Corrupt and Contented," *McClure's Magazine*, July 1903, 249–63; and Bonnie R. Fox, "The Philadelphia Progressives: A Test of the Hofstadter-Hays Thesis," *Pennsylvania History* 34 (October 1967): 372–94.

94. Mandlebaum, *Boss Tweed's New York*; Shefter, "The Electoral Foundation of the Political Machine," in *The History of American Electoral Behavior*, ed. Joel H. Silbey, Allan G. Bogue, and William H. Flanigan (Princeton, N.J.: Princeton University Press, 1978), 263–98; and "Emergence of the Political Machine: An Alternative View," in *Theoretical Perspectives on Urban Politics*, ed. Willis D. Hawley and Michael Lipsky (Englewood Cliffs, N.J.: Prentice-Hall, 1976), 14–44; McCormick, *From Realignment to Reform*, 263–98; and Leo Hershkowitz, *Tweed's New York: Another Look* (Garden City, N.J.: Anchor Books, 1978).

95. See chapter 6.

NOTES TO CHAPTER 4

1. Presidential turnout in 1900 was 94.7 percent in Indiana, 91.0 percent in Wisconsin, and 91.4 percent in West Virginia. See table 1.2 for late-nineteenth-century peak turnout levels.

2. See figures 4.1 to 4.8.

3. John J. Stucker, "The Impact of Women's Suffrage on Patterns of Voter Participation in the U.S.: Quasi-Experimental and Real-Time Analysis, 1890–1920" (Ph.D. dissertation, University of Michigan, 1973), 51–4, 161–3; Richard Carlson, "The Effects of Voter Registration Systems on Presidential Turnout in Non-Southern States: 1912–1924" (Ph.D. dissertation, University of Illinois at Urbana-Champaign, 1976): 19.

4. In New England as well, turnout declined gradually from late-nineteenth-century peaks, but the falloff in this region occurred earlier. See figure 4.1.

5. The simple regression equation is $Y = BX + A$, where Y = turnout and X = time. B, the regression coefficient, is the slope of the regression line and indicates the expected change in turnout for each one-unit change in time (one year). R^2 is the amount of variation in turnout explained by the passage of time, and F is a measure of the statistical significance of the relationship between the two variables.

6. These steep downward slopes contrast vividly with the period 1880 to 1896, when only the South experienced a significant trend in voter participation. The consistency is a reflection of the fact that mass participation had been relatively stable in most of the country during the late nineteenth century.

7. The R^2 for the north central region was also strong. In other regions, the R^2 was weak, indicating that cross-state differences explain more of the variation in turnout than change over time.

8. The slopes were obtained with regression analysis using the same regression equation described above.

9. Indiana, Ohio, Wisconsin, and Michigan.

10. The falloff in Illinois was magnified by the enfranchisement of women for the 1916 presidential election. By 1912, however, turnout in the state had already fallen 21.3 percent. From 1896 to 1916, voting declined 18 percent in Ohio, 22.3 percent in Michigan, and 25.3 percent in Wisconsin.

11. None of these states exhibited secular trends in turnout during the 1880s and 1890s, although turnout had increased slightly in each from 1880 to 1896.

12. Iowa, Kansas, Minnesota, Nebraska, South Dakota, Maryland, Tennessee, West Virginia, Colorado, Utah, California, Oregon, and Washington each experienced significant secular declines in voter participation.

13. Likewise, although some of the sparsely settled mountain states displayed anomalous patterns, turnout fell off in most of these states after 1900.

14. Iowa, Kansas, Minnesota, and South Dakota all experienced declines of close to or over 1 percent per year, as did Maryland and Kentucky in the border region and California and Washington in the West.

15. In Maine, New Hampshire, Vermont, and New York, the slopes of these declines were significant.

16. Compare figures 4.1 and 4.2 with figures 4.3 and 4.4.

17. Only two New England states, Connecticut and Massachusetts, had significant downward trends in turnout during the early twentieth century, and these slopes were mild. On the other hand, New Jersey, New York, and Pennsylvania all experienced significant secular declines. In New York the early-twentieth-century decline was .8 percent per year, whereas in New Jersey and Pennsylvania turnout fell at an annual rate of 1 percent.

18. From 1880 to 1916 turnout declined by over 25 percent in nine of the ten southern states. The decline in Arkansas was 20.3 percent. See table 4.5.

19. Six of the ten states—Alabama, Louisiana, North Carolina, South Carolina, Texas, and Virginia—experienced significant downward secular trends in voting in this period.

20. For similar views, see Walter Dean Burnham, "Rejoinder to 'Comments' by Philip Converse and Jerrold Rusk," *American Political Science Review* 68 (September 1974): 1055; and "The System of 1896: An Analysis," in *The Evolution of American Electoral Systems*, ed. Paul Kleppner (Westport, Conn.: Greenwood Press, 1981), 190; J. Morgan Kousser, *The Shaping of Southern Politics: Suffrage Restriction and the Establishment of the One-Party South, 1880–1910* (New Haven, Conn.: Yale University Press, 1974), 45; and Paul Kleppner, *Who Voted? The Dynamics of Electoral Turnout, 1870–1980* (New York: Praeger, 1982), 66.

21. Stein Rokkan and Jean Meyriat, *International Guide to Electoral Statistics* (The Hague: Mouton, 1969); Thomas T. Mackie and Richard Rose, *The International Almanac of Electoral History* (New York: Free Press, 1974).

22. Congressional Quarterly, *Guide to U.S. Elections* (Washington, D.C.: Congressional Quarterly, 1975), 320.

23. See chapter 1 for a discussion of the concept of a core electorate.

24. Walter Dean Burnham, "The Changing Shape of the American Political Universe," *American Political Science Review* 59 (March 1965): 7–28.

25. In contrast, no region exhibited a significant trend in off-year participation during the 1880s and 1890s.

26. In constructing figures 4.8 through 4.13, I used mean off-year congressional turnout to represent the size of the core electorate, and the difference between mean presidential turnout and mean off-year congressional turnout to estimate the size of the marginal electorate. The proportion of eligible voters who did not cast ballots in presidential elections was assumed to be nonvoters. This three-way division is in effect an aggregate measure of the composition of the electorate. As with all aggregate measures, individual-level behavior cannot be directly inferred from these figures. Nonetheless, partitioning the electorate in this way is a valuable heuristic tool that enables us to visualize clearly the full extent of the post-1896 transformation of the mass electorate.

27. Using regression analysis of county-level presidential turnout, Kleppner estimates that the composition of the northern electorate was 67.7 percent core voters, 16.2 percent marginal voters, and 15.6 percent nonvoters from 1876 to 1890 and 61.7 percent core voters, 16.8 percent marginal voters, and 21.4 percent nonvoters from 1900 to 1916. In the South he estimates that 46.7 percent of the late-nineteenth-century electorate were core voters, 22.7 percent were marginal voters, and 30.4 percent were nonvoters, whereas the composition of the early-twentieth-century southern electorate was 23.5 percent core voters, 9.3 percent marginal voters, and 67 percent nonvoters; Kleppner, *Who Voted?* 24.

28. Philip E. Converse, "Change in the American Electorate," in *The Human Meaning of Change*, ed. Angus Campbell and Philip E. Converse (New York: Russell Sage Foundation, 1972), 263–337; and Jerrold Rusk, "Comment: The American Electoral Universe: Speculation and Evidence," *American Political Science Review* 68 (September 1974): 1028–49.

29. See table 1.4.

30. Mean roll-off in New England was actually negative for this period, indicating that fewer people cast votes for presidential candidates than for congressional or gubernatorial candidates on the same ballot.

31. Jerrold Rusk, "The Effect of the Australian Ballot Reform on Split-Ticket Voting: 1876–1908" (Ph.D. dissertation, University of Michigan, 1968), 188.

32. Some states gave voters the option of voting for all of a party's candidates with one check-off.

33. Drop-off is a measure of the percentage of active voters who are core voters, whereas off-year turnout figures reveal the percentage of the electorate who are core voters. See Appendix 2.

34. This change in the composition of the voting electorate was not as simple or straightforward as the change in the size of the active electorate. Regression analysis of drop-off figures reveals that only the mid-Atlantic states experienced a significant trend toward increasing drop-off after 1896 ($B = .5$). During the 1880s and 1890s, drop-off decreased significantly in both the north central and midwestern regions, and this trend ended after 1896. In neither of these regions was there a significant trend in drop-off from 1898 to 1918. There is no reason to expect, however, that the increase in the proportion of marginal voters would be linear. As the size of the voting electorate was contracting, the level of voter participation in particular contests fluctuated according to idiosyncratic circumstances.

35. Jerrold Rusk and John Stucker, "Legal-Institutional Factors in American Voting" (unpublished paper, revised June 1975), 22a; and U.S. Department of Commerce, Bureau of the Census, "Voter Participation in Presidential Elections: 1824–1968" (Series Y 27–28), in *Historical Statistics of the United States: Colonial Times to 1970*, part 2 (1975), 1068.

36. See Appendix 1 on measuring turnout.

37. Stucker, "Impact of Women's Suffrage." See also Rusk and Stucker, "Legal-Institutional Factors in American Voting"; Richard John Carlson, "Effects of Voter Registration Systems," 19.

38. Ecological regression analysis cannot be used effectively to determine the relative participation rates of men and women, since the gender composition of county electorates does not vary significantly; Stucker, "Impact of Women's Suffrage," 86–127.

39. For example, we can control for women's suffrage while conducting regression analysis on turnout over time. The results indicate that turnout from 1880 to 1916 was depressed by 10.1 percent in northern states that enfranchised women. (Because of the low turnout levels in the South, where women could not vote, regression analysis of the entire nation showed no effect for women's suffrage.) These results are very similar to Stucker's but are of questionable value. Since almost the only states to enact women's suffrage before 1920 were mountain and western states, the effect of women's suffrage on turnout is confounded by regional differences.

40. See chapter 1.

41. Paul Kleppner, "Were Women to Blame? Female Suffrage and Voter Turnout," *Journal of Interdisciplinary History* 12 (Spring 1982): 637.

42. Not surprisingly, this cohort of women thus participated at lower rates for their entire political lives; Glenn Firebaugh and Kevin Chen, "Voter Turnout

of Nineteenth Amendment Women: The Enduring Effect of Disenfranchisement," *American Journal of Sociology* 100 (January 1995): 972–96.

43. Kousser, *Shaping of Southern Politics*, 14–5, 224–6; Kleppner, *Who Voted?* 65.

44. Kousser, *Shaping of Southern Politics*, 26. See also Kleppner, *Who Voted?* 65.

45. Kousser, *Shaping of Southern Politics*, 237, 229–36. See also Kleppner, *Who Voted?* 66.

46. See table 4.2.

47. Kleppner, *Who Voted?* 64.

48. Angus Campbell, Philip E. Converse, Warren E. Miller, and Donald E. Stokes, *The American Voter* (New York: John Wiley and Sons, 1960), 184–210; Lester W. Milbraith, *Political Participation: How and Why Do People Get Involved in Politics?* (Chicago: Rand McNally, 1965), 114–28; Sidney Verba and Norman H. Nie, *Participation in America: Political Democracy and Social Equality* (New York: Harper and Row, 1972), 125–37; Robert R. Alford and Roger Friedland, "Political Participation and Public Policy," *Annual Review of Sociology*, vol. 1, ed. Alex Inkeles (Palo Alto: Annual Review, 1975); Kevin V. Mulcahy and Richard S. Katz, *America Votes: What You Should Know about Elections Today* (Englewood Cliffs, N.J.: Prentice-Hall, 1976); William H. Flanigan, *Political Behavior of the American Electorate*, 2d ed. (Boston: Allyn and Bacon, 1972), 22; and Arend Lijphart, "Unequal Participation: Democracy's Unresolved Dilemma," *American Political Science Review* 91 (March 1997): 1–14.

49. John F. Reynolds, *Testing Democracy: Electoral Behavior and Progressive Reform in New Jersey, 1880–1920* (Chapel Hill: University of North Carolina Press, 1988), 179. In a landmark study of nonvoting in the 1923 mayoral race in Chicago, Charles S. Merriam and Harold F. Gosnell also find especially low turnout in black wards; Merriam and Gosnell, *Non-Voting: Causes and Methods of Control* (Chicago: University of Chicago Press, 1924), 25–6.

50. Alien suffrage was repealed in Michigan (1894), Minnesota (1896), North Dakota (1898), Colorado (1902), Wisconsin (1910), Oregon (1914), Nebraska (1918), South Dakota (1918), and Kansas (1918). Texas and Missouri followed suit in 1920 and Indiana in 1922; in 1925 Arkansas became the last state to enact a citizenship requirement for voter eligibility. Rusk and Stucker, "Legal-Institutional Factors in American Voting," 19–20a; U.S. Department of Commerce, Bureau of the Census, "Voter Participation in Presidential Elections," 1068.

51. Kleppner, *Who Voted?* 64.

52. Reynolds, *Testing Democracy*, 179.

53. Ibid., 149.

54. Gary W. Cox and J. Morgan Kousser, "Turnout and Rural Corruption: New York as a Test Case," *American Journal of Political Science* 25 (November 1981): 652; Richard McCormick, *From Realignment to Reform: Political Change in New York State, 1893–1910* (Ithaca, N.Y.: Cornell University Press, 1981), 2–22.

55. Reynolds, *Testing Democracy*, 112, 149–50, 193; and Burnham, "Changing Shape of the American Political Universe," 15.

56. Kleppner's *Who Voted?* is an important first step in this direction.

57. For example, though there is abundant evidence that immigrants generally voted at lower rates than native-stock voters, this apparently was not the case

in Chicago, where the Democratic party remained a powerful political organization capable of mobilizing immigrant voters; see Merriam and Gosnell, *Non-Voting*, 25–6. See chapter 5 for a discussion of the relationship between party organization and electoral demobilization.

58. Michael Avey, *The Demobilization of American Voters: A Comprehensive Theory of Voter Turnout* (New York: Greenwood Press, 1989), 13; and William R. Shaffer, *Computer Simulations of Voting Behavior* (New York: Oxford Univeristy Press, 1972), 36.

59. Kleppner, *Who Voted?* 63–70; and Reynolds, *Testing Democracy*, 148–53.

60. Not all the new additions to the eligible voter pool in the early twentieth century were young voters. Immigrants gained the right to vote as they were naturalized. However, the same forces that militated against the mobilization of young voters affected newly naturalized voters as well.

61. Walter Dean Burnham, "Theory and Voting Research," *American Political Science Review* 68 (November 1974): 1012. Paul Kleppner and Stephen Baker pursue this idea in "The Impact of Voter Registration Requirements on Electoral Turnout," *Journal of Political and Military Sociology* 8 (Fall 1980): 218–20.

62. Kleppner, *Who Voted?* 66–8; and Kleppner and S. Baker, "Impact of Voter Registration," presented to the annual meeting of the American Political Science Association, September 1969, 53–4.

63. Turnout of voters aged twenty to thirty was 59.1 percent; thirty to forty, 64 percent; forty to fifty, 64.9 percent; fifty to sixty, 69.8 percent; sixty to seventy, 81.2 percent; and seventy and older, 56.5 percent; Ben A. Arneson, "Non-Voting in a Typical Ohio Community," *American Political Science* Review 19 (November 1925): 818.

64. Merriam and Gosnell, *Non-Voting*.

65. Ibid., x, 30.

66. In contrast, the generation of voters who came of age in the 1930s was far more fully mobilized; Kleppner, *Who Voted?* Kristi Anderson, "Generation, Partisan Shift, and Realignment: A Glance Back at the New Deal," in *The Changing American Voter*, ed. Norman H. Nie, Sidney Verba, and John R. Petrocik (Cambridge, Mass.: Harvard University Press, 1976), 74–95.

67. A. Campbell, Converse, Miller, and Stokes, *American Voter*, 261–5; and Raymond E. Wolfinger and Steven J. Rosenstone, *Who Votes?* (New Haven, Conn.: Yale University Press, 1980), 37–60.

68. H. S. Gilbertson, "Elements of the County Problem," *Annals of the American Academy of Political and Social Science* 47 (May 1913): 10. For details on the movement to reduce the number of elected offices, see Richard S. Childs, *Short-Ballot Principles* (Boston: Houghton and Mifflin, 1911); and *Civic Victories: The Story of an Unfinished Revolution* (New York: Harper and Row, 1952), 83–92; and John Porter East, *Council-Manager Government: The Political Thought of Its Founder Richard S. Childs* (Chapel Hill: University of North Carolina Press, 1965), 43–55.

69. See chapter 5.

70. Michael McGerr, *The Decline of Popular Politics: The American North, 1865–1928* (New York: Oxford University Press, 1986), 145–51.

71. McGerr, *Decline of Popular Politics*, 146. On primary legislation, see chapter 5.

72. McGerr, *Decline of Popular Politics*, 146–7.

73. Ibid., 146; Paula Baker, "The Domestication of Politics: Women and American Political Society," *American Historical Review* 89 (June 1984): 639; and Reynolds, *Testing Democracy*, 108, 114.

74. Richard Jensen, "Armies, Admen, and Crusaders: Types of Presidential Campaigns," *History Teacher* 2 (January 1969); and *The Winning of the Midwest: Social and Political Conflict, 1888–1896* (Chicago: University of Chicago Press, 1971), 165–77; McGerr, *Decline of Popular Politics*, 138–83; Reynolds, *Testing Democracy*, 95; and Robert B. Westbrook, "Politics as Consumption: Managing the Modern American Election," in *The Culture of Consumption: Critical Essays in American History*, ed. Richard Wrightman Fox and T. J. Jackson Lears (New York: Pantheon Books, 1983), 143–74.

75. As quoted in McGerr, *Decline of Popular Politics*, 184–5. See also Reynolds, *Testing Democracy*, 108, 114–6.

76. Reynolds, *Testing Democracy*, 114–6.

77. Robert S. Lynd and Helen Merrell Lynd, *Middletown* (New York: Harcourt, Brace, and World, 1956), 416.

78. Ibid., 417; Lewis Atherton, *Main Street on the Middle Border* (Bloomington: Indiana University Press, 1954), 306–7.

79. Merriam and Gosnell, *Non-Voting*, 33.

80. William E. Dugan and William A. Taggart, "The Changing Shape of the American Political Universe Revisited," *Journal of Politics* 57 (May 1995): 469–82.

81. The historical literature on the social changes that America underwent from 1890 to 1916 is vast. I rely most heavily on works by Robert Wiebe, especially *The Search for Order, 1877–1920* (New York: Hill and Wang, 1967) and *The Segmented Society: An Introduction to the Meaning of America* (New York: Oxford University Press, 1975); and Samuel Hays, especially in *American Political History as Social Analysis: Essays* (Knoxville: University of Tennessee Press, 1980).

82. Robert D. Marcus, *Grand Old Party: Political Structure in the Gilded Age, 1880–1896* (New York: Oxford University Press, 1971), 254–5; McGerr, *Decline of Popular Politics*, 148–9; Reynolds, *Testing Democracy*, 117; and Jensen, "Armies, Admen, and Crusaders," 45.

83. John Higham, "The Reorientation of American Culture in the 1890s," in *Writing American History: Essays on Modern Scholarship* (Bloomington: Indiana University Press, 1970), 74–102; Gunther Barth, *City People: The Rise of Modern City Culture in Nineteenth-Century America* (New York: Oxford University Press, 1980); John F. Kasson, *Amusing the Million: Coney Island at the Turn of the Century* (New York: Hill and Wang, 1978); Lynd and Lynd, *Middletown*, 485; Alan Trachtenberg, *The Incorporation of America: Culture and Society in the Gilded Age* (New York: Hill and Wang, 1982), 123.

84. McGerr, *Decline of Popular Politics*, 107–37; Jensen, "Armies, Admen, and Crusaders," 44; and Marcus, *Grand Old Party*, 254–5.

85. McGerr, *Decline of Popular Politics*, 125–30; and Barth, *City People*, 79–88, 105–6.

86. P. Baker, "Domestication of Politics," 639; and *The Moral Framework of Public Life: Gender, Politics, and the State in Rural New York, 1870–1930* (New York: Oxford University Press, 1991), xvi.

87. Gerson Harry Smoger, "Organizing Political Campaigns: A Survey of Nineteenth and Twentieth Century Trends" (Ph.D. dissertation, University of Pennsylvania, 1982), 207.

88. Atherton, *Main Street*, 290–3; Barth, *City People*, 164–91.

89. Kleppner, *Who Voted?* 80; see also *The Cross of Culture: A Social Analysis of Midwestern Politics, 1850–1900* (New York: Free Press, 1970), 316–75; and *The Third Electoral System, 1853–1892: Parties, Voters, and Political Cultures* (Chapel Hill: University of North Carolina Press, 1979), 357–82.

90. Kleppner, *Who Voted?* 79–80; and Paul Kleppner, *Continuity and Change in Electoral Politics, 1893–1928* (New York: Greenwood, 1987), 183–213. For a criticism of Kleppner's analysis, see J. Morgan Kousser, "Review Essay: Voters, Absent and Present," *Social Science History* 9 (Spring 1985): 215–26.

91. Kleppner, in my view, describes this process much too narrowly.

92. See chapter 6 for a discussion of the shift from electoral to interest-group politics.

93. Wiebe, *Search for Order*, 129.

94. Samuel Hays, "Society and Politics: Politics and Society," *Journal of Interdisciplinary History* 15 (Winter 1985): 261; and P. Baker, "Domestication of Politics," 639.

95. McGerr, *Decline of Popular Politics*, 149; and Paula Baker, "The Culture of Politics in the Late Nineteenth Century: Community and Political Behavior in Rural New York," *Journal of Social History* 18 (Winter 1984): 182.

NOTES TO CHAPTER 5

1. See chapter 6.

2. Some scholars of voting behavior emphasize only the partisan stability of the period; see Jerome M. Clubb, William J. Flanigan, and Nancy H. Zingale, *Partisan Realignment: Voters, Parties, and Government in American History* (Beverly Hills: Sage, 1980). On the other hand, scholars who stress the breakdown of partisan loyalty in these decades frequently overstate their case; see for example Walter Dean Burnham, "The Changing Shape of the American Political Universe," *American Political Science Review* 59 (March 1965): 7–28; Paul Kleppner, "Critical Realignments and Electoral Systems," in *The Evolution of American Electoral Systems*, ed. Paul Kleppner (Westport, Conn.: Greenwood Press, 1981), 3–32; and John F. Reynolds, *Testing Democracy: Electoral Behavior and Progressive Reform in New Jersey, 1880–1920* (Chapel Hill: University of North Carolina Press, 1988), 97–105. The key here is to recognize the emergence of new patterns while explaining the persistence of old ones.

3. Twentieth-century survey research shows that partisan voters are ex-

tremely slow to defect to the opposing party; Angus Campbell, Philip E. Converse, Warren E. Miller, and Donald E. Stokes, *The American Voter* (New York: John Wiley and Sons, 1960), 86–7, 93–6.

4. William G. Shade, Stanley D. Hooper, David Jacobson, and Stephen E. Moiles, "Partisanship in the United States Senate," *Journal of Interdisciplinary History* 4 (Autumn 1973): 204.

5. This time lag is a key to understanding mass political behavior in the early twentieth century. For example, writing about post-1896 shifts in partisan alignments, Kleppner concludes that "new patterns emerge slowly, almost incrementally, because it is not primarily the behavior of habituated partisans that are affected but that of new cohorts of coming-of-age voters." Paul Kleppner, *Who Voted? The Dynamics of Electoral Turnout, 1870–1980* (New York: Praeger, 1982), 76.

6. For similar findings, see Burnham, "Changing Shape of the American Political Universe"; and "Communications to the Editor," *American Political Science Review* 65 (December 1971): 1149–52; Jerrold Rusk, "The Effect of the Australian Ballot Reform on Split-Ticket Voting: 1876–1908," *American Political Science Review* 64 (December 1970): 1220–38; and Reynolds, *Testing Democracy,* 97–100.

7. Lee Benson, Joel H. Silbey, and Phyllis F. Field, "Toward a Theory of Stability and Change in American Voting Patterns: New York State, 1792–1970," in *The History of American Electoral Behavior,* ed. Joel H. Silbey, Allan G. Bogue, and William H. Flanigan (Princeton, N.J.: Princeton University Press, 1978), 96–7.

8. Since third-party voting averaged over 6 percent in every northern state except Delaware during the early twentieth century, I could not divide the states on this basis to analyze party-vote instability in two-party states. For comparison see chapter 2.

9. For similar findings, see Paul Kleppner, "Critical Realignments and Electoral Systems," 22–3; and Reynolds, *Testing Democracy,* 100–5.

10. A. Campbell, Converse, Miller, and Stokes, *American Voter,* 86–7, 93–6; and Sidney Verba and Norman H. Nie, *Participation in America: Political Democracy and Social Equality* (New York: Harper and Row, 1972), 209–28.

11. Burnham, "Changing Shape of the American Political Universe"; *Critical Elections and the Mainsprings of American Politics* (New York: W. W. Norton, 1970), 91–135; and "The End of Party Politics," *Trans-Action* 7 (December 1969): 12–22.

12. Historians often distinguish between "structural" and "democratic" reforms. Structural reforms include such innovations as Civil Service, nonpartisan elections, and municipal reforms aimed at removing political decision making from direct popular influence; democratic reforms, such as the initiative, the referendum, and the recall, involved the general public directly in political decisions. See John D. Buenker, John C. Burnham, and Robert M. Crunden, *Progressivism* (Cambridge, Mass.: Schenkman, 1977), 53–4; Melvyn Holli, "Urban Reform in the Progressive Era," in *The Progressive Era,* ed. Lewis L. Gould (Syracuse, N.Y.: Syracuse University Press, 1974), 132–52. This distinction is problematic, however, since both "structural" and "democratic" reforms were

designed to weaken the power of the political parties, and both impacted nega-
tively upon mass participation in electoral politics. The distinctions made by political
scientists between procedural and substantive legal changes are equally artificial,
because procedural reforms almost always had substantive effects on the political
process. See Jerrold G. Rusk and John J. Stucker, "Legal-Institutional Factors in
American Voting" (unpublished paper, revised June 1975); John J. Stucker, "The
Impact of Women's Suffrage on Patterns of Voter Participation in the U.S.:
Quasi-Experimental and Real-Time Analysis, 1890–1920" (Ph.D. dissertation,
University of Michigan, 1973), 65; and Richard John Carlson, "The Effects of
Voter Registration Systems on Presidential Turnout in Non-Southern States:
1912–1924" (Ph.D. dissertation, University of Illinois at Urbana-Champaign,
1976), 54.

13. Chester Lloyd Jones, "The County in Politics," *Annals of the American
Academy of Political and Social Science* 47 (May 1913): 89.

14. Spencer D. Albright, *The American Ballot* (Washington, D.C.: American
Council on Public Affairs, 1942), 26–30; Joseph B. Bishop, "The Secret Ballot in
Thirty-Five States," *Forum* 2 (January 1892): 592; Eldon C. Evans, *A History of
the Australian Ballot System in the United States* (Chicago: University of Chicago
Press, 1917), 46; and Reynolds, *Testing Democracy*, 49–70.

15. Peter Argersinger, "'Place on the Ballot': Fusion Politics and Antifusion
Laws," *American Historical Review* 85 (April 1980): 287–306; and "Regulating
Democracy: Election Laws and Dakota Politics, 1889–1902," *Midwest Review* 5
(Spring 1983): 1–19; Richard McCormick, *From Realignment to Reform: Political
Change in New York State, 1893–1910* (Ithaca, N.Y.: Cornell University Press,
1981), 114–8; and Reynolds, *Testing Democracy*, 137–45.

16. Evans, *History of the Australian Ballot System*, 29–31; M. Ostrogorsky,
Democracy and the Organization of Political Parties, 2 vols., trans. Frederick Clarke
(New York: McMillan Co., 1902), 501–2; Charles C. Binney, "The Merits and
Defects of the Pennsylvania Ballot Law of 1891," *Annals of the American Academy
of Political and Social Science* (May 1892): 758–9; and Argersinger, "Regulating
Democracy," 2.

17. Reynolds, *Testing Democracy*, 64–5.

18. John F. Reynolds and Richard McCormick, "'Outlawing Treachery': Split
Tickets and the Ballot Laws in New York and New Jersey, 1880–1910," *Journal of
American History* 72 (March 1986): 838–41; David Hammack, *Power and Society:
Greater New York at the Turn of the Century* (New York: Russell Sage Foundation,
1982), 120–9; Ostrogorsky, *Democracy and the Organization of Political Parties*,
506–7.

19. Fusion was undermined in two ways. In the first place, partisan voters,
many of whom refused to contemplate the possibility of defecting, could cooper-
ate with voters from other parties when candidates ran on fusion tickets. The
prohibition on double listing of candidates made such cooperation impossible.
Second, for parties to agree to fusion tickets meant that one or both parties had
to give up their own place on the ballot. This was the equivalent of committing
political suicide, since their place on future ballots was now based on the vote
they had received in the previous election; Argersinger, "'Place on the Ballot'";

"Regulating Democracy"; and "To Disfranchise the People: The Iowa Ballot Law and the Election of 1897," *Mid-America* 63 (January 1981): 18–35.

20. Argersinger, "Regulating Democracy," 16; Arthur S. Link and Richard L. McCormick, *Progressivism* (Arlington Heights, Ill.: Harlan Davidson, 1983), 51–3; and Reynolds, *Testing Democracy*, 171.

21. Rusk, "Effect of the Australian Ballot Reform," *American Political Science Review.*

22. Evans, *History of the Australian Ballot*, 46, 36–46; Rusk, "Effect of the Australian Ballot Reform," *American Political Science Review*, 1222; and Robert C. Brooks, *Political Parties and Electoral Problems* (New York: Harper and Brothers, 1923), 389–408.

23. Ostrogorsky, *Democracy and the Organization of Political Parties*, 503–6; Rusk, "Effect of the Australian Ballot Reform," *American Political Science Review*; Argersinger, "Regulating Democracy"; Bishop, "Secret Ballot," 589–98; and McCormick, *From Realignment to Reform*, 114–8.

24. Lionel E. Fredman, *The Australian Ballot: The Story of an American Reform* (East Lansing: Michigan State University Press, 1968), 46; Evans, *History of the Australian Ballot System*, 53; Reynolds, *Testing Democracy*, 143–4; and J. Morgan Kousser, *The Shaping of Southern Politics: Suffrage Restriction and the Establishment of the One-Party South, 1880–1910* (New Haven, Conn.: Yale University Press, 1974), 51–6.

25. Evans, *History of the Australian Ballot System*, 46, 53; and Kousser, *Shaping of Southern Politics*, 52–3.

26. McCormick, *From Realignment to Reform*, 115; and Kousser, *Shaping of Southern Politics*, 51–6.

27. George Frederick Miller, *Absentee Voters and Suffrage Laws* (Washington, D.C.: Daylion, 1948).

28. Paul F. Bourke and Donald A. Debats, "Individuals and Aggregates: A Note on Historical Data and Assumptions," *Social Science History* 4 (May 1980): 229–50.

29. Burnham, "Changing Shape of the American Political Universe," 20; McCormick, *From Realignment to Reform*, 136; Clinton R. Woodruff, "Municipal Progress: 1904–1905," *Annals of the American Academy of Political and Social Science* 27 (January–June 1906): 191–9; and Argersinger, "Regulating Democracy," 15.

30. Nineteenth-century parties had made frequent use of primaries in choosing candidates, but they were generally utilized as part of a larger process that included both caucuses and conventions. By 1899 two-thirds of the states had passed laws to regulate primary elections. None of those laws, however, had established mandatory uniform primaries. Despite the growth of primary legislation during the Gilded Age, primaries as well as party conventions remained "almost wholly under party control"; Charles Merriam and Louise Overacker, *Primary Elections* (Chicago: University of Chicago Press, 1928), 22, 20–59; V. O. Key, Jr., *American State Politics: An Introduction* (New York: Alfred A. Knopf, 1956), 85–169; Ernst Christopher Meyer, *Nominating Systems: Direct Primaries versus Conventions in the United States* (Madison, Wisc.: State Journal

Printing, 1902); John T. Salter, ed., "The Direct Primary," *Annals of the American Academy of Political and Social Science* 106 (March 1923); and Lamart Beman, ed., *The Direct Primary*, vol. 6 of *The Reference Shelf* (New York: H. W. Wilson, 1926).

31. Direct-primary legislation spread rapidly through the nation between 1907 and 1917. By 1917 all but five states had adopted some variant of the direct primary. Thirty-two of the forty-four states had instituted mandatory direct primaries for all state offices; Merriam and Overacker, *Primary Elections*, 66 (see 359–404 for the laws of each state); Ostrogorsky, *Democracy and the Organization of Political Parties*, 510–20; Boyd Archer Martin, *The Direct Primary in Idaho* (Stanford, Calif.: Stanford University Press, 1947), 10–1.

32. James W. Davis, *Presidential Primaries: Road to the White House* (New York: Thomas Y. Crowell, 1967), 26–8; and Merriam and Overacker, *Primary Elections*, 141–95.

33. Ralph S. Boots, "Party Platforms in State Politics," in "The Direct Primary," ed. John T. Salter, *Annals of the American Academy of Political and Social Science* 106 (March 1923): 72–82; and Frank J. Sorauf, *Political Parties in the American System* (Boston: Little, Brown, 1964), 47.

34. See chapter 6.

35. Key, *American State Politics*, 85–169.

36. Merriam and Overacker, *Primary Elections*, 212–3, 238–9; Salter, "Direct Primary"; Beman, *Direct Primary*; Hammack, *Power and Society*, 128–9; and Link and McCormick, *Progressivism*, 52.

37. Reynolds, *Testing Democracy*, 171.

38. Key, *American State Politics*, 169, 85–13; Sorauf, *Political Parties in the American System*, 110–3.

39. Brooks, *Political Parties*, 342–3.

40. These were usually called "corrupt practices" acts. In total, twenty-three states limited campaign expenditures; Link and McCormick, *Progressivism*, 52; John F. Reynolds, "The 'Silent Dollar': Vote Buying in New Jersey," *New Jersey History* 98 (Fall–Winter 1980): 204–8; Richard McCormick, "The Discovery that 'Business Corrupts Politics': A Reappraisal of the Origins of Progressivism," *American Historical Review* 86 (April 1981): 266–7; Brooks, *Political Parties*, 329–53; and Clinton R. Woodruff, "The Municipal League of Philadelphia," *American Journal of Sociology* 11 (September 1905): 336–58.

41. Sorauf, *Political Parties in the American System*, 109; Reynolds, *Testing Democracy*, 129–30; Richard Jensen, "Armies, Admen, and Crusaders: Types of Presidential Campaigns," *History Teacher* 2 (January 1969): 43; and Gil Troy, *See How They Ran: The Changing Role of the Presidential Candidate* (New York: Free Press, 1991), 108–32.

42. Fifteen states permitted constitutional initiatives as well as statutory ones; Link and McCormick, *Progressivism*, 58; Lloyd Sponholtz, "The Initiative and Referendum: Direct Democracy in Perspective, 1898–1920," *American Studies* 14 (Fall 1973): 43–64; Brooks, *Political Parties*, 460–1, 490–1; Ellias Paxson Oberholtzer, *The Referendum in America Together with Some Chapters on the Initiative and the Recall* (New York: Charles Scribner's Sons, 1912), 391–426, 454–70;

Bradley Robert Rice, *Progressive Cities: The Commission Movement in America, 1901–1920* (Austin: University of Texas Press, 1977), 72–83.

43. For a discussion of the controversy surrounding direct election, see David J. Rothman, *Politics and Power: The United States Senate, 1869–1901* (Cambridge, Mass.: Harvard University Press, 1966), 243–67.

44. Edward Banfield and James Wilson, *City Politics* (New York: Vintage Books, 1966), 87–96; and Samuel Hays, "The Politics of Reform in Municipal Government in the Progressive Era," *Pacific Northwest Quarterly* 55 (October 1964): 157–69.

45. The city-commission plan, which originated in Galveston in 1901, was adopted by 160 cities—almost all small to medium-sized—before 1911. By 1920 it had spread to nearly 500 cities; Holli, "Urban Reform," 147; and Rice, *Progressive Cities*, xiv, 113–25.

46. See chapter 6 for an extended discussion of this issue.

47. Stephen Skowronek, *Building a New American State: The Expansion of National Administrative Capacities, 1877–1920* (New York: Cambridge University Press, 1982), 177–211; Martin Shefter, "Party, Bureaucracy, and Political Change in the United States," in *Political Parties: Development and Decay*, ed. Louis Maisel and Joseph Cooper (Beverly Hills: Sage Publications, 1978), 228–9; and Gerson Harry Smoger, "Organizing Political Campaigns: A Survey of Nineteenth and Twentieth Century Trends" (Ph.D. dissertation, University of Pennsylvania, 1982): 83–4.

48. In his essays, Samuel Hays emphasizes this shifting locus of political power; Hays, *American Political History as Social Analysis: Essays* (Knoxville: University of Tennessee Press, 1980).

49. See chapter 4.

50. John D. Buenker, "The Urban Political Machine and Woman Suffrage: A Study in Political Adaptability," *Historian* 33 (February 1971): 265–8; Aileen S. Kraditor, *The Ideas of the Woman Suffrage Movement, 1890–1920* (New York: Columbia University Press, 1965), esp. 41, 52–74, 124–62; Alan P. Grimes, *The Puritan Ethic and Women's Suffrage* (New York: Oxord University Press, 1967), 78–98; Andrew Sinclair, *The Better Half: The Emancipation of the American Woman* (New York: Harper and Row, 1965), 241–53, 298–300; and Richard Hofstadter, *The Age of Reform: From Bryan to FDR* (New York: Alfred A. Knopf, 1955), 265.

51. As quoted in Nancy F. Cott, *The Grounding of Modern Feminism* (New Haven, Conn.: Yale University Press, 1987), 102.

52. See chapter 4.

53. For specific poll tax laws in each southern state, see Jerrold G. Rusk and John J. Stucker, "The Effect of the Southern System of Election Laws on Voting Participation: A Reply to V. O. Key, Jr.," in *The History of American Electoral Behavior*, ed. Joel H. Silbey, Allan G. Bogue, and William H. Flanigan (Princeton, N.J.: Princeton University Press, 1978), 208–13; and Frederick Ogden, *The Poll Tax in the South* (University: University of Alabama Press, 1958), 32–58. See also Kousser, *Shaping of Southern Politics*, 63–72.

54. John B. Phillips, "Educational Qualifications of Voters" *University of Colorado Studies*, gen. ser. A (1906): 59; Rusk and Stucker, "Effect of the Southern

System," 214–9; Dudley O. McGovney, *The American Suffrage Medley: The Need for a National Uniform Suffrage* (Chicago: University of Chicago Press, 1949), 59–79; and Kousser, *Shaping of Southern Politics*, 56–62.

55. The passage of restrictive legislation began in Florida and Mississippi, in 1889 and 1890 respectively, and had spread to Arkansas and South Carolina by 1896. After Bryan's defeat, all the remaining southern states rapidly adopted mechanisms to restrict voter participation. The federal elections in which poll taxes were first used by each southern state are as follows: Alabama, 1902; Arkansas, 1894; Florida, 1890; Georgia, 1872; Louisiana, 1898; Mississippi, 1890; North Carolina, 1900; South Carolina, 1896; Texas, 1904; and Virginia, 1904. Literacy tests took effect in the following years: Alabama, 1902; Georgia, 1908; Louisiana, 1898; Mississippi, 1892; North Carolina, 1902; South Carolina, 1896; and Virginia, 1902. In the border states, Tennessee instituted a poll tax in 1890, and Oklahoma required a literacy test beginning in 1912; Kousser, *Shaping of Southern Politics*, 45–62; and Rusk and Stucker, "Effect of the Southern System," 208–23.

56. See chapter 4.

57. In establishing property and literacy restrictions on the franchise, the various southern states invented numerous escape clauses for white voters. These included the "grandfather clause," which permitted men to register to vote if they legally could have voted in 1867 or if they were descendants of 1867 voters, and the "fighting grandfather clause," which allowed anyone to vote who had fought for the Union or the Confederacy or was descended from someone who had. Both of these provisions were intended to exclude blacks while reassuring southern whites that they could continue to vote regardless of whether they met the new property and literacy requirements. Grandfather clauses were declared unconstitutional by the Supreme Court in 1915, but by then most states had turned to subtler techniques of discriminating on the basis of race. These included the "understanding" clause of the literacy tests, which could be as readily used to enfranchise illiterate whites as to disfranchise literate blacks, and a "good character provision" that allowed local registrars to enfranchise voters of "good character" and with a clear understanding of the obligations of citizenship; Kousser, *Shaping of Southern Politics*, 58–60; Rusk and Stucker, "Effect of the Southern System," 208–23; and McGovney, *American Suffrage Medley*, 67–8.

58. Rusk and Stucker, "Effect of the Southern System," 223–47; and Kousser, *Shaping of Southern Politics*. Both of these studies convincingly show that suffrage restriction fundamentally altered southern electoral behavior.

59. James Bryce, *The American Commonwealth*, 2 vols., 2d ed., rev. (London: MacMillan, 1892), 1:464–5; Kirk H. Porter, *A History of Suffrage in the United States* (Chicago: University of Chicago Press, 1969), 110–1; Rusk and Stucker, "Legal-Institutional Factors in American Voting," 6–10; and Kousser, *Shaping of Southern Politics*, 57–8.

60. The first federal election years in which literacy tests were required in northern states were Connecticut, 1856; Massachusetts, 1858; Wyoming, 1890; Maine, 1894; California, 1896; Washington, 1898; Delaware, 1898; New Hampshire, 1906; and Arizona, 1912. In addition, New York instituted a literacy test in

1922, as did Oregon in 1926; Rusk and Stucker, "Legal-Institutional Factors in American Voting," 27–27b; Carlson, "Effects of Voter Registration Systems," 85; McGovney, *American Suffrage Medley*, 59–79; Phillips, "Educational Qualification of Voters," 59; and Bryce, *American Commonwealth*, 1:465.

61. By 1880 twenty-eight of the thirty-eight states had adopted some form of voter registration; Carlson, "Effects of Voter Registration Systems," 93–120; Rusk and Stucker, "Legal-Institutional Factors in American Voting," 23–5; Philip E. Converse, "Change in the American Electorate," in *The Human Meaning of Change*, ed. Angus Campbell and Philip E. Converse (New York: Russell Sage Foundation, 1972), 282–4; Paul Kleppner and Stephen Baker, "Impact of Voter Registration," presented to the annual meeting of the American Political Science Association, September 1979, 4–8; Joseph P. Harris, *Registration of Voters in the United States* (Washington, D.C.: Brookings Institution, 1929), 65–93.

62. Kleppner, *Who Voted?* 60; Kousser, *Shaping of Southern Politics*, 47–50; Kleppner and S. Baker, "Impact of Voter Registration," presented to the annual meeting of The American Political Science Association, 7–9; Rusk and Stucker, "Legal-Institutional Factors in American Voting," 25–6; and Frances Fox Piven and Richard A. Cloward, *Why Americans Don't Vote* (New York: Pantheon Books, 1988), 88–94.

63. The United States is the only major democracy that requires individuals to register to vote; Piven and Cloward, *Why Americans Don't Vote*, 17; Kevin P. Phillips and Paul H. Blackman, *Electoral Reform and Voter Participation; Federal Registration: A False Remedy for Voter Apathy* (Washington, D.C.: American Enterprise Institute for Public Policy Research), 1975.

64. Kleppner, *Who Voted?* 87.

65. Ibid., 60; and Converse, "Change in the American Electorate," 290–2.

66. Reynolds, *Testing Democracy*, 142.

67. Kousser, *Shaping of Southern Politics*, 47–50.

68. Converse, "Change in the American Electorate"; Jerrold Rusk, "Comment: The American Electoral Universe: Speculation and Evidence," *American Political Science Review* 68 (September 1974): 1028–49; and Rusk and Stucker, "Legal-Institutional Factors in American Voting"; Walter Dean Burnham, "Theory and Voting Research: Some Reflections on Converse's 'Change in the American Electorate,'" *American Political Science Review* 68 (September 1974): 1002–23; and Kleppner and S. Baker, "Impact of Voter Registration," presented to the annual meeting of the American Political Science Association.

69. See Appendix 1 on measuring voter turnout.

70. Kleppner and S. Baker, "Impact of Voter Registration," presented to the annual meeting of the American Political Science Association; and Carlson, "Effects of Voter Registration Systems."

71. Piven and Cloward, *Why Americans Don't Vote*; Converse, "Change in the American Electorate"; Rusk and Stucker, "Legal-Institutional Factors in American Voting."

72. Burnham, "Theory and Voting Research," 1004–13.

73. Kleppner and S. Baker, "Impact of Voter Registration," presented to the annual meeting of the American Political Science Association; Kleppner, *Who*

Voted? 58–63. For similar findings, see Carlson, "Effects of Voter Registration Systems."

74. Burnham, "Communications to the Editor," 1150–1; McCormick, *From Realignment to Reform*, 115–7; Reynolds and McCormick, "'Outlawing Treachery'"; and Reynolds, *Testing Democracy*, 64–70.

75. Reynolds, *Testing Democracy*, 152.

76. Ibid., 168–73; Carlson, "Effects of Voter Registration Systems"; Kleppner and S. Baker, "Impact of Voter Registration," presented to the annual meeting of the American Political Science Association; Walter Dean Burnham, *The Current Crisis in American Politics* (New York: Oxford University Press, 1982); and Key, *American State Politics*, 15–6.

77. John M. Allswang, *Bosses, Machines, and Urban Voters: An American Symbiosis* (Port Washington, N.Y.: Kennikat Press, 1977); Fred I. Greenstein, "The Changing Pattern of Urban Party Politics," *Annals of the American Academy of Political and Social Science* 353 (May 1964): 1–13; Buenker, "Urban Political Machine"; Walter Dean Burnham, "The Appearance and Disappearance of the American Voter," in *The Current Crisis in American Politics* (New York: Oxford University Press, 1982), 121–65; Charles S. Merriam and Harold F. Gosnell, *Non-Voting: Causes and Methods of Control* (Chicago: University of Chicago Press, 1924); and Gosnell, *Machine Politics: Chicago Model* (Chicago: University of Chicago Press, 1937).

NOTES TO CHAPTER 6

1. Although the election of 1896 provides a chronological dividing line between the late-nineteenth- and early-twentieth-century electoral systems, this single election did not cause the evaporation of electoral competition. The late-nineteenth-century party system collapsed during the mid-1890s, the exact timing of the transformation varying throughout the nation; J. E. Budgor, A. Capell, D. A. Flanders, N. W. Polsby, M. C. Westyle, and J. Zaller, "The Election of 1896 and the Modernization of Congress," presented to the annual meeting of the Social Science History Association, Ann Arbor, Michigan, 1977, 9.

2. Walter Dean Burnham, "The System of 1896: An Analysis," in *The Evolution of American Electoral Systems*, ed. Paul Kleppner (Westport, Conn.: Greenwood Press, 1981), 171–88; Paul Kleppner, "Critical Realignments and Electoral Systems," in *The Evolution of American Electoral Systems*, ed. Paul Kleppner (Westport, Conn.: Greenwood Press, 1981), 20–4; and *Who Voted? The Dynamics of Electoral Turnout, 1870–1980* (New York: Praeger, 1982), 71–3; and E. E. Schattschneider, "United States: The Functional Approach to Party Government," in *Modern Political Parties: Approaches to Comparative Politics*, ed. Sigmund Neumann (Chicago: University of Chicago Press, 1956), 201–4.

3. Burnham, "System of 1896," 173–6; and "Periodization Schemes and 'Party Systems': The 'System of 1896' as a Case in Point," *Social Science History* 10 (Fall 1986): 293–6.

4. In every region except the border states, competition between the two

parties fell off in 1896. The four-election means from 1880 to 1892 are significantly higher than the five-election means from 1880 to 1896. Thus, table 6.1 understates the change in electoral competitiveness that occurred during the early twentieth century. See table 3.2 above for 1880–1892 competitiveness means.

5. Because of the anomalous nature of electoral contests in the mountain region, which did not experience close electoral competition during the 1880s and 1890s, the full extent of the decline in electoral competitiveness is partially obscured in these summary measures of northern and national competition. Since these figures are state-level averages, the influence of the mountain states is magnified far beyond its importance. Elections in this sparsely populated region, in fact, had little effect on presidential contests.

6. The mean competitiveness scores of the ten southern states during the first five twentieth-century presidential elections were Alabama, 51.9; Arkansas, 72.9; Florida, 49.3; Georgia, 49.5; Louisiana, 27.9; Mississippi, 15.6; North Carolina, 79.8; South Carolina, 9.2; Texas, 48.7; and Virginia, 71.5.

7. Between 1898 and 1916 electoral competition in congressional and gubernatorial contests in the South averaged just over 30 on the competitiveness index. This means that the average margin of victory was 70 percent of the total vote. In congressional elections, over 60 percent of the vote separated the two parties in every state except Virginia and North Carolina.

8. Electoral politics in a state is generally considered competitive if the average margin of victory is less than 10 percent of the total vote. See chapter 3.

9. Compare table 6.2 with table 3.2.

10. Electoral competition fell off in congressional, gubernatorial, and presidential elections in California and Oregon; both states were decidedly less competitive after 1896.

11. These states were also the first to experience the decline in mass participation. See chapter 4.

12. The mean competitiveness score in New England for the four presidential elections, 1880–1892, was 85.7 as compared to a score of 79.6 from 1900 to 1916. All six states in New England experienced noncompetitive politics from 1900 to 1910, but the situation changed with the split in the Republican party during the second decade.

13. Mean regional competitiveness scores from 1898 to 1918 for gubernatorial and congressional elections respectively were New England, 84.5 and 82.9; mid-Atlantic states, 86.5 and 88.4; north central states, 87.7 and 82.2; Midwest, 82.8 and 78.9; South, 30.3 and 30.4; border states, 90.7 and 88.1; mountain states, 88.8 and 83.2; and West, 83.5 and 84.1.

14. Electoral competitiveness was comparably uneven in gubernatorial contests. Only two of the settled northern states, New Jersey and Pennsylvania, failed to exceed 90 on the competitiveness index in at least one gubernatorial election, and electoral competitiveness in both of these states peaked at 88. Twenty-two of these twenty-eight states had gubernatorial elections decided by less than 4 percent of the vote (all except Vermont, New Jersey, Pennsylvania, Kansas, Tennessee, and Nevada), but twenty-three experienced at least one

election in which the winner won by over 20 percent of the total vote (all except Connecticut, New Jersey, New York, Ohio, and Missouri).

15. The percentage of state elections in which minor parties held the balance of power in presidential, gubernatorial, and congressional elections respectively were, for 1880–1896, 23 percent, 32 percent, and 26 percent and, for 1898–1918, 26 percent, 32 percent, and 22 percent. For the North, the comparable figures were, for 1880–1896, 29 percent, 40 percent, and 33 percent and, for 1898–1918, 34 percent, 40 percent, and 29 percent.

16. States are classified as competitive states if the vote margin between the major parties in all state-level presidential, gubernatorial, and congressional elections from 1898 to 1918 combined averaged less than 10 percent; see Appendix 2.

17. Burnham, "System of 1896," 176.

18. Ibid., 177–80.

19. Building on the insights of E. E. Schattschneider, Burnham argues persuasively that Democratic hegemony in the South helped to ensure Republican national dominance. Because of its strength in Dixie, the Democratic party "could be truncated but not displaced." Although "indestructible," "the Democratic party was not a nationally acceptable alternative." The Republican party thus faced an opposition that had little chance of winning; Burnham, "System of 1896," esp. 197. See also Schattschneider, "United States: The Functional Approach," 202.

20. Only Taft and Hoover—the latter because he presided over the nation's worst economic depression—suffered electoral defeat.

21. H. Douglas Price, "Careers and Committees in the American Congress: The Problem of Structural Change," in *The History of Parliamentary Behavior*, ed. William O. Aydelotte (Princeton, N.J.: Princeton University Press, 1977), 38–40.

22. Price, "Congress and the Evolution of Legislative Professionalism," in *Congress in Change: Evolution and Reform*, ed. Norman Ornstein (New York: Praeger, 1975), 16.

23. H. Douglas Price, "The Congressional Career, Then and Now," in *Congressional Behavior*, ed. Nelson W. Polsby (New York: Random House, 1971), 16–7; and "Careers and Committees," 36–9; Nelson W. Polsby, "The Institutionalization of the House of Representatives," *American Political Science* Review 62 (March 1968): 145–8; and Morris P. Fiorina, David W. Rohde, and Peter Wissel, "Historical Change in House Turnover," in *Congress in Change: Evolution and Reform*, ed. Norman J. Ornstein (New York: Praeger, 1975), 25–38.

24. Price, "Careers and Committees," 31–6.

25. Kleppner, *Who Voted?* 184.

26. Compare tables 6.4 and 6.5 with tables 3.7 and 3.8 above.

27. Overviews of the historiography on this subject are provided by Arthur S. Link and Richard L. McCormick, *Progressivism* (Arlington Heights, Ill.: Harlan Davidson, 1983), 58–66; and Daniel T. Rodgers, "In Search of Progressivism," *Reviews in American History* 10 (December 1982): 113–32. My understanding of this transformation is particularly informed by Stephen Skowronek, *Building a*

New American State: The Expansion of National Administrative Capacities, 1877–1920 (New York: Cambridge University Press, 1982); Gabriel Kolko, *The Triumph of Conservatism: A Reinterpretation of American History, 1900–1916* (New York: Free Press, 1963); Grant McConnell, *Private Power and American Democracy* (New York: Vintage Books, 1966); Samuel Hays, *American Political History as Social Analysis: Essays* (Knoxville: University of Tennessee Press, 1980); Robert Wiebe, *The Search for Order, 1877–1920* (New York: Hill and Wang, 1967); Robert McCormick, *From Realignment to Reform: Political Change in New York State, 1893–1910* (Ithaca, N.Y.: Cornell University Press, 1981); Carl V. Harris, *Political Power in Birmingham, 1871–1921* (Knoxville: University of Tennessee Press, 1977); Polsby, "Institutionalization of the House of Representatives"; and Burnham, "System of 1896."

28. Burnham, "System of 1896"; Walter Dean Burnham, "The Changing Shape of the American Political Universe," *American Political Science Review* 59 (March 1965): 7–28; Jerome M. Clubb and Santa A. Traugott, "Partisan Cleavage and Cohesion in the House of Representatives, 1861–1974," *Journal of Interdisciplinary History* 7 (Winter 1977): 375–401; Robert R. Alford and Roger Friedland, "Political Participation and Public Policy," *Annual Review of Sociology*, vol. 1, ed. Alex Inkeles (Palo Alto: Annual Review, 1975); Robert D. Marcus, *Grand Old Party: Political Structure in the Gilded Age, 1880–1896* (New York: Oxford University Press, 1971), 250–65; and McCormick, "Prelude to Progressivism: The Transformation of New York State Politics, 1890–1910," *New York History* 59 (July 1978): 253–76.

29. See chapter 3.

30. Polsby, "Institutionalization of the House of Representatives"; Nelson W. Polsby, Miriam Gallaher, and Barry Spencer Rundquist, "The Growth of the Seniority System in the House of Representatives," *American Political Science Review* 63 (September 1969): 787–807; Michael Abram and Joseph Cooper, "The Rise of Seniority in the House of Representatives," *Polity* 1 (Fall 1968): 52–85; Price, "Careers and Committees"; "Congressional Career"; and "Congress and the Evolution of Legislative Professionalism"; George Goodwin, Jr., "The Seniority System in Congress," *American Political Science Review* 53 (June 1959): 412–37; David Brady, Joseph Cooper, and Patricia A. Hurley, "The Decline of Party in the U.S. House of Representatives, 1887–1968," *Legal Studies Quarterly* 4 (August 1979): 381–407; Alan G. Bogue, Jerome M. Clubb, Carroll R. McKibbin, and Santa A. Traugott, "Members of the House of Representatives and the Processes of Modernization, 1789–1960," *Journal of American History* 63 (September 1976): 275–302; Clubb and Traugott, "Partisan Cleavage and Cohesion"; and Budgor, Capell, Flanders, Polsby, Westyle, and Zaller, "Election of 1896."

31. Clubb and Traugott, "Partisan Cleavage and Cohesion," 399; Brady, Cooper, and Hurley, "Decline of Party"; and David Brady and Philip Althoff, "Party Voting in the U.S. House of Representatives, 1890–1910: Elements of a Responsible Party System," *Journal of Politics* 36 (August 1974): 753–75.

32. Price, "Congress and the Evolution of Legislative Professionalism," 17–8; and "Congressional Career"; Polsby, Gallaher, and Rundquist, "Growth of the Seniority System," 194–5; Polsby, "Institutionalization of the House of

Representatives"; Abram and Cooper, "Rise of Seniority"; Budgor, Capell, Flanders, Polsby, Westyle, and Zaller, "Election of 1896"; Goodwin, "Seniority System in Congress"; James Holt, *Congressional Insurgents and the Party System, 1909–1916* (Cambridge, Mass.: Harvard University Press, 1967), esp. 16–28; Price, "Congress and the Evolution of Legislative Professionalism"; Polsby, Gallaher, and Rundquist, "Growth of the Seniority System," 184–9; and Abram and Cooper, "Rise of Seniority," 78.

33. Polsby, "Institutionalization of the U.S. House of Representatives."

34. Wiebe, *Search for Order,* 192–5; and George B. Galloway, *History of the House of Representatives* (New York: Thomas Y. Crowell, 1962), 249–54.

35. Burnham, "System of 1896," 175; and Marcus, *Grand Old Party,* 8–10, 256–7.

36. Skowronek, *Building a New American State,* 177–211. Brian Balogh, by contrast, argues that administrative politics did not reach its fruition until a half-century later; "Reorganizing the Organizational Synthesis: Federal-Professional Relations in Modern America," *Studies in American Political Development* 5 (Spring 1991): 119–72. See also Theda Skocpol and Gretchen Ritter, "Gender and the Origins of Modern Social Policies in Britain and the United States," *Studies in American Political Development* 5 (Spring 1991): 36–93.

37. Naomi Lamoreaux, "Regulatory Agencies," in *Encyclopedia of American Political History,* ed. Jack P. Greene (New York: Charles Scribner and Sons, 1984), 1114–5; Kolko, *Triumph of Conservatism,* 255–78; Thomas K. McCraw, "Regulation in America: A Review Article," *Business History Review* 49 (Summer 1975): 159–83.

38. Lamoreaux, "Regulatory Agencies," 1114; and Skowronek, *Building a New American State,* 248–84.

39. Link and McCormick, *Progressivism,* 26–66; and Wiebe, *Search for Order,* 164–95.

40. Samuel Hays, "The Politics of Reform in Municipal Government in the Progressive Era," *Pacific Northwest Quarterly* 55 (October 1964): 157–69; Melvyn Holli, "Urban Reform in the Progressive Era," in *The Progressive Era,* ed. Lewis L. Gould (Syracuse, N.Y.: Syracuse University Press, 1974), 132–52; Martin J. Schiesl, *The Politics of Efficiency: Municipal Administration and Reform in America, 1880–1920* (Berkeley: University of California Press, 1977); Bradley Robert Rice, *Progressive Cities: The Commission Movement in America, 1901–1920* (Austin: University of Texas Press, 1977); Richard Joseph Stillman II, *Rise of the City Manager: A Public Professional in Local Government* (Albuquerque: University of New Mexico Press, 1974); and Edward Banfield and James Wilson, *City Politics* (New York: Vintage Books, 1966). Two excellent case studies, David Hammack's *Power and Society: Greater New York at the Turn of the Century* (New York: Russell Sage Foundation, 1982) and Carl Harris's *Political Power in Birmingham, 1871–1921* (Washington D.C.: Brookings Institution, 1929), explore the shifting locus of urban power during this period.

41. Richard McCormick, "The Discovery That 'Business Corrupts Politics': A Reappraisal of the Origins of Progressivism," *American Historical* Review 86 (April 1981): 268.

42. Wiebe, *Search for Order,* 180.

43. McCormick, "Discovery That Business Corrupts Politics," 268.

44. Marcus, *Grand Old Party,* 256–7.

45. Kolko, *Triumph of Conservatism;* James Weinstein, *The Corporate Ideal in the Liberal State, 1900–1918* (Boston: Beacon Press, 1968); Hays, "Politics of Reform"; and Wiebe, *Search for Order.*

46. McCormick, *From Realignment to Reform;* Rodgers, "In Search of Progressivism," 113–32; Buenker, "The Progressive Era: A Search for a Synthesis," *Mid-America* 51 (July 1969): 175–93; and Link and McCormick, *Progressivism.*

47. Richard Hofstadter, *The Age of Reform: From Bryan to FDR* (New York: Alfred A. Knopf, 1955), 131–271; McConnell, *Private Power and American Democracy,* 30–50; McCormick, "Discovery That Business Corrupts Politics," 274; and *From Realignment to Reform;* and Argersinger, "From Political Management to Administrative Politics, Review of *From Realignment to Reform: Political Change in New York State, 1895–1910,* by Richard L. McCormick," *Reviews in American History* 10 (September 1982): 391–5.

48. Wiebe, *Search for Order,* 111–95; and Balogh, "Reorganizing the Organizational Synthesis," 119–72.

49. Hays, *American Political History as Social Analysis,* 66–86, 293–325; and Louis Galambos, "The Emerging Organizational Synthesis in Modern American History," *Business History Review* 44 (Autumn 1970): 279–90.

50. This is also the conclusion that Skowronek reaches in *Building a New American State.*

51. Congress, for example, debated this course of action when contemplating the creation of the Federal Trade Commission; see Kolko, *Triumph of Conservatism,* 255–78.

52. See chapter 3.

53. Skowronek, *Building a New American State.*

54. McConnell, *Private Power and American Democracy;* Hays, *American Political History as Social Analysis;* Wiebe, *Search for Order;* Rodgers, "In Search of Progressivism," 113–7; Buenker, "Progressive Era"; John D. Buenker, John C. Burnham, and Robert M. Crunden, *Progressivism* (Cambridge, Mass.: Schenkman, 1977), 31–63; and Link and McCormick, *Progressivism,* 47–66.

55. Wiebe emphasizes the extent to which government officials became dependent on professional lobbying for the day-to-day management of government; Wiebe, *Search for Order,* 183–5.

56. In a pioneering study, *Private Power and American Democracy,* Grant McConnell explored this process by which interest groups through pressure politics "captured" control over independent administrative agencies.

NOTES TO APPENDIX 1

1. The two most frequently cited sources on nineteenth-century fraud are Joseph Harris and Clinton Woodruff, both political scientists and active proponents of electoral reform. Joseph P. Harris, *Registration of Voters in the United*

States (Washington D.C.: Brookings Institution, 1929); Clinton R. Woodruff, "Election Methods and Reforms in Philadelphia," *Annals of the Academy of Political and Social Science* 27 (March 1901): 181–204; and "Philadelphia's Election Frauds," *Arena* 24 (October 1900): 397–404. See also M. Ostrogorski, *Democracy and the Organization of Political Parties*, 2 vols., trans. Frederick Clarke (New York: McMillan Co., 1902), 2:343–50; and Joseph Lincoln Steffens's widely read indictment, *The Shame of the Cities* (New York: Peter Smith, 1948). For an extensive bibliography of contemporary charges of fraud, see Howard W. Allen and Kay Warren Allen, "Vote Fraud and the Validity of Election Data," in *Analyzing Electoral History*, ed. Jerome M. Clubb, William H. Flanigan, and Nancy H. Zingale (Beverly Hills, Calif.: Sage, 1981), 153–91.

2. Converse argues that perhaps as many as a million fraudulent votes were counted in nationwide elections during the 1890s, out of an electorate of around seventeen million. For example, extensive rural vote fraud was held responsible for high turnouts in Indiana, and massive corruption explained Philadelphia's participation rate; Philip E. Converse, "Change in the American Electorate," in *The Human Meaning of Change*, ed. Angus Campbell and Philip E. Converse (New York: Russell Sage Foundation, 1972), 286–91, 299.

3. The historical literature in this vein is extensive. For some examples, see Samuel P. Orth, *The Boss and the Machine: A Chronicle of the Politicians and Party Organization* (New Haven, Conn.: Yale University Press, 1919); Harold F. Gosnell, *Boss Platt and His New York Machine* (Chicago: University of Chicago Press, 1924); and *Machine Politics: Chicago Model* (Chicago: University of Chicago Press, 1937); Richard P. McCormick, *The History of Voting in New Jersey: A Study in the Development of Election Machinery, 1664–1911* (New Brunswick, N.J.: Rutgers University Press, 1953), 158–63; Matthew Josephson, *The Politicos, 1865–1896* (New York: Harcourt, Brace and World, 1963); and John F. Reynolds, *Testing Democracy: Electoral Behavior and Progressive Reform in New Jersey, 1880–1920* (Chapel Hill: University of North Carolina Press, 1988). McCormick and Reynolds, in particular, stress that fraud in the Garden State was as much a rural as an urban phenomenon.

4. Howard and Kay Allen demonstrate that the evidence of election fraud was almost wholly "anecdotal . . . unsystematic, impressionistic, and by and large inconclusive"; Allen and Allen, "Vote Fraud," 167, 153–91. See also James L. Baumgardner, "The 1888 Presidential Election: How Corrupt?" *Presidential Studies Quarterly* 14 (Summer 1984): 416–27.

5. Paul Kleppner and Stephen C. Baker, "Impact of Voter Registration," presented to the annual meeting of the American Political Science Association, September 1979, 38–46; and Walter Dean Burnham, "Theory and Voting Research: Some Reflections on Converse's 'Change in the American Electorate,'" *American Political Science Review* 68 (September 1974): 1017.

6. The use of violence, intimidation, and fraud in the South has been well documented. C. Vann Woodward, *Origins of the New South 1877–1913* (Baton Rouge: Louisiana University Press, 1951), 259–63, 321–50; and V. O. Key, Jr., *Southern Politics in State and Nation* (New York: Vintage Books, 1949), 533–54.

7. Allen and Allen, "Vote Fraud," 176; Burnham, "Those High Nineteenth-

Century American Voting Turnouts: Fact or Fiction?" *Journal of Interdisciplinary History* 16 (Spring 1986): 617–9; Richard Jensen, *The Winning of the Midwest: Social and Political Conflict, 1888–1896* (Chicago: University of Chicago Press, 1971), 34–57; and Reynolds, *Testing Democracy*, 50–2.

8. A compilation of all congressional election challenges is provided in Allen and Allen, "Vote Fraud," 176–8. See also Jensen, *Winning of the Midwest*, 36.

9. Peter Argersinger's claim that "an indulgent political culture encouraged and made possible election fraud in the Gilded Age" finds no confirmation in recent work on nineteenth-century political culture; Argersinger, "New Perspectives on Election Fraud in the Gilded Age," *Political Science Quarterly* 100 (Winter 1986): 687. See, for example, Jean Baker, *Affairs of Party: The Political Culture of Northern Democrats in the Mid-Nineteenth Century* (Ithaca, N.Y.: Cornell University Press, 1983); William E. Gienapp, "Politics Seemed to Enter into Everything: Political Culture in the North, 1840–1860," in *Essays in Antebellum American Politics, 1840–1860*, ed. Stephen E. Maizlish and John J. Kushma (College Station: University of Texas Press, 1982), 14–69; and Michael McGerr, *The Decline of Popular Politics: The American North, 1865–1928* (New York: Oxford University Press, 1986), 3–42.

10. Even while arguing that historians have not paid sufficient attention to fraud, Argersinger concludes that "the reality of election fraud in the Gilded Age was its strategic, not massive, nature." Such fraud would not seriously distort estimates of the size of voter participation; Argersinger, "New Perspectives on Electoral Fraud in the Gilded Age," 672.

11. Allen and Allen, "Vote Fraud," 166. See also Reynolds, *Testing Democracy*, 53–6.

12. See Allen and Allen, "Vote Fraud," 166; Reynolds, "The 'Silent Dollar': Vote Buying in New Jersey," *New Jersey History* 98 (Fall–Winter 1980): 191–211; and John M. Allswang, *Bosses, Machines, and Urban Voters: An American Symbiosis* (Port Washington, N.Y.: Kennikat Press, 1977), 34. Furthermore, not all inducements increased voter turnout. Parties could and did reward opponents for not voting; see Gary W. Cox and J. Morgan Kousser, "Turnout and Rural Corruption: New York as a Test Case," *American Journal of Political Science* 25 (November 1981): 646–62.

13. U.S. Department of Commerce, Bureau of the Census, "Voter Participation in Presidential Elections: 1824–1968" (Series Y 27–28), *Historical Statistics of the United States: Colonial Times to 1970*, part 2 (1975): 1068–79; Burnham, "Those High Nineteenth-Century American Voting Turnouts," 625–44; and Paul Kleppner, *Who Voted? The Dynamics of Electoral Turnout, 1870–1980* (New York: Praeger, 1982), 163–5; Gerald Ginsberg, "Computing Antebellum Turnout: Methods and Models," *Journal of Interdisciplinary History* 16 (Spring 1986): 579–611.

14. I followed the procedures laid out by U.S. Department of Commerce, Bureau of the Census, "Voter Participation in Presidential Elections," which was written by Walter Dean Burnham. See also Walter Dean Burnham, "Estimates of the Potential Electorate," in *Historical Statistics of the United States: Colonial Times to 1970* (Washington, D.C.: U.S. Department of Commerce, Bureau of the

Census, 1975): part 2, 1068–79; and "Those High Nineteenth-Century American Voting Turnouts," 613–44.

15. Women achieved the vote for federal and state elections on the following dates: Wyoming, 1890; Colorado, 1893; Utah, 1896; Idaho, 1897; California and Washington, 1911; Arkansas, Kansas, and Oregon, 1913; Illinois, 1913 for presidential elections; Montana and Nebraska, 1914; and New York, 1917.

16. The states were Indiana, Michigan, Wisconsin, Minnesota, Nebraska, South Dakota, Arkansas, Colorado, Oregon, Kansas, Texas, and Missouri. In total, alien suffrage accounted for less than 1 percent of the national electorate; Paul Kleppner, *Continuity and Change in Electoral Politics, 1893–1928* (New York: Greenwood Press, 1987), 165–6.

17. Burnham estimates the potential electorate in the same manner, although my figures differ from his in several cases where he failed to adjust for alien suffrage; U.S. Department of Commerce, Bureau of the Census, "Voter Participation in Presidential Elections." See also Burnham, "Those High Nineteenth-Century American Voting Turnouts," 628–31. The census tables I used were the following: U.S. Department of Commerce, Bureau of the Census, *Compendium of the Eleventh Census: 1890*, part 2, "Foreign Born Population, Table Four, Foreign Born Males 21 Years of Age and Over, Classified according to Citizenship, by States and Territories: 1890," 683; and U.S. Department of Commerce, Bureau of the Census, *Compendium of the Fifteenth Census: 1930*, vol. 2, "Population, table 12, Citizenship of the Foreign-Born White Population 21 Years Old and Over, by Sex, by Divisions and States: 1900–1930," 414–8. Since the 1880 census did not classify the foreign-born by citizenship status, figures for the 1880s were estimated using the growth of the foreign-born population between 1890 and 1900.

18. Burnham estimates that this error is "well under 1 percent"; U.S. Department of Commerce, Bureau of the Census, "Voter Participation in Presidential Elections," 1069.

19. See Burnham's discussion of this issue in U.S. Department of Commerce, Bureau of the Census, "Voter Participation in Presidential Elections," 1067. See also Jerrold G. Rusk and John J. Stucker, "Measuring Patterns of Electoral Participation in the United States," *Micropolitics* 3 (Winter 1984): 470–4.

20. Peter R. Knights, "A Method for Estimating Census Under-Enumeration," *Historical Methods Newsletter* 3 (December 1969): 5–8. Using a random sampling of city directories to check census figures for Boston during 1850 and 1860, Knights estimates that the census undercounted Bostonians by 7.6 percent, of which half had been missed because they had relocated.

21. Ray M. Shortridge, "Estimating Voter Participation," in *Analyzing Electoral History: A Guide to the Study of American Voter Behavior*, ed. Jerome M. Clubb, William H. Flanigan, and Nancy H. Zingale (Beverly Hills, Calif.: Sage, 1981), 137–52.

22. Kleppner, *Who Voted?* 165.

23. To date, the scholarly debate over the accuracy of nineteenth-century turnout estimates has not paid much attention to the impact of geographic mobility on census underenumeration, voter eligibility, or participation rates.

24. Case studies of western and midwestern farming areas find that only one-quarter to one-third of the population in a given county or township remained in the same area from one census to the next. See Stephen Thernstrom and Peter R. Knights, "Men in Motion: Some Data and Speculations about Urban Population Mobility in Nineteenth-Century America," *Journal of Interdisciplinary History* 1 (Summer 1970): 7–35; Gordon W. Kirk, Jr., and Carol Tyirin Kirk, "Migration, Mobility, and the Formation of the Occupational Structure in an Immigrant Community: Holland, Michigan, 1850–1880," *Journal of Social History* 7 (Winter 1974): 142–64; Peter J. Coleman, "Restless Grant County: Americans on the Move," *Wisconsin Magazine of History* 46 (Autumn 1962): 16–20; Richard J. Hopkins, "Occupational and Geographic Mobility in Atlanta, 1870–1890," *Journal of Southern History* 34 (May 1968): 200–13. For a dissenting view, see Donald H. Parkerson, "How Mobile Were Nineteenth-Century Americans?" *Historical Methods* 15 (Summer 1982): 99–109.

25. Knights, "Method for Estimating Census Under-Enumeration." For the decade 1850–1860, Knights estimates that census underenumeration was 7.6 percent and the annual mobility rate was 30 percent.

26. There is no historical compilation of state residency laws. The best summary of state election laws is found in Jerrold G. Rusk and John J. Stucker, "Legal-Institutional Factors in American Voting" (unpublished paper, revised June 1975). Kleppner concludes that the "modal" state residency requirement in the late nineteenth century was one year; Kleppner, *Who Voted?* 33.

27. Americans mostly moved within a given locality rather than undertaking long-distance migration. These transients were only minimally affected by residency restrictions, but their ability to participate in electoral politics was still hampered.

28. George Frederick Miller, *Absentee Voters and Suffrage Laws* (Washington, D.C.: Daylion, 1948).

29. Voter survey research invariably finds a strong relationship between community ties and political participation. More settled residents vote more often; see Lester W. Milbraith, *Political Participation: How and Why Do People Get Involved in Politics?* (Chicago: Rand McNally, 1965), 53; and Peverill Squire, Raymond E. Wolfinger, and David P. Glass, "Residential Mobility and Voter Turnout," *American Political Science Review* 81 (March 1987): 45–65.

30. I used election returns and census material provided by the Inter-University Consortium for Political and Social Research in computer-readable form. The material was originally aggregated to the state level in a project coordinated by Walter Dean Burnham, Jerome Clubb, and William Flanigan. The file was partially checked against published records, and several minor corrections were made. Neither the collectors of the data nor the consortium bear any responsibility for the analysis or interpretations presented here. The variables that are used to analyze voting behavior are my own and are described in Appendix 2. Election returns for the Senate are excluded because much of the time period studied here predates direct election of senators.

31. See Rusk and Stucker, "Measuring Patterns of Electoral Participation in the United States," 479–80. Most scholars who work with county-level data have

been forced to limit themselves to an examination of one state. See for example Reynolds's excellent study of New Jersey politics during this same period; Reynolds, *Testing Democracy*. In contrast, Paul Kleppner conducts national studies using county-level data. However, he has published the results of his analysis in the most summary of forms and has provided other scholars with little information about how he navigated his way through the pitfalls of this level of analysis on a large scale; Kleppner, *Who Voted?* and *Continuity and Change*. See Allan J. Lichtman's review of the latter work in the *Journal of American History* 75 (September 1988): 642–3.

32. Ira Sharkansky, *Regionalism in American Politics* (Indianapolis: Bobbs-Merrill, 1970).

33. The use of standard regional divisions also avoids the problem of grouping cases according to the dependent variables, which we are trying to explain.

NOTES TO APPENDIX 2

1. Burnham was the first to develop a roll-off index, but he does not explain explicitly how he computes his figures; Walter Dean Burnham, "The Changing Shape of the American Political Universe," *American Political Science Review* 59 (March 1965): 9.

2. John J. Stucker, "The Impact of Women's Suffrage on Patterns of Voter Participation in the U.S.: Quasi-Experimental and Real-Time Analysis, 1890–1920" (Ph.D. dissertation, University of Michigan, 1973), 49.

3. Philip Loring Allen, "Ballot Laws and Their Working," *Political Science Quarterly* 21 (1906): 38–58; Jerrold Rusk, "Effect of the Australian Ballot Reform on Split-Ticket Voting: 1876–1908" (Ph.D. dissertation, University of Michigan, 1968); and "Effect of the Australian Ballot Reform on Split-Ticket Voting: 1876–1908," *American Political Science Review* 64 (December 1970): 122–38.

4. Drop-off, like roll-off, was first used by Burnham in "The Changing Shape of The American Political Universe," 9. His measure of drop-off is based on the total number of votes cast in succeeding elections and fails to control for increases in the voting population over time. This problem is avoided here by using turnout figures when calculating drop-off.

5. Stucker, "Impact of Women's Suffrage," 49. Stucker calculates drop-off by simply subtracting off-year turnout figures from presidential turnout. See also Jerrold G. Rusk and John J. Stucker, "Measuring Patterns of Electoral Participation in the United States," *Micropolitics* 3 (Winter 1984): 486–9.

6. Andrew T. Cowart, "A Cautionary Note on Aggregate Indicators of Split-Ticket Voting," *Political Methodology* 1 (Winter 1974): 110–2, 121.

7. This way of measuring ticket splitting is used by Burnham in "The Changing Shape of the American Political Universe," 11. Rusk utilizes the same index, except that he chooses to eliminate all elections in which minor parties receive more than 6 percent of the vote. These elections are not eliminated here so that we can analyze the difference between elections with third-party challenges and

those without; Rusk, "Effect of the Australian Ballot Reform," *American Political Science Review*, 1224–5.

8. John F. Reynolds and Richard McCormick, "'Outlawing Treachery': Split Tickets and the Ballot Laws in New York and New Jersey, 1880–1910," *Journal of American History* 72 (March 1986): 838–41.

9. Jerome M. Clubb, William H. Flanigan, and Nancy H. Zingale, *Partisan Realignment: Voters, Parties, and Government in American History* (Beverly Hills, Calif.: Sage, 1980), 55–74.

10. J. Morgan Kousser, "Ecological Regression and the Analysis of Past Politics," *Journal of Interdisciplinary History* 4 (Autumn 1973): 237–62; David Waterhouse, "Estimation of Voting Behavior from Aggregated Data: A Test," *Journal of Social History* 16 (Spring 1983): 35–53; Allan J. Lichtman, "The End of Realignment Theory? Toward a New Research Program for American Political History," *Historical Methods* 15 (Fall 1982): 170–88; and "Correlation, Regression, and the Ecological Fallacy," *Journal of Interdisciplinary History* 4 (Winter 1974): 417–33; John L. Shover and John J. Kushma, "Retrieval of Individual Data from Aggregate Units of Analysis: A Case Study Using Twentieth-Century Urban Voting Data," in *The History of American Electoral Behavior*, ed. Joel H. Silbey, Allan G. Bogue, and William H. Flanigan (Princeton, N.J.: Princeton University Press, 1978), 327–39; and E. Terrence Jones, "Ecological Inference and Electoral Analysis," *Journal of Interdisciplinary History* 2 (Winter 1972): 249–62.

11. Gudmund R. Iverson, "Recovering Individual Data in the Presence of Group and Individual Effects," *American Journal of Sociology* 79 (September 1973): 426.

12. Kousser, "Ecological Regression," 246–7; Dale Baum, "Know-Nothingism and the Republican Majority in Massachusetts: The Political Realignment of the 1850s," *Journal of American History* 64 (March 1978): 965; and William H. Flanigan and Nancy H. Zingale, "Alchemists's Gold: Inferring Individual Relationships from Aggregate Data," *Social Science History* 9 (Winter 1985): 71–91.

13. This is clear evidence that the underlying assumption of strictly individual-level effects is inappropriate; Kousser, "Ecological Regression," 250; and Iverson, "Recovering Individual Data," 426. Both 3 x 3 tables using the percent Democrat, Republican, and third-party of the total votes cast and 4 x 4 tables using the percent Democrat, Republican, third-party, and nonvoters of all eligible voters were examined for paired elections and for a series of elections in various time periods for each region, the North, and the nation as a whole. In every case some estimates of partisan persistence or defection were logically impossible. Controlling for group-level effects by "categorical separation," as Jones suggested, did not improve the results; "Ecological Inference." In fact, disaggregating to the regional level had the opposite effect of producing even more outlandish estimates. On the national level, apparently, some of the group-level effects balance each other out, so the overall estimates were closer to acceptable limits.

14. This index is similar to one used by Paul Kleppner, *Who Voted? The Dynamics of Electoral Turnout, 1870–1980* (New York: Praeger, 1982), 25.

15. Mark Stern, "Measuring Inter-Party Competition: A Proposal and a Test of a Method," *Journal of Politics* 39 (August 1972): 889–904. For different measures of competition, see C. Anthony Broh and Mark S. Levine, "Patterns of Party Competition," *American Politics Quarterly* 6 (July 1978): 357–84; David J. Elkins, "The Measurement of Party Competition," *American Political Science Review* 68 (June 1974): 682–700; Paul T. David, *Party Strength in the United States, 1872–1970* (Charlottesville: University Press of Virginia, 1972); Richard E. Zody and Norman R. Luttbeg, "An Evaluation of Various Measures of State Party Competition," *Western Political Quarterly* 21 (December 1968): 723–4; David G. Pfeiffer, "The Measurement of Inter-Party Competition and Systemic Stability," *American Political Science Review* 61 (June 1967): 457–67; Richard I. Hofferbert, "Classification of American State Party Systems," *Journal of Politics* 26 (August 1964): 550–67; Joseph A. Schlesinger, "A Two-Dimensional Scheme for Classifying the States according to Degree of Inter-Party Competition," *American Political Science Review* 49 (December 1955): 1120–8; and Austin Ranney and Willmore Kendall, "The American Party System," *American Political Science Review* 48 (June 1954): 477–85.

16. For example, a vote division of 52 percent to 48 percent would usually be classified as highly competitive, but if that division were stable across offices and over time, the majority party could so dominate office-holding that indices based on this factor would indicate a noncompetitive electoral situation. Likewise, a political situation where repeated landslide victories—first for one party, then for the other—produced continuous alternations in office would appear highly competitive on an office-holding index but noncompetitive on a vote-division one.

17. Zody and Luttbeg, "Evaluation of Various Measures," 723–4; Pfeiffer, "Measurement of Inter-Party Competition," 658.

18. Whereas indices of office-holding are more relevant to studies of government, measures of vote division are most useful for analysis of mass politics. Some measures of competitiveness are based directly on the percentage of the vote received by the dominant party; see Pfeiffer, "Measurement of Inter-Party Competition." The problem with this way of measuring competition is that minor-party voting in the United States in the late nineteenth century fluctuated widely, and therefore the percentage of the total vote received by one party is not necessarily a good indicator of the closeness of elections.

19. Since state-level election returns were used, this index of competitiveness in congressional elections is actually an aggregate-level measure based on the mean state-level vote received by each major party. As with all aggregate indices, there is no necessary relationship between this measure and the actual level of competitiveness in individual congressional contests. Lopsided races won by candidates from opposing parties can balance each other out on the state level. This is not a problem with these indices of presidential and gubernatorial competitiveness, which are not aggregate indices but measures of the actual closeness of these races on the state level.

20. Paul David's commonly used index also measures increasing electoral competitiveness on a scale of 0 to 100. To determine competitiveness, however, David calculates the runner-up's percentage of one-half the two-party vote. For

example, if a vote divides 55 percent to 45 percent, his index produces a competitiveness rating of 90, identical to the one produced by our index. But on a vote divided 45 percent Republican, 35 percent Democratic, and 10 percent Populist, David's formula produces a score of 87.5 since the Democratic vote is 43.75 percent of the two-party vote. On our index, the competitiveness score is still 90 since 10 percent of the total vote separates the two major parties. David's index thus presents a 45 percent to 35 percent to 20 percent vote division as less competitive than a 55 percent to 45 percent division, whereas our index presents the two races as equally competitive. David's index has this effect because it has the built-in assumption that third-party votes are not available to the major parties. This assumption is both unnecessary and, for this period, incorrect. See David, *Party Strength*.

21. For example, although a 46 percent Republican, 28 percent Democrat, 26 percent Populist division of the vote produces a competitiveness rating of only 82, the possibility of a Democratic-Populist alliance made the outcome of such an election much more uncertain than that score would indicate.

Index

About the Author

Mark Lawrence Kornbluh is Associate Professor of History and Director of MATRIX: The Center for Humane Arts, Letters and Social Sciences Online at Michigan State University. Kornbluh received his B.A. from the University of California, Berkeley, and his Ph.D. from The Johns Hopkins University. His research interests have focused on a wide range of issues related to political and cultural participation and democracy. Recently, Kornbluh's interests have increasingly focused on the revolution in communication and educational technology. As Executive Director of H-Net: Humanities and Social Sciences OnLine, he has been involved in a wide range of international initiatives to utilize the Internet to increase access and exchange of knowledge.

Kornbluh teaches both graduate and undergraduate courses in American history at Michigan State and lives in Okemos, Michigan, with his wife, Miriam Joy Behar, and two children, Evan and Allie Kornbluh.